THE POLITICS OF

WEAPONS INNOVATION:

THE THOR-JUPITER

CONTROVERSY

The Politics of Weapons Innovation: The Thor-Jupiter Controversy is one of a series of studies sponsored by the Institute of War and Peace Studies of Columbia University. *Defense and Diplomacy* by Alfred Vagts; *Man, the State and War* by Kenneth N. Waltz; *The Common Defense* by Samuel P. Huntington; *Strategy, Politics and Defense Budgets* by Warner R. Schilling, Paul Y. Hammond, and Glenn H. Snyder; *Political Unification* by Amitai Etzioni; *Stockpiling Strategic Materials* by Glenn H. Snyder; *The Politics of Military Unification* by Demetrios Caraley; *NATO and the Range of American Choice* by William T. R. Fox and Annette Baker Fox; *A World of Nations* by Dankwart A. Rustow; *Asia and United States Policy* by Wayne A. Wilcox; *The American Study of International Relations* by William T. R. Fox; and *Alliances and Small Powers* by Robert L. Rothstein are other volumes in the series. *Theoretical Aspects of International Relations,* edited by William T. R. Fox; *Inspection for Disarmament,* edited by Seymour Melman; and *Changing Patterns of Military Politics,* edited by Samuel P. Huntington are all volumes of essays planned and edited by Institute members. The Institute of War and Peace Studies jointly sponsored the publication of the following: *Political Power: USA/USSR* by Zbigniew Brzezinski and Samuel P. Huntington, with the Russian Institute of Columbia University; *Foreign Policy and Democratic Politics* by Kenneth N. Waltz, with the Center for International Affairs, Harvard University; *To Move a Nation* by Roger Hilsman, with the Washington Center of Foreign Policy Research, Johns Hopkins University; *Western European Perspectives on International Affairs* by Donald J. Puchala and Richard L. Merritt, with the Yale Political Data Program; *How Nations Behave* by Louis Henkin, with the Council on Foreign Relations; and *Soviet Perspectives on International Relations, 1956–67* by William Zimmerman, with the Russian Institute of Columbia University.

THE POLITICS OF
WEAPONS INNOVATION:

THE THOR-JUPITER CONTROVERSY

BY MICHAEL H. ARMACOST

Columbia University Press / New York and London

1969

Copyright © 1969 Columbia University Press
SBN 231-03206-4
Library of Congress Catalog Card Number: 70-90213
Printed in the United States of America

To my wife
Bonny

FOREWORD

After two decades of scholarship in the politics of defense policy-making, it is no longer news that "Washington" is a jungle of quasi-sovereignties in which conflict is continuous but not total. The ideal of a national decision-making process in which a wise President, after giving due weight to all relevant considerations, makes "right" decisions on national security within the limits set by Congress and the Constitution is far from the reality. Improved methods of coordinating the flow of advice to the top of the government and improved methods of identifying the critical decisions, as for example by cost-benefit analysis, may move the policy process in the direction of the ideal; but the field remains wide in which adversary processes more than presidential directives shape outcomes. None of the adversaries need yield in patriotism and devotion to the national interest to any of the others for the politics of policy-making on occasion to be protracted and bitter.

A number of my present and former colleagues at Columbia University, most of them also colleagues in its Institute of War and Peace Studies, have contributed greatly to our understanding of the national security policy process. Among them are Demetrios Caraley, Paul Y. Hammond, Roger Hilsman, Samuel P. Huntington, Richard E. Neustadt, Warner R. Schilling and Glenn H. Snyder. In his study of the Thor-Jupiter missile controversy, Michael H. Armacost reports on a significant controversy in defense politics. Decision-making under conditions of strategic indeterminacy, in which the facts are complex and poorly understood and the goals are multiple, is often agonizing and drawn out. An inherently difficult choice was, in the missile controversy, further complicated by parochial service loyalties and perspectives and by the interplay of conflicting military and non-military pressures. Whether the story which Professor Armacost has to tell illustrates the wastefulness of inter-service squabbling and duplicating weapons development or the efficiency of the adversary process and competitive weapons development, the reader may decide for himself.

William T. R. Fox

ACKNOWLEDGMENTS

The research for this book—in its original form as a doctoral dissertation—was undertaken at a time when the nation was still preoccupied with the "missile gap." It is being published at a moment of national soul searching over the wisdom of deploying an anti-ballistic missile defense system. In the early 1960s some questioned whether the United States could compete effectively in an on-going qualitative arms race. Today many question the necessity and prudence of continuing such competition. To recount the Thor-Jupiter controversy now may seem rather like reciting the ancient history of the missile age. But while the case materials of this book have been dated by the development of new technology and the emergence of new policy struggles, it is hoped that the method of analysis employed may prove relevant to more contemporary issues.

I am delighted to be able to acknowledge the assistance received from many teachers, colleagues, and friends. Above all, I wish to thank Professor William T. R. Fox, Director of the Institute of War and Peace Studies, Columbia University, for many personal kindnesses as well as professional counsel. He advised, warned, and encouraged me at each stage in the preparation of the manuscript. Professors Warner R. Schilling, Roger Hilsman, Lewis Henkin, and Donald Keesing, all of Columbia University, read and made many helpful suggestions and criticisms on one or another draft. General James N. Gavin read and offered useful comments on an early version of Chapter II. For their assistance I am grateful. For the sins of commission or omission which remain, I bear sole responsibility.

A number of former defense officials gave generously of their time to discuss their recollections of the Thor-Jupiter controversy with me. These included the late President Eisenhower, Admiral Arthur Radford, General James N. Gavin, General John B. Medaris, General Lauris Norstad, Mr. Neil McElroy, Mr. Wilfred McNeil, Mr. Trevor Gardner, Mr. Simon Ramo, Mr. Wilbur Brucker, Mr. William Holaday, Mr. Alvin G. Waggoner, Mr. William Schaub, and Mr. Thomas Morrow. What follows is, of course, my version of that controversy, not theirs. For its shortcomings I alone am accountable.

Research for this book was facilitated by a grant from the Haynes Foundation. Revisions of my dissertation were initiated during a stint with the Institute of War and Peace Studies in the summer of 1965. Completion of the revised manuscript was made possible by a Pomona College Faculty Summer Research Fellowship.

Mrs. Shirley Martin, Miss Lee Ann Wilson and Mrs. Janet Tanner typed the various drafts. The book is dedicated to my wife, Bonny, who suffered graciously through the whole interminable process.

March 1, 1969
Tokyo, Japan

CONTENTS

(1) INTRODUCTION

Throughout much of America's history, national security has been a natural condition rather than an explicit aim of foreign and military policy. A geographic location remote from the European centers of power, the political equilibrium on the Continent, the fortuitous interposition of the British fleet, the weakness of neighbors to the north and south, the impotence of Asia, and a rich endowment of natural resources served to reinforce American liberal presuppositions that peace and security were normal, conflict and strife annoying aberrations. Since World War II, however, fundamental changes in the structure of world politics and a revolution in military technology have radically transformed the nature of the United States security position. Mobilization strategies are hardly adequate in an era when the decisive phases of a general war might occur in the first hours or days of such a conflict. Forces-in-being based upon the latest qualitative advances in weaponry loom preeminent in the balance of terror. Indeed, it is precisely these forces which determine the precariousness of that balance.

"Every up-to-date dictionary," William James wrote in 1911, "should say that 'peace' and 'war' mean the same thing, now *in posse*, now *in actu*. It may even reasonably be said that the intensely sharp competitive preparation for war by the nation is the real war, permanent, unceasing; and that battles are only a sort of public verification of mastery gained during the 'peace' intervals." [1] James' observation is even more timely in the 1960s as former buffers of time and space have been eliminated

[1] William James, *Memories and Studies* (New York, Longmans Green, and Co., 1911), p. 273.

by the development of ballistic missile systems capable of delivering thermonuclear warheads almost instantaneously over intercontinental distances. Military policy and diplomacy have indeed become "intertwined as never before." [2]

The necessity of permanent preparedness has made participation in the arms race a persistent concern of American military and civilian officials since 1945. A level of affluence permitting the diversion of vast resources into the military budget, a dramatic acceleration in the rate of progress in scientific research and military technology, and the sustained relationship of enmity between the Soviet Union and the United States have encouraged this preoccupation. Nor is the disposition to innovate generally inhibited by a technically illiterate and conservative military leadership. Having witnessed the decisive impact of novel weapons on the battlefield in World War II, and having been entrusted with the responsibility for maintaining a continuing deterrence, generals and admirals have been transformed "from being the most traditional element in any national society—hanging on to their horses, or their sailing ships, for as long as possible—into the boldest innovators." [3]

Yet even though the formulation and implementation of national security policy has been the most significant responsibility of top officials in the government for more than two decades, the myth that national security policies are devised through some uniquely apolitical process has, as Professor William T. R. Fox has noted, "died hard." [4] Certain constraints on party politics operate, to be sure, "at the water's edge," although even there the extent of genuine nonpartisanship has often been overstated. But the process by which strategy, defense budgets, and weapons policies are conceived and implemented cannot be more accurately described than political in the most fundamental sense of the term.

[2] Raymond Aron, *The Great Debate* (New York, Doubleday & Co., Inc., 1965), p. 146.

[3] Alastair Buchan, "The Age of Insecurity," *Encounter,* XX (June, 1963), 5.

[4] Warner R. Schilling, Paul Y. Hammond, and Glenn H. Snyder, *Strategy, Politics, and Defense Budgets* (New York, Columbia University Press, 1962), p. viii.

Politics, after all, is the process by which the scarce goods and values of the community are distributed among competing institutions, interests, individuals and groups. It is a method "for resolving through the interplay of power, those questions that do not lend themselves to intellectual resolution."[5] Questions concerning national security policy are preeminently of this kind. The objectives of security policy are numerous; the resources available to support their achievement are relatively scarce. Thus the need to ration power among competing aims and the necessity of deciding among competing strategic programs.

Inevitably discussions of national security policy will disclose serious differences of opinion among policy makers. Those differences exist, as Warner R. Schilling has pointed out, "because no one can demonstrate to the satisfaction of all concerned that his theories about how present and future weapons can be used to prevent and win wars are the predictions that reality could or will prove correct."[6] Conflicting opinions and interests on these matters cannot be left simply unresolved. Nor is persuasion alone sufficient to affect their resolution. Since the problems are political, in attempting to predict their outcome one must consider *who* is contending with *whom,* as well as *what* are the issues in contention.

In recent years a great deal has been learned about the political aspects of national security policy making. It has been demonstrated that security policy is anything but a series of discrete acts unfolding in majestic progression with clear-cut decisions based invariably upon exhaustive analysis and unfailing good judgment;[7] that the diffusion of power and responsibility within the Executive Branch insures the prevalence of legisla-

[5] Charles E. Lindblom, *The Intelligence of Democracy* (New York, The Free Press, 1965) , p. 187.

[6] Warner R. Schilling, "The Politics of National Defense: Fiscal 1950," in *Strategy, Politics, and Defense Budgets,* p. 226. For a discussion of the factors which frustrate agreement upon a single "technically correct" solution of the national security equation, see pp. 10–15.

[7] Roger Hilsman, *To Move A Nation: The Politics of Foreign Policy in the Administration of John F. Kennedy* (New York, Doubleday & Co., Inc., 1967) , pp. 3–13 and *passim.*

tive techniques for policy formulation despite the executive locale of decisions on most strategic issues; [8] that conflicting analyses of those problems, "institutionally grounded" biases, and personal idiosyncrasies all contribute to the competitive relationships among the policy making elites; [9] that policy is a ratification of existing power relationships, as well as a substantive program designed to meet external exigencies; [10] that policies formulated without specific reference to the politically feasible, or informed by pertinent aspects of the prevailing "climate of opinion," will be largely irrelevant; [11] that politics is a prominent feature not only of policy making but of the struggles to revise the process by which policy is made; [12] and that in the light of uncertainties which surround security policy issues, rational policy making may well be a "science of muddling through" rather than a process of clear-cut aims, explicit and quantitative weighing of alternatives, and decisive choice. [13] The list could be extended, of course, since the number of scholars toiling in the vineyards of national security policy research is substantial; their productivity impressive.

Considering the growing importance of decisions relating to weapons innovation, the political facets of military-technological policy making have received relatively little attention.[14]

[8] Samuel P. Huntington, "Strategic Planning and the Political Process," *Foreign Affairs,* XXXVIII (January, 1960), 285–99.

[9] William T. R. Fox, "Civilians, Soldiers, and American Military Policy," *World Politics,* VI (April, 1955), 402–18; Schilling, "Fiscal 1950," pp. 21–22.

[10] Samuel P. Huntington, *The Common Defense: Strategic Programs in National Politics* (New York, Columbia University Press, 1961), p. 167. This point was also developed by Roger Hilsman, "Congressional-Executive Relations and the Foreign Policy Consensus," *American Political Science Review,* LI (September, 1958), p. 732.

[11] Paul Y. Hammond, "NSC-68: Prologue to Rearmament," in Schilling, Hammond, and Snyder, *Strategy, Politics, and Defense Budgets,* pp. 267–368.

[12] Demetrios Caraley, *The Politics of Military Unification: A Study of Conflict and the Policy Process* (New York, Columbia University Press, 1966).

[13] Charles E. Lindblom, "The Science of 'Muddling Through,'" *Public Administration Review,* XIX (Spring, 1959), 79–88.

[14] A useful bibliography of materials on weapons, technology, and military policy is to be found in Samuel P. Huntington, *Changing Patterns*

The most comprehensive analysis of this aspect of defense policy has been attempted by economists interested in rationalizing program decisions in terms of the criterion of cost effectiveness." [15] Merton Peck and Frederic Scherer, authors of the impressive study, *The Weapons Innovation Process*,[16] have illumined some of the political features of that process, though this was not the primary focus of their three-volume work. Warner R. Schilling has written a fascinating case study of the events and deliberations leading to the U. S. decision to develop thermonuclear weapons.[17] Still, the political character of weapons innovation is deserving of more specific and detailed study than it has thus far received.

It is quite apparent that at every stage in the weapons innovation process—from the formulation of a research and development program to the incorporation of finished hardware into the strategic arsenal—the nature and variety of the participating individuals and groups, the diversity of their objectives, and the imponderables of technology, intelligence, and strategy combine to produce a pattern of policy making that is essentially political; that is, it is marked by bargaining as well

---

of *Military Politics* (New York, The Free Press of Glencoe, 1962), pp. 258–60. One especially useful addition is David W. Tarr, "Military Technology and the Policy Process," *The Western Political Quarterly*, XVIII (March, 1965), 135–48.

[15] See, for example, Alain Enthoven and Henry Rowen, "Defense Planning and Organization," in *Public Finances: Needs, Sources, and Utilization* (Princeton, Princeton University Press, 1961), pp. 365–417; Charles Hitch and Roland McKean, *Economics and Defense in the Nuclear Age* (Cambridge, Harvard University Press, 1960); Alain Enthoven, "Defense and Disarmament: Economic Analysis in the Department of Defense," *American Economic Review*, LIII (May, 1963), 413–23; Carl Kaysen, "Improving the Efficiency of Military Research and Development," *Public Policy*, XII (Cambridge, Harvard University Press, 1963), pp. 219–73; Sterling J. Livingston, "Decision-Making in Weapons Development," *Harvard Business Review*, XXXVI (January–February, 1958), 127–36; and Burton Klein, "A Radical Proposal for R. and D.," *Fortune*, LVII (May, 1958), 112 ff.

[16] Merton Peck and Frederic Scherer, *The Weapons Innovation Process* (Cambridge, Harvard University Press, 1962).

[17] Warner R. Schilling, "The H-Bomb Decision: How to Decide Without Actually Choosing," *Political Science Quarterly*, LXXVI (March, 1961), 24–46.

as analysis. An irreducible element of conjecture is intrinsic in most weapons decisions. Knowledge of enemy capabilities and intentions is at best incomplete and ambiguous. Attempts to anticipate the main lines of scientific advance is always a hazardous enterprise. While the element of unpredictability in advanced engineering is less dramatic, precise calculations of cost and lead time, as well as the operational utility of new weapons, have again and again defied systematic attempts at prediction.[18] Equally difficult to foresee are the strategic implications of novel weapons, and their impact upon established divisions of labor among the services.

Under these circumstances the fact that differences of opinion frequently arise among the services over weapons development priorities and procurement policies is hardly surprising. Interservice rivalries are not, to be sure, restricted to competition for new weapons. Nor does the prospect of novel weapons technology invariably unleash spirited competition among the services. During the 1950s, however, the reciprocal influences of interservice rivalry and weapons innovation upon one another were especially evident.[19]

Naturally the rate and direction of technological innovation is conditioned by the strategic perspectives and proprietary interests of the services. Service partisans recognize that the development of novel weapons will facilitate the execution of

[18] See T. A. Marschak, "The Role of Project Histories in the Study of R & D," *RANDP-2850* (January, 1964), 115.

[19] Interservice rivalry has flourished persistently since World War II. Clearly, its frequency and intensity are to some extent a product of postwar measures of unification introduced in Defense Department organization. Discord among the Army and Navy had earlier been less acute and more sporadic when they enjoyed clearly distinguishable missions, required different weapons systems, and were coddled by separate Congressional committees, responsive to different sectional or economic constituencies. Within a more unified Defense Department the zone of competition among the services has regularly centered upon the annual budgetary struggle, occasional revisions of roles and missions assignments, and the quest for access to the most modern weapons. For a provocative discussion of interservice politics, see Samuel P. Huntington, "Interservice Competition and the Political Roles of the Services," in Harry L. Coles (ed.), *Total War and Cold War* (Columbus, Ohio University Press, 1962).

established assignments. In a situation in which three and a half autonomous services compete within a single Defense Department for functional roles in the implementation of a single national strategy, moreover, the expectation is widely shared that successful weapons development efforts may enhance a service's claims for both additional money and missions. Reflecting on the incentives for innovation in military technology, one Air Force colonel observed:

Today we must recognize that the only constant is that technical changes will continue at an ever accelerating rate. To resist this is suicidal, while intelligent accommodation to it can yield many benefits. The criterion of success for a military service has become the ability to conceive, develop, and to exploit efficiently the ever increasing rate of scientific advance.[20]

Frictions are bound to arise occasionally among services acting upon such premises. It is plausible to assume that the intensity of such frictions will depend upon whether defense expenditures are rising or falling, whether the prevailing strategic concept emphasizes a balanced arsenal or seeks deterrence of a wide range of contingencies through reliance upon a single military instrument, e.g., the Strategic Air Command, and whether or not new military technology renders ambiguous the established "treaties" among the services on roles and missions.

All the conditions encouraging rivalry among the services were present during the years 1953 to 1960. Divergent doctrinal legacies, unique combat experiences, distinctive professional competences, particular technological capabilities, and clashing proprietary interests all stimulated the services' competitive efforts to develop and exploit missile technology. In the struggles to reconcile their conflicting perspectives and interests, the services were as energetic in the mobilization of allies, the activation of clients, the embarrassment of rivals, and the negotiation of compromise settlements as they were in their efforts to persuade other partisans of the merits of their preferred policies.

Since weapons policies are framed within a political environ-

[20] Col. Edward N. Hall, "Industry and the Military in the United States," *Air University Quarterly Review,* X (Fall, 1958) , 35.

ment, the analytical tools of the political scientist are clearly
relevant to a description and evaluation of that process. The
sources of power, the techniques by which power is pooled,
the conditions under which it may be employed effectively, the
channels through which influence may be exerted, and the prevailing perspectives toward politics and technology which inform the outcome of those decisions are all relevant data which
merit examination.

The purpose of this study is, therefore, to contribute to an
understanding of how the content of weapons policies is influenced by the character of the political process through which
those decisions are made. Specifically, this study presents an
analysis of the ways in which interservice competition affected
the development, production, and deployment of the novel
weapon system: the intermediate-range ballistic missile.

The Thor-Jupiter controversy between the Air Force and
Army provides the case study material for this analysis. Both
services coveted the responsibility for developing and producing
an operational IRBM system. In 1955, both advanced plausible
and promising technical proposals—the Army for the Jupiter
Missile System, the Air Force for its Thor system. During 1956,
each sought to design a weapon system which would advance its
qualifications for the deployment assignment. After the Air
Force successfully obtained sole responsibility for deployment
of an IRBM in November, 1956, the focus of service rivalry
shifted in anticipation of future struggles, to the organizational
arrangements which would govern subsequent research and development efforts in the space field. Detailed study of the rival
Army and Air Force efforts to design, develop, produce, and
deploy an IRBM system should shed some light on the political
dimensions of the choices between competing weapons systems.

The nature of such choices naturally varies from case to case.
Some features of the Thor-Jupiter controversy were undoubt-
edly unique. Army and Air Force differences were projected
into the public realm with an extraordinary virulence. The
blurring of established divisions of functions by the develop-

ment of missile delivery capabilities was unusual. The guided missile was not a direct derivative of either the airplane or of field artillery, Air Force and Army rhetoric to the contrary notwithstanding. It had characteristics similar to both. If the intrinsic technical characteristics of the IRBMs implied no obvious jurisdictional assignment, the stakes which the services invested in a favorable decision were such as to compound the difficulties of choice. Since long-range missiles could be efficiently employed only with nuclear warheads, moreover, the proprietary issue of control over the nuclear stockpile was also reopened.

More than simply the jurisdictional question of who would design, produce, and deploy the IRBM was at issue. Competing patterns of contractor relations contributed to the dynamics of contention. The controversy set not only the Army and Air Force against one another, but the airframe industry against other industrial aspirants for a major role in missile development as well. It also involved a spirited contest between sponsors and supporters of the "arsenal system" and those who advocated reliance upon the "weapon system manager" concept of development. In the former, government scientists, engineers, and technicians were at times engaged in the in-house fabrication and assembly of military weaponry, as well as being participants in the research, design, and component development stages of weapons innovation. In the latter, a military service provided managerial surveillance while contracting out to industry the responsibility for systems engineering, technical direction, and component production and assembly on new weapon systems. In the convergence of jurisdictional conflicts among the services with these industrial and administrative rivalries, the case is perhaps unique.

An element of generality is imparted to the conclusions, however, since the Thor-Jupiter controversy revealed the variable reactions of the services to novel strategic delivery capabilities made possible by rocket technology. While each technological revolution will be differently appreciated and exploited by the

services, the differential impact of technical advance upon their
fortunes, the forceful disruption of the prevailing distribution
of power and responsibility among them by technological change,
and the expectation that political-technological efforts may be
undertaken on behalf of proprietary as well as strategic interests
are predictable aspects of every revolutionary advance in military weaponry.

PRESSURE GROUP POLITICS, INTERSERVICE RIVALRY,
AND WEAPONS INNOVATION

Understanding of the process by which strategic decisions are
formulated has been enriched by applying analogies from the
fields of both international politics and legislative bargaining.
The relevance of those analogies is amply confirmed in the case
of the Thor-Jupiter controversy. The relations among the services, as among sovereign states, are marked by the existence of
both conflict and accommodation. The formulation and execution of alliance policies, the application of limited reprisals, the
persistent conduct of negotiations among quasi-sovereign entities, and efforts to arrange compromises through the activities of
third party mediators are all to be found in the IRBM dispute.
Such analogies call attention to the relative autonomy of the
participants and their consequent need voluntarily to coordinate their interests, moderate their ambitions, and mitigate their
differences in the search for a mutually acceptable policy.[21]

Limits to such analogies inhere in the fact that the bureaus,
agencies, and departments engaged in the politics of weapons
innovation are only "quasi-sovereign." While bargaining among
them is pervasive, the potential for authoritative decision is
greater in administrative than in international politics. Consequently the "strain toward agreement"—enhanced by the existence of shared objectives and the natural desire of bureaucrats

[21] Comparisons between international politics and the domestic policy
making process have long been noted by Professor William T. R. Fox in
his lectures at Columbia University. They were also discussed in Roger
Hilsman's early explorations of consensus-building in the making of
policy. See his "The Foreign Policy Consensus: An Interim Report,"
Conflict Resolution, III (December, 1959), 367-71.

to get on with the job—is strengthened by the knowledge that policy may be imposed if it cannot be freely negotiated.[22]

The techniques of legislative politics are also much in evidence in the Thor-Jupiter controversy. Difficult choices are invariably postponed. Responsibility for them is regularly devolved upon committees. Agreements are often facilitated by compromise and logrolling, and policies frequently reflect the lowest common denominator of consensus—occasionally achieved upon the basis of unrealistic assumptions.[23]

One would not want to overemphasize the lateral relationships in defense politics, however, at the expense of an awareness of hierarchical elements. As Paul Y. Hammond has noted, even the highest ranking committees in the U.S. Government, such as the Joint Chiefs of Staff and the National Security Council, though they are bedeviled by the familiar failings of committees, contain intrinsically hierarchical elements. This is due to the fact that they serve the President. His sense of priorities, his idiosyncrasies, and his administrative style are thus "reflected in the problems they take up, the staff work they do, the deliberative acts they perform, and the recommendations they offer." [24]

In the search for an appropriate model of service politics, one must therefore account for both the pervasiveness of bargaining among semiautonomous agencies and departments, and the residual elements of hierarchy to be found in the bureaucratic

[22] The suggestive phrases "quasi-sovereign" and "strain toward agreement" were coined by Professors William T. R. Fox and Warner R. Schilling respectively. While a consensus among the services will generally be easier to arrange than among nation states, Secretary of Defence Charles Wilson's plaintive exhortation to the services to "at least . . . treat each other like allies" contains a useful reminder that this is not inevitably the case. Cited by Harry Howe Ransom, *Can American Democracy Survive Cold War?* (New York, Doubleday & Co., Inc., 1964), p. 80.

[23] The similarities between legislative politics and strategy making were most clearly developed by Samuel P. Huntington, "Strategic Planning and the Political Process," *Foreign Affairs*, XXXVIII (January, 1960), 291–92. See also Charles E. Lindblom, *The Intelligence of Democracy* (New York, The Free Press, 1965).

[24] Paul Y. Hammond, "Foreign Policymaking: Pluralistic Politics or Unitary Analysis?" *RAND P-2961-1* (February, 1965), 20.

politics of the Pentagon. Defense politics in the 1950's certainly was marked by the aggressive maneuvering of rather autonomous service departments eager to maximize their share in the distribution of budgets, roles and missions, and research and development assignments. At the same time, those vested with formal authority for the management of the Department of Defense struggled to discipline the efforts of the services to a single strategic policy. In the Thor-Jupiter controversy the service departments performed prodigious feats of lobbying. The activities of the Secretary of Defense and his assistants more nearly resembled the interest aggregation functions of political party leaders. Thus one may hazard the hypothesis that in the realm of weapons innovation the services act as powerful *institutional* interest groups.[25]

The services, in this context, articulate and aggregate demands and present them as a program to those legally endowed and politically capable of authorizing action. They attempt to mobilize support for their programs through persuasion and bargaining. They seek to transform their recommendations into policy through the various channels of influence in the policy making process. Like interest group activity in any political system, interservice politics is likely to be conditioned by the substance of existing policy, by the prevailing procedures for policy making, and by those cultural norms which constitute the ground rules for politics in a particular environment.[26]

The pressure group model appears especially attractive, since it emphasizes the interaction and interdependence between a relatively homogeneous group of public officials endowed with the legal responsibility to formulate policy and a network of

[25] Institutional interest groups are to be distinguished from anomic, associational, and non-associational groups which also engage in interest articulation. Institutional interest groups are formal organizations with designated political functions or legal responsibilities other than simply the articulation of interests, which nevertheless lobby as corporate groups on behalf of their own interests or those of other groups in society. See Gabriel Almond and Bingham Powell, Jr., *Comparative Politics: A Developmental Approach* (Boston, Little, Brown and Co., 1966), p. 77.

[26] Harry Eckstein has analyzed the influence these variables exerted on British pressure group politics in his study *Pressure Group Politics* (Stanford, Stanford University Press, 1960), esp. pp. 15–39.

lobby groups, each seeking to implement its own "partial view
of the public interest." This implies that weapons policies are
not merely discrete contractual bargains negotiated by free-
wheeling and selfish partisans under the surveillance of Presidential or Congressional politicians who serve as "referees."
On the contrary, the administrative politics of weapons innovation contain a "mixture of authoritarian *and* equalitarian
elements, the lateral relationships, and the hierarchy of authority." [27] In short, the emphasis is neither upon an undis-
ciplined pluralism nor upon transcendent central direction, but
upon the dialectic between the services as pressure groups and
the politically accountable leaders of the Pentagon as managers
of a diffuse defense establishment. It is thus appropriate to inquire: in what ways, and to what extent do strategic ideas, the
distribution of power and responsibility implicit in Defense
Department organizational arrangements, and the climate of
opinion regarding both technical innovations and interservice
politics influence the pattern of bargaining and its results?

If the services assume the role of pressure groups in the area
of weapons policy, it follows that their political activities are
characterized by partisan behavior. Partisanship, however,
should not be understood as a pejorative term. Service leaders
are not motivated exclusively by any selfish urge to aggrandize
themselves at others' expense. While an air of special pleading
permeates some service perspectives and proposals, this can be
easily overemphasized. Partisanship is not to be equated with
parochialism, an excessively narrow outlook, or a tendency to
engage in feuds with other bureaus, agencies, or departments.
Every pluralistic system of decision making will tend to shape
personnel to distinctive viewpoints. As various decision makers
promote their own unique conceptions of what national security requires, they inevitably act as partisans.[28]

The interaction of partisans produces an "adversary system"
of policy making. It encourages the articulation of a maximum

[27] Hammond, "Foreign Policymaking: Pluralistic Politics or Unitary
Analysis?" *RAND P-2961-1*, 21.
[28] These points are taken up in Lindblom, "The Science of 'Muddling
Through,'" *Public Administration Review*, XIX, p. 86; and Lindblom,
The Intelligence of Democracy, p. 29. In this case study the perceptions,

number of values with candor and clarity. It provides a measure
of insurance that if important objectives are carelessly overlooked by one group of decision makers, another group will
attend to their advocacy. In the market place of policy making,
the system provides incentives for the mobilization of the most
salient arguments for and against each specific policy alternative.

Within these terms of reference the Secretary of Defense and
his staff are accurately described as partisans. Since, however,
there is a greater likelihood that all the most relevant information concerning broad policy matters may be organized at the
highest levels of government, their location in the structure of
policy making will offer the possibility of a broader conception
of policy, even as the Secretary, by virtue of his authority and
the divisions among the services, is likely to enjoy a significantly
more favorable bargaining position than, for example, the representatives of the service departments.

THE CLOSED POLITICS OF WEAPONS INNOVATION

If this model of interservice politics as pressure group activity within a somewhat decentralized policy making structure is
accurate, it suggests that one widely discussed description of the
weapons development process requires substantial modification.

One of the chief characteristics of the development of military technology in the advanced countries, Sir Charles P. Snow
(now Lord Snow of Leicester) observed in the Godkin Lectures

---

calculations, and proprietary interests which influence service strategies
for obtaining weapons, budgets, and roles and missions have been
stressed to the possible neglect of their divergent strategic conceptions.
This is not an accurate reflection of their significance as sources of service
rivalry. On the contrary, doctrinal differences are often deep and profoundly significant. In the day-to-day activities of the services, however,
the need to meet the ongoing requirements of running a vast defense
establishment inhibits the discussion of principles which upset organizations and promise no easy resolution. Nor are service doctrines to be
merely understood as *ex post facto* rationalizations of policies adopted
on other grounds, though strategic preferences may be rooted in proprietary interests. Doctrine will also reflect divergent experiences in past
wars, disparate expectations of future wars, and the "distinctive competences" institutionalized in the separate services. For a discussion of
this point, see Philip Selznick, *Leadership in Administration* (Evanston,
Row, Peterson and Company, 1957), pp. 9, 14, 42.

he delivered at Harvard in 1960, "is that the cardinal choices have to be made by a handful of men; in secret; and at least in legal form, by men who cannot have a first-hand knowledge of what those choices depend upon or what their results may be." [29] The "committee, court, and hierarchical" politics which significantly affect those cardinal choices were termed by Snow, "closed politics."

Compared with the formulation of agricultural policy, tax policy, or other domestic legislation, the politics of weapons innovation is evidently closed.[30] Yet does Snow's description of closed politics as "any kind of politics in which there is no appeal to a larger assembly . . . in the sense of a group of opinion, or an electorate, or on an even bigger scale what we call loosely 'social forces' " accurately characterize the politics of competitive weapons innovation? [31] To what extent, one may inquire, are the chief features of Snow's model—namely, limited participation in policy making, the absence of an informed and attentive audience to monitor discussions among the principals, the anonymity of decision makers, and the monopoly of choice by either politically unaccountable experts or scientifically illiterate politicians—likely to be significantly modified under the determined pressures of service lobbying, at least when the innovation of a novel weapon is marked by interservice competition?

INTERSERVICE POLITICS AND THE CRITERIA
OF RATIONALITY FOR SELECTING WEAPONS SYSTEMS

If weapons innovation is acknowledged to be a political process and if the services are viewed as lobbying groups jealous

[29] Sir Charles P. Snow, *Science and Government* (Cambridge, Harvard University Press, 1960) , p. 1.
[30] Professor Samuel P. Huntington has described the political process by which "structural" as opposed to "strategic" decisions are reached as "open politics." In making such decisions the "political processes of arousing support or opposition are directed toward these multiple decision-making foci in Congress." Huntington, *The Common Defense,* p. 125. By "structural" decisions he refers to those which deal with the "procurement, allocation, and organization of the men, money, and material which go into the strategic units and uses of forces." *Ibid.,* p. 4.
[31] Snow, *Science and Government,* p. 56.

of and aggressively defending their institutional interests, what insurance is there that the weapons proposals they advance to assure their organizational survival or expansion will necessarily serve the strategic and foreign policy interests of the nation? What criteria are to be applied in evaluating service weapons proposals? What procedures of policy making will enhance the likelihood that intelligent choices will be made among competing projects?

In seeking standards and procedures to insure an optimum rationality in weapons decisions, it must be admitted at the outset that the standards of rationality are not easily stated. They must surely be framed with a clear recognition of the uncertainties facing those who allocate scarce funds, scientific personnel, engineering and production facilities, and managerial talents among the various research and development programs of the services. Respect for such uncertainties, as well as a passion to minimize them as far as is possible, must shape an intelligent research and development strategy. Indeed, research and development are essentially stages in a learning process in which the gradual accumulation of information and technical experience renders intelligent decision making possible.[32]

If a technical problem urgently demands solution, duplicative efforts may be warranted in order to accelerate this learning process. By temporarily deferring a choice between competitive projects, time and information may be obtained, and the flexibility to adjust the design for a finished weapon system to changing circumstances and greater technical experience sustained. In short, the very nature of research and development choices encourages incrementalist decision making, a postponement of the drastic choices between projects, and an attempt to maximize the technical and informational yield from project competition.

Duplication is by no means always intelligent. It may be wasteful, as critics of defense spending frequently contend. Since

[32] See Richard R. Nelson, "Uncertainty, Learning and the Economics of Parallel Research and Development Efforts," *The Review of Economics and Statistics,* XLIII (November, 1961), 351–64.

deferred choice between competing projects permits not only the accumulation of knowledge but the development of vested interests in the maintenance of programs, political obstacles to clear-cut decisions emerge as the intellectual obstacles are being removed.

If the context of uncertainty renders the development of standards of *rationality* in weapons policy making elusive, the *reasonableness* of certain policies certainly can be improved through a more careful elaboration of the available options, a more systematic evaluation of costs and strategic benefits, and a constant effort to identify the role which prejudice, intuition, outdated postulates, and doctrinaire methods play in reaching important decisions.[33] In other words, however speculative weapons decisions may be, it is assumed that more and better analysis and improved procedures of policy making may assist politicians and administrators in asking and answering the right questions. One objective of this analysis of the Thor-Jupiter controversy is to examine the Army-Air Force competition in terms of its technical productiveness, and in order to evaluate those techniques of defense management which facilitate or hinder timely and intelligent decisions between parallel programs.

METHODS OF PROCEDURAL CONTROL OVER
WEAPONS INNOVATION AND INTERSERVICE RIVALRY

Within the framework of this study, the civilian leaders of the Defense Department were preoccupied both with the maintenance of a satisfactory rate of technological innovation and the management of inter-service rivalry occasioned by the development of new weapons. A variety of managerial techniques appear relevant for the accomplishment of these twin objectives. Strategic *doctrine* may provide a referent for the design criteria of novel weapons, as well as defining the appropriate functions for military services and commands. The negotiation of roles and missions *treaties* provides a means of revising the division

---

[33] See William T. R. Fox, "Frederick Sherwood Dunn and the American Study of International Relations," *World Politics*, XV (October, 1962), 6.

of labor among the services, ameliorating conflicts among them, and redirecting their weapons development efforts. The *centralization* of decision-making authority over research and development programs may promise the elimination of waste, unnecessary duplication, hazardous delays, and bureaucratic inefficiency. More and better *analysis* may serve as a helpful antidote to precipitate or ill-considered decisions.

Each of these methods of procedural control was utilized to a greater or lesser extent in the course of the Thor-Jupiter controversy. What does the experience of this case suggest regarding their relative merits in containing service rivalries within manageable limits while maximizing the technological yield of project competition among them?

A NOTE ON MATERIALS

This study is the product of a systematic review of published materials bearing upon the U.S. missile programs in the 1950s. Investigations into those programs conducted by Congressional committees and Executive agencies constitute the primary materials out of which this case study was fashioned. Especially useful were: the Airpower hearings conducted by a subcommittee of the Senate Armed Services Committee in 1956; [34] the inquiry into the satellite and missile programs undertaken by the Preparedness Investigation Subcommittee of the Senate Armed Services Committee in 1957–1958; [35] the probe into national defense missiles conducted by the House Committee on Armed Services in 1958; [36] and the examination of the organization and management of the space and missile programs taken up by the House Committee on Government Operations in 1959.[37] In addition, numerous reports, committee prints, the

[34] U.S. Senate, Committee on Armed Services, *Hearings, Study of Airpower,* 84th Cong., 2nd Sess., 1956.

[35] U.S. Senate, Committee on Armed Services, *Hearings, Inquiry into Satellite and Missile Programs,* 85th Cong., 2nd Sess., 1957–1958.

[36] Investigation of National Defense Missiles, 85th Cong., 2nd Sess., 1958.

[37] U.S. House of Representatives, Committee on Government Opera-

memoirs of leading participants, interviews with some of the principals, and books and articles dealing with the missile programs of the service departments were employed.

This is a study of interservice rivalry. Just as these rivalries served as a spur to technical innovation, they stimulated competitive revelations about the problems and prospects of the various service programs. Such a study was made possible by the welter of claims, counterclaims, indiscreet "leaks," furious public relations campaigns, and frequently conflicting testimony of service partisans before Congressional committees eager to exacerbate competitiveness if it would increase their knowledge about (or yield them leverage over) the expensive missile development projects.

Certain limitations are intrinsic in the materials. In the first place, some materials relevant to this case study remain classified; for example, those portions of Congressional hearings conducted in executive session. Nor was it possible to cover all gaps in the materials by interviewing "participant-observers" to these events. At the time the research for this book was initially undertaken, several of the most prominent officials involved in these decisions—above all, former Secretary of Defense Charles Wilson and Deputy Defense Secretary Reuben Robertson—had passed away. Several others were either unavailable for interviews, not inclined to discuss their involvement in the missile programs with candor, or unable to reconstruct the events recounted here in sufficient detail as to be helpful. Needless to add, some interviews proved immensely helpful in supplementing information derived from published sources. Thus, the best that can be claimed for this record of the Thor-Jupiter controversy is that it represents as complete an account as can be compiled from the public record.

Secondly, it is important to keep in mind the fact that much of the evidence cited below was the product of a cross-examination of Defense Department officials and representatives of the

_____

tions, *Hearings, Organization and Management of Missile Programs,* 86th Cong., 1st Sess., 1959.

services by Congressional committees. Such testimony probably overemphasizes the competitiveness of the services without doing full justice to the cooperation which characterizes their relations in many endeavors.

Thirdly, this situation of "advocacy by adversaries" before Congressional committees posed obvious incentives to the services to present as united a front as was possible. This tended to obscure the conflicting opinions and interests of individuals within each service department. Likewise, this situation encouraged civilian and military officials alike to rationalize the most arbitrary and whimsical decisions as the consequences of logical processes of management, or rigorous analysis of the alternatives.

Fourthly, because the record of the Thor-Jupiter controversy is not entirely available to the researcher at this time, it has been necessary to orient the analysis toward questions which permit answers. It is not possible to evaluate the precise financial costs or technological benefits of the Thor-Jupiter controversy. One can merely cite "ball park" figures for those costs and record some of the apparent benefits. If one cannot describe completely the factors influencing the important decisions relating to IRBM development, production, and deployment, it is possible to generate and illuminate hypotheses regarding the dynamics of interservice rivalries, the efficacy of various methods of procedural control for disciplining such competition, and the extent to which these features of interservice competition compromise the closed politics of weapons innovation and enhance or detract from the rationality of weapons decisions.

Finally, it must be acknowledged that there are limits intrinsic in the case study method. The purpose of this analysis, as in any such study, is not to prove anything, but rather to illustrate the usefulness of certain hypotheses as they bear upon a significant problem. There is obviously the danger of imposing a neatness upon the process of decision making which is misleading and highly artificial. As one historian who had the experience of close proximity to an incumbent president has noted,

"The historian tends in retrospect to make the processes of decision far more tidy and rational than they are: to assume that people have fixed positions and represent fixed interests and to impose a pattern on what is actually a swirl if not a chaos." [38] Despite these shortcomings, however, this case study may still increase the fund of data on national security policy while shedding further light on the relationship between interservice rivalry and weapons innovation.

[38] Henry Brandon, "Schlesinger at the White House," *Harper's Magazine*, CCXXIX (July, 1964), 56.

(2) INCENTIVES
FOR INNOVATION

In 1952–1953, the hydrogen bomb tests conducted in the Pacific confirmed the fact that a quantum jump in the destructive force of military weaponry had been achieved. This development made long-range ballistic rockets a vastly intriguing and potentially efficient method of delivering thermonuclear warheads to distant enemy targets in the event of general war. Thus technological advance disclosed a practical use for long-range missiles which seemed to warrant the massive expenditures which development and production would entail. Meanwhile, the elaboration of the Eisenhower Administration's New Look military doctrine, with its emphasis upon strategic retaliation and its relative downgrading of other conventional capabilities, induced an intense preoccupation by all of the services with weapons which permitted access to this high priority mission. Finally, the policy making system and the methods of management which emerged in the Pentagon under the leadership of Secretary of Defense Charles Wilson were permissive of vigorous competition among the Army, Air Force, and Navy for the right to develop qualitatively similar intermediate-range ballistic missiles. It is the purpose of this chapter to analyze these technological, strategic, and organizational sources of service rivalry in the innovation of long-range missile delivery systems.

LONG-RANGE MISSILE PROGRAMS TO 1953

The American ICBMs and IRBMs are the lineal descendants of ballistic rockets developed by German missile scientists and engineers during World War II.[1] Despite the marginal value of these rockets to the German war effort,[2] the Peenemunde rocket experts achieved an extraordinary record of technological breakthroughs. In addition to the development of Operational V-1 and V-2 rockets, they laid the scientific and engineering foundations for future improvements in the range, performance, and reliability of such missiles. Their plans even included the development of a multistage rocket of transoceanic range.

At war's end, Americans and Russians alike demonstrated considerable interest in the technical exploits of the German missile scientists. The U.S. Army Ordnance Technical Intelligence Branch in Europe, under the command of Colonel H. N. Toftoy and Major J. P. Hamill, quickly confiscated enough parts from the underground Nordhausen rocket fabricating plant for the assembly and test firing of one hundred V-2

[1] For a detailed account of the German wartime efforts, see Walter Dornberger, *V-2* (New York, Ballantine, 1954). Impressive theoretical and experimental work on liquid-fuel ballistic rockets had been independently carried out by Robert Goddard in the United States. It received, however, little support and elicited little interest from the War Department. The American military was not without men of prescience, however, as James R. Randolph predicted in the January, 1930, issue of *Ordnance,* the future feasibility and likely utilization of ultralong-range bombardment rockets. George C. Reinhardt and William Kintner, *The Haphazard Years* (New York, Doubleday & Co., Inc., 1960), p. 160.

[2] The actual military value of both the V-2 and V-1 lay largely in the realm of psychological strategy. Spectacular as was the technological achievement apparent in the V-2, its accuracy was unpredictable, its reliability low, and its payload small. Moreover, as Joseph Angel observed, "The weapon had been committed to battle too late, its military effectiveness was more limited than had been anticipated, and reliable intelligence reports indicated that the Germans had not produced sufficient quantities of the weapon to make it a long-continuing danger of great significance." See his "Guided Missiles Could Have Won," in Eugene M. Emme (Ed.), *The Impact of Air Power* (New York, Van Nostrand Company, Inc., 1959), p. 265.

rockets.[3] One hundred and twenty-seven carefully selected scientists, engineers, and technicians were also brought to the United States to constitute the nucleus of an Army "in-house" technical capability in the field of ballistic missilery.[4]

After the Soviet Union's initial space triumphs, Dr. Werner von Braun asserted that the United States might easily have developed an initial ICBM capability in the early 1950s had a vigorous research program been undertaken in 1945 and pressed with the relentlessness of the Manhattan Project.[5] Under prevailing postwar conditions, however, this was impossible. The Army had neither the requirement nor the funds for such a program. Consequently, the former Peenemunde group of rocket experts occupied themselves at Fort Bliss, Texas, translating and sorting documents, assisting in the test firing of V-2s at the White Sands Proving Grounds, developing telemetry and data reduction processes for high altitude research probes, and making themselves available for consultations with Air Force, Navy, and industrial contractor personnel interested in missile technology.[6]

The Army Air Corps, the direct antecedent of the U.S. Air Force, initially displayed only sporadic interest in long-range surface-to-surface ballistic rockets. In a pamphlet published shortly after World War II, Theodore von Karman surveyed the implications of new technology for the future of air power. He concluded that substantial advances in the state of the art would have to be made before ballistic missile development

[3] Major General H. N. Toftoy (Ret.), Correspondence to the author, August 10, 1963.

[4] The Russians were equally interested in the Peenemunde complex. Less fortunate than the Americans in the acquisition of outstanding missile scientists and engineers, they captured many production experts, V-2 components, and blueprints of existing and projected missiles. By 1947, assisted by hundreds of German engineers, technicians, and workers, the Russians were producing V-2's in their own factories at a rate comparable to the Peenemunde level of 1944. See G. A. Tokaty, "Soviet Rocket Technology." in Eugene M. Emme (ed.), *The History of Rocket Technology* (Detroit, Wayne State University Press, 1964), pp. 271–84.

[5] "The Seer of Space," *Life*, XLIII (November 18, 1957), 136.

[6] Major General H. N. Toftoy, Correspondence, August 10, 1963.

would become very promising.[7] Although his estimate was vastly more encouraging than that of Vannevar Bush,[8] his report reflected no genuine sense of urgency about such developments.

In the spring of 1946 the Consolidated Vultee Aircraft Corporation did receive a modest contract (MX-774) to explore the theoretical possibilities and design problems of a mammoth, liquid-fueled, multistaged, intercontinental ballistic missile.[9] Conditions were not favorable for such a radical innovation, however, and funds for the project were precipitately curtailed during the economy drive of mid-1947.[10] Before the termination of the Convair contract, construction of several prototype models had begun. Three were eventually completed and test fired. Although the tests did not yield dramatic results, they did confirm the fact that significant advances had been achieved in the reduction of structural weights of the airframe, the development of multistaged rockets, the introduction of gimballing engines for improved guidance and stability, and the feasibility of separating reentry bodies.[11] Impressive as these advances were, the projected accuracies at intercontinental ranges, the enormous thrust requirements demanded to power such vast loads of liquid fuel, and the unwieldy and inefficient warheads then

[7] Von Karman's appraisal was included in a paper entitled "Where We Stand," later published under the title *Toward New Horizons*. For a detailed history of Air Force efforts to develop ballistic missiles, see Ernest Schwiebert, *A History of the U.S. Air Force Ballistic Missiles* (New York, Frederick A. Praeger, 1965).

[8] Bush wrote in 1949 of practical intercontinental ballistic rockets as mere "fantasy." He clearly felt that in view of their dubious accuracy and their enormous expense they could not for the foreseeable future meet the test of "cost-effectiveness." See his *Modern Arms and Free Men* (New York, Simon & Schuster, 1949), pp. 86–87, 121.

[9] U.S. *Congressional Record,* 85 Cong., 2nd Sess., 1958, CIV, pp. 683–86.

[10] Suspension of work on the ICBM contract was consonant with Air Force priorities in the guided missiles field. "Operational Requirements for Guided Missiles," issued in June, 1947, placed long-range, surface-to-surface missiles behind air defense missiles and rockets which might enhance the striking power of fighters and bombers. Schwiebert, *Air Force Ballistic Missiles,* p. 45.

[11] John C. Chapman, *Atlas: The Story of a Missile* (New York, Harper & Bros., 1960), pp. 32–4.

available made the project appear a dubious technical venture of questionable military value.[12]

By 1949 the Air Force was spending almost $3 billion annually for the development and procurement of manned airplanes; only $39 million supported their sundry missile projects.[13] Those funds were directed exclusively to aerodynamic missiles, a preference which was perhaps related to the fact that such missiles resembled "their familiar aircraft, flew at comparable speeds, and could be controlled by guidance they understood." [14] Aside from certain component development work, the only funds devoted to long-range ballistic rockets between 1947 and 1951 were those modest sums supplied by Convair Corporation out of their private investment budget.[15]

When war in Korea stimulated dramatic increases in defense spending, financial support for the MX-774 project—redesignated MX-1539 and named Atlas—was resumed. Yet the technical difficulties of developing an operationally useful ICBM were still of such a magnitude that the Air Force chose to proceed conservatively with feasibility studies and component development, postponing decisions on the technical specifications of a missile until the horizons of guidance, reentry, and warhead technology were broadened.

Meanwhile, in 1950 the Army team of missile engineers had been transferred to the Huntsville Arsenal in Huntsville, Alabama. Early in 1951 they began design work on a tactical ballistic missile for the Army. While no range restrictions were

[12] When Air Force scientists sought to reorient the MX-774 project as a high-altitude research vehicle, the objections of the Research and Development Board toward duplicative projects—a thoroughly understandable objection in terms of the limited budgets available to them—forced a technical competition in which the Convair proposal was overruled in favor of the Navy's Viking program. The Viking was a high altitude sounding rocket developed jointly by the Naval Research Laboratory and Martin Company of Baltimore. It later became the first stage booster rocket for the Navy Vanguard satellite project. See Milton W. Rosen, *The Viking Rocket* (New York, Harper & Bros., 1955).

[13] Paul Jacobs, "Pilots, Missilemen, and Robots," *The Reporter,* XVIII (February 6, 1958), 15.

[14] Schwiebert, *Air Force Ballistic Missiles,* p. 56.

[15] *Congressional Record,* CIV, 1958, p. 683.

imposed on the Army's efforts, roles and mission assignments were clarified somewhat on March 15, 1950, when the Joint Chiefs of Staff recommended exclusive Air Force jurisdiction over long-range strategic missiles. This assignment was confirmed on March 21 by Secretary of Defense Louis Johnson.[16]

More significantly, the combination of the Russian detonation of an atomic weapon in 1949, and the demonstration of their hostile intentions in Korea a year later precipitated deliberations which ultimately led to the development by the United States of the hydrogen bomb.[17] Subsequently, light, high-yield thermonuclear warheads would be available and would transform even relatively inaccurate ballistic missiles into efficient strategic weapons. Nonetheless, at the time of President Eisenhower's inauguration, no stated requirement for the ICBM existed, missile technology was primitive, a missile industry existed only in embryo form, and no service had committed itself to the acquisition of such a weapon.[18]

THE NEW LOOK AND THE ARMY

The intensity of Army interest in the Jupiter IRBM project and its subsequent resentment when the Air Force was assigned responsibility for its deployment were directly related to the Eisenhower Administration's New Look military policy. That policy represented an adjustment of the American military posture to the prospect of protracted cold war. It constituted a

[16] U.S. Congress, House, Committee on Science and Astronautics, *A Chronology of Missile and Astronautic Events*, 87th Cong., 1st Sess., p. 14.

[17] For a detailed discussion of the factors bearing on those deliberations, see Warner R. Schilling, "The H-Bomb Decision: How to Decide Without Actually Choosing," *Political Science Quarterly*, LXXVI, 24–26.

[18] Actually, from 1945 to 1953 the three services initiated 114 separate missile projects. By the end of 1953, however, only 25 survived as hardware projects, while 9 were being sustained as study contracts. Interest in ballistic missiles was persistent, yet erratic, and the combination of budgetary constraints, the preoccupation with the unification struggle, the energy channeled into the creation of the Strategic Air Command, and misleading intelligence on Soviet efforts in the missile field produced a fragmented, leisurely, and uninspired program. See Trevor Gardner, "How We Fell Behind in Guided Missiles," *The Airpower Historian*, Vol. V, No. 1 (January, 1958), 3–13.

considerable shift in both *preparedness* and *declaratory* policy.
President Eisenhower later described it as "first, a reallocation
of resources among the five categories of forces, [nuclear retaliatory or strike forces, forces deployed overseas, forces to keep the
sea lanes open in the event of emergency, forces to protect the
United States from air attack, reserve forces], and second, the
placing of greater emphasis than formerly on the deterrent and
destructive power of improved nuclear weapons, better means
of delivery, and effective air-defense units." [19] Such a policy
would capitalize on the clear preponderance of the United
States in nuclear weapons and the means for their delivery. It
was consonant with the conviction that the threat to American
security was both economic and military; above all, it would
establish a viable level of preparedness that could be sustained
over the long haul. Deterrence, as Glenn Snyder has suggested,
may be enforced either by denial or punishment.[20] Emphasis
upon denial tends to lead to the maintenance of surface forces
capable of preventing an enemy from achieving his territorial
objectives. Emphasis upon punishment, on the other hand,
tends to lead to the procurement of strategic nuclear air power
sufficient to manipulate an enemy's will to fight by promising
unacceptable costs. The New Look was a clear and unmistakable victory for the advocates of deterrence through nuclear
retaliation.[21]

Initially the New Look policy enjoyed a very broad base of
public support, since the underlying premises of that doctrine
were congenial to many widely shared and deeply felt perspectives of the American people.[22] The reliance upon atomic air

[19] Eisenhower, *Mandate for Change,* p. 451.

[20] See Glenn H. Snyder, *Deterrence by Denial and Punishment* (Research Monograph No. 1, Center of International Studies, Princeton University, 1959).

[21] To be sure, a strategy of deterrence was implicit in the American
military posture from 1945 on. The novelty of the New Look lay in the
magnitude of the threats invoked and the geographic scope of their possible application.

[22] For an account of the innovation of the New Look strategic doctrine,
see Glenn H. Snyder, "The 'New Look' of 1953," in Warner R. Schilling,
Paul Y. Hammond, and Glenn H. Snyder, *Strategy, Politics, and Defense
Budgets,* pp. 379–524.

power for retaliatory purposes was consistent with the desire for economies in defense spending and the conscious effort to limit outlays to only the highest priority missions. The promise of interventions "at times and places of our own choosing" implied a reassertion of American initiative. In offering a plausible deterrent to surprise attack, the New Look perhaps alleviated fears deeply rooted in the experience of Pearl Harbor. Certainly a strategy of retaliation neatly accommodated the instincts of a people inclined to engage in war as a punitive crusade rather than to employ military instruments in quest of limited and attainable political objectives.[23]

Since one or another feature of the New Look doctrine evoked the sympathy and support of various liberals *and* conservatives, the "security conscious" *and* the "solvency conscious," internationalists *and* isolationists, the Army, for whom it contained ominous implications, was virtually alone in expressing opposition. Their resistance was based upon reservations toward the policy's assumptions, resentment against its mode of adoption, and recognition of its potentially disastrous consequences for Army programs, budgets, and morale.

The assumptions of the New Look appeared especially vulnerable to Army strategists.[24] A disproportionate reliance upon nuclear deterrence could scarcely appeal to those who bore the responsibility for protecting American security interests should deterrence fail. Framed in the aftermath of the Korean War, it appeared to be a "one weapon strategy" portending a drastic deemphasis upon land, naval, and tactical air power. Army strategists were convinced that the assumption that all wars could be

[23] For an analysis of the American "civilian mind" which is much in evidence in various facets of the New Look doctrine, see William T. R. Fox, "Representativeness vs. Efficiency: Dual Problem of Civil-Military Relations," *Political Science Quarterly,* LXXVI (June, 1961), 354–66.

[24] Army reactions to the New Look doctrine were vigorously expressed in the writings of several eminent Army officers in the late 1950s. See, for example, General Matthew Ridgway, *Soldier* (New York, Harper & Bros., 1956); General Maxwell Taylor, *The Uncertain Trumpet* (New York, Harper & Bros., 1959); and James M. Gavin, *War and Peace in the Space Age* (New York, Harper & Bros., 1958). Their views and those of like-minded officers were regularly published in the *U.S. Army Combat Forces Journal,* especially from 1954 to 1956.

deterred by a single implement of destruction was manifestly belied by the experience of Korea.

Army partisans also found the emphasis upon financial solvency disturbing. Stability of fiscal support was much to be preferred to the "feast-famine" cycle of the past. Still they found it difficult to reconcile sharp reductions in the overall level of defense spending with the evident expansion in American mutual defense commitments undertaken by Secretary of State John Foster Dulles. In the growing imbalance between foreign policy commitments and the power to support them, they discerned diplomatic insolvency. They feared that overemphasis upon stabilizing defense expenditures for the long haul would bring a loss of sensitivity to shorter range dangers.

The manpower policies implicit in the New Look similarly appeared to be based upon dubious assumptions.[25] The new strategy represented an attempt to substitute technology for manpower. It sought to exploit what was thought to be the West's comparative advantage. Where cutbacks in personnel were called for, they would be offset by reorganization and modernization of the reserve program in which Secretary of Defense Wilson placed great faith. But pilot studies undertaken by Army staff planners suggested that tactical nuclear war would require more, rather than less, manpower. Furthermore, since the wars of the future would be struggles among elite troops and genuine professionals, reserve forces appeared irrelevant to their needs, and a needless drain on their budget.

So strong were these reservations that the Army Chief of Staff, General Matthew B. Ridgway, was prepared to acquiesce in the major premises of the New Look, even for tentative planning purposes, only on condition that the optimistic foreign policy assumptions upon which they were based be kept continuously under review and remain valid. Ridgway's provisional approval was interpreted by Secretary Wilson, however, as unequivocal agreement. Subsequent developments confirmed the Chief of

[25] For a critique of Secretary of Defense Wilson's manpower policies, see Samuel P. Huntington, "Men at Arms?" *Air Force and Space Digest,* XLIII (March, 1960), 46–53. See also Ridgway, *Soldier,* pp. 290–91.

Staff's suspicion that those assumptions had been excessively sanguine, but this did not ease the task of revising programs based upon them.[26]

To make matters worse, the President was disposed to consider public expressions of dissent from official policy as special-interest pleading. Implementation of the New Look required a greater subservience of the military command to civil policies and politics.[27] Public expressions of skepticism from the Chiefs were clearly not welcomed by the White House. Unexpressed grievances regarding both the *content* of policy and the *method* of policy making smoldered.

The New Look rejected a posture of balanced forces in favor of a strategy of high priorities. Resources were available for only the most essential military tasks. It was the definition of essential that the Army found disturbing. Graduated deterrence and limited war strategies, appropriate in their view to the post-Korea situation, and in which they enjoyed significant roles, were rejected. Emphasis upon strategic air power left them undernourished in the continuing scramble for scarce funds. The impact of the New Look upon Army programs is evident from the following figures. In the budget for the 1954 fiscal year, the first prepared by the Eisenhower Administration, the Army absorbed 76 per cent of the overall decrease in spending.[28] At the same time General Ridgway was told to reduce uniformed troops from 1,500,000 to 1,000,000 by mid-1956. The Army budget declined from a postwar high of $21.4 billion in 1952 to $7.1 billion in the 1955 fiscal year.[29] The budgetary implications of the New Look were especially disturbing to the Army since not only was their base budget figure reduced from Korean War levels, but they no longer were to obtain what they had come to consider their *fair share* of the defense budget.[30]

Within the framework of diminishing resources, faltering

[26] Snyder, "The 'New Look' of 1953," p. 443.

[27] Walter Millis, *Arms and the State* (New York, The Twentieth Century Fund, Inc., 1958), p. 378.

[28] Ridgway, *Soldier*, p. 273.   [29] Ibid, p. 288.

[30] See Aaron Wildavsky, *The Politics of the Budgetary Process* (Boston, Little, Brown and Company, 1964), p. 17.

morale, and declining responsibilities, some Army planners became convinced that their future as an important independent combat force depended upon their success in acquiring tactical and air defense missiles and major responsibilities in outer space. Yet the priorities of the New Look made it difficult for the Army to obtain the requisite research and development funds for such ambitious programs.

One of the great ironies of the New Look was the implication of fiscal austerity for military research and development. Geared to the long haul, and relying upon American technological supremacy, the logical corollary should have been a heavy increase in the proportion of funds directed toward research and development projects. Such an emphasis could be sustained within the framework of stable or declining military budgets only if the top civilian leaders in the Pentagon fostered such priorities and created an atmosphere sympathetic to them.

Secretary of Defense Wilson's industrial experience, however, had not given him a research orientation. Budgetary allocations for research and development did not substantially increase. On the contrary, their stability veiled a subtle decline in fiscal support. Maintenance and operations expenses of the research and development agencies formerly supported by other funds were now assimilated into the research and development budgets.[31] Inflation further diminished the real value of their allocations. Research and development money was most readily available, moreover, for projects which promised a payoff in the form of

[31] As General Gavin explained the problem to the Senate Special Preparedness Investigation Subcommittee, "We have gone along on a steady level of effort, we have absorbed operation and management costs and other costs that in effect have reduced steadily the amounts going into research and development." U.S., Congress, Senate, Committee on Armed Services, *Hearings, Inquiry into Satellite and Missile Programs,* 85th Cong., 2nd Sess., 1957–1958, p. 259. (Hereafter referred to as *Satellite and Missile Program Hearings.*) Army complaints were echoed by Air Force representatives as well. See, for example, the testimony of General Donald A. Putt of the Air Research and Development Command, in U.S. Congress, Senate, Committee on Armed Services, *Hearings, Study of Airpower,* 84th Cong., 2nd Sess., 1956, p. 670. (Hereafter referred to as *Airpower Hearings.*)

hardware in the not too distant future. At this point the quest for knowledge confronted the quest for budgets, doctrine, and roles and missions.

After World War II, the gamesmanship of budgetary infighting was gradually transformed. Traditionally, the debates focused upon numbers. Typical slogans were the "Two ocean Navy" or the "70 group Air Force." As the pace of technical change quickened, quality became the chief currency of competition. The service which mastered the most advanced technologies could expect corresponding rewards when funds were distributed. In the mid-1950s, the major new technology was guided missile delivery systems. It was here that the battle for budgets would be won or lost.

To relate the predicament of the Army simply to their declining fortunes in the scramble for funds, however, would be rather misleading. They were concerned about more than their own institutional interests. Their actions reflected anxious reservations toward prevailing military policy. Moreover, the consequences of fiscal austerity were the more pronounced in view of the fact that Army leaders were simultaneously producing their own doctrinal New Look containing an ambitious reassessment of their matériel requirements.

THE ARMY NEW LOOK

The prospect of "nuclear plenty" occasioned a rethinking by Army staff planners of the tactical possibilities of nuclear weaponry. Hitherto, most had simply assumed that the limited stockpile of fissionable materials precluded their use for other than strategic targets.[32] Others, aware that the B-29 had had to be

---

[32] Gavin, *War and Peace in the Space Age,* p. 112. Indeed, so secret was the information on the atomic weapons stockpile that early in 1947, Commissioner Lewis Strauss of the Atomic Energy Commission discovered that James Forrestal, Secretary of the Navy, whose task it was to instruct the President on numbers of atomic bombs to be produced, had not been informed of the size of the existing stockpile and their rate of production. The Chief of Naval Operations and the Secretary of War were equally uninformed. Subsequently, Admirals Ramsey, Sherman, Nimitz, and Secretary Forrestal were briefed by Rear Admiral Parsons, the only Navy

redesigned to accommodate the early atomic bombs, assumed that they were too unwieldy for tactical use.

Preoccupied with their own struggles over Universal Military Training, the Army did not initiate any major jurisdictional conflict with the Air Force over control of the stockpile of fissionable materials. This did not mean, to be sure, that all leading officers were insensitive to the battlefield consequences of the new technology. As early as 1947, those who witnessed the Bikini tests were persuaded that the amphibious invasion had been outdated, and that Army tactics would have to be revised in light of the possibility of a tactical use of atomic weapons.[33] Among officers like James M. Gavin, Maxwell Taylor, and Matthew Ridgway, the potentialities of air mobility employed in conjunction with tactical nuclear strikes began to be discussed.[34] They gradually acquired valuable support from the scientific community, especially from those who rejected what they considered an overemphasis upon the strategic offensive.[35] In 1951, the Army bid successfully for the atomic cannon, a weapon already obsolescent and unsuited for their tactical needs, yet a glamour implement, and one which enhanced their proprietary access to fissionable materials.[36]

---

officer in Washington possessing such information. Lewis L. Strauss, *Men and Decisions* (New York, Doubleday & Co., Inc., 1962) , p. 264.

[33] Gavin, *War and Peace in the Space Age*, p. 112.

[34] Gavin was assigned to the Weapon Systems Evaluation Group in March, 1949, and spent the summer studying possible tactical employment of nuclear weapons. In his report, he recommended a reevaluation of the national policy of assigning all fissionable material to strategic uses. That portion of his report, however, was stricken from the final copy. In the earliest plans drawn up for European defense, atomic weapons were limited to several hundred for SAC, while those assigned to tactical objectives in Europe were "a grudging handful." *Ibid.*, p. 129.

[35] Among the scientists engaged on Project Vista—undertaken at the California Institute of Technology early in 1951 under the joint sponsorship of the Army, Navy, and Air Force, and directed to study both ground and air tactical nuclear warfare—there was considerable support for Army planes to use atomic weapons for tactical purposes. Charles J. V. Murphy, "Hidden Struggle for the H-Bomb," *Fortune*, XLVII (May, 1953) , 109.

[36] Henry A. Kissinger, *Nuclear Weapons and Foreign Policy* (New York, Doubleday & Co., Inc., 1957) , p. 233.

The reappraisal of Army problems and requirements in the nuclear age began in earnest under the auspices of Chief of Staff Matthew Ridgway in late 1953. Early in January, 1954, Lieutenant General James M. Gavin, one of the most original and imaginative Army Strategists, joined G-3 as Assistant Chief of Staff of Plans and Operations. Gavin had begun analyzing problems of tactical mobility prior to World War II. More recently he had been concerned with problems of European defense arising out of the use of tactical nuclear weapons. Encouraged by General Ridgway,[37] he now produced a description of the battlefield of the future, which would necessitate radical changes in both Army doctrine and matériel.

He anticipated a battlefield of great depth; a war of dynamic tempo; and the need for weapons of unprecedented range, accuracy, and firepower.[38] In order to survive, military units would have to be capable of instantaneous dispersal and reconcentration in response to the tactical situation. A premium would thus be placed upon mobile and self-sufficient battlefield units. Aerial and ground maneuvers would have to be integrated to an unprecedented degree. Negotiations for interdiction strikes would pose intolerable delays when the enemy was equipped with nuclear weapons. Coherent improvisation in such a fluid environment would also require major improvements in command, control, and communication arrangements within the Army.

Army leaders were by no means uniformly concerned with the problems of tactical nuclear warfare. The experiences of Korea showed that a serious preoccupation with the tactical and logistic problems of limited conventional war was imperative.

[37] Ridgway, *Soldier,* pp. 297–98.
[38] For descriptions of the battlefield of the future, and estimates of the Army's requirements to survive in it, see Gen. Matthew B. Ridgway, "An Army on its Toes," *Army* (December, 1954), 10–11; Gavin, *War and Peace in the Space Age,* p. 138; Gavin's testimony in Senate Committee on Armed Services, *Airpower Hearings, 1956,* pp. 809–11; Gen. Maxwell Taylor, "The Changing Army," *Army* (October, 1955), 10; and Theodore H. White, "The Atomic Battlefield: Conversation with a Soldier," *The Reporter,* XII (February 10, 1955), 29–32.

Those whose primary tasks were related to defense against such limited, nonatomic challenges were apprehensive lest the Army succumb to the same one weapon strategy of which they accused the Air Force.[39]

General Maxwell Taylor, who succeeded Ridgway as Chief of Staff in 1955, reconciled such differences by calling for an Army with a dual capability: "This dual requirement for the big war and the small war means that we must constantly develop two fundamental capabilities: firepower and mobility." [40]

Taylor's statement aroused some dissent from Army officers exclusively concerned with one or the other capability. It also set the service on a collision course with the Air Force. Mobility was to be improved through emphasis on Sky Cavalry and greater procurement of tactical assault and transport airlift. Improvements in firepower were sought through a vigorous development program for surface-to-surface missiles. The former clashed with Air Force procurement priorities for strategic delivery systems and air defense interceptors; the latter constituted an implicit assault on Air Force roles and missions and was interpreted as a brazen attempt to slice into the nuclear stockpile.

That Army leaders sought to redefine their tasks in ways which enhanced their future prospects is to be understood more as a tactic of organizational survival than an exercise in empire building. Nor was their rivalry with the Air Force a product of simple personal egotism. Army leaders, like their counterparts in the other services, were engaging in the perfectly legitimate effort to defend those values which it was their mandate to safeguard. It could be argued, to be sure, that the growing preoccupation with long-range ballistic missiles diverted the Army from their traditional responsibilities in limited war and conventional combat for which they possessed a distinctive competence. The Chief of Staff and his advisers more likely formulated these doctrinal innovations in order to adjust Army capabilities to an age of nuclear plenty and to defend the in-

[39] See, for example, Lt. Col. M. L. Crosthwaite, "The True Deterrent," *Army* (August, 1955), 46–47.
[40] Taylor, "An Army on Its Toes," *Army* (December, 1954), 10.

tegrity of the Army at a time when the policy environment was in flux and the future significance of the Army's traditional contributions to national defense were being severely questioned.

It seems apparent, in any event, that interservice competition encouraged an intense preoccupation with the revision and explication of service doctrine. The Air Force published a comprehensive statement of the United States Air Force Basic Doctrine in 1953. The Army replied in its 1955 edition of Field Manual 100-5, which included a statement later elaborated in a 65-page pamphlet entitled, "A Guide to Army Philosophy." The Army statement was probably more than a mere rejoinder to the earlier Air Force formulation. A service down on its luck is as likely to turn to ideology as a new and crusading group needing intellectual justification for its existence. As Philip Selznik has observed: "A well-formulated doctrine is remarkably handy for boosting internal morale, communicating the bases for decisions, and rebuffing outside claims and criticisms." [41]

THE ARMY AND THE QUESTION OF
ROLES AND MISSIONS

The functional allocation of military roles and missions has been a focal point of service rivalry since the Unification Act of 1947. This appears inevitable when three and a half proud and powerful services vie for responsibility, influence, and status within a single strategy which is either the product of reluctant compromise among the Chiefs of Staff or a concept imposed by the Chairman of the JCS and his civilian superior upon acquiescent or dissenting colleagues.

The basic assignment of roles and missions was painstakingly negotiated at Key West and Newport in 1947.[42] Needless to say, those agreements were not immune from criticism; nor did

[41] Philip Selznick, *Leadership in Administration* (Evanston, Row, Peterson and Co., 1957), p. 14.

[42] See Walter Millis (ed.), *The Forrestal Diaries* (New York, Viking Press, 1951), pp. 169, 225, 392, 464, 476, and *passim*. See also Arnold A. Rogow, *James Forrestal, A Study of Personality, Politics, and Policy* (New York, Macmillan Co., 1963), pp. 286–88.

they permanently settle service controversies. Service functions were divided at Key West roughly according to the maxim: "Armies walk, navies sail, and air forces fly." Yet this expressed an arbitrary fragmentation of responsibilities on the basis of weapons specifications. Ironically, this came at the very moment when war was becoming both more complex and more inter-related.

Since the Key West Agreement encouraged the conviction that weapons would be assigned according to combat medium rather than combat mission, the services considered their primary and overriding mission to be the destruction and defeat of their enemy counterparts. This stimulated service hopes for self-sufficiency in weapons, supporting organizations, and intelligence services, as well as a correlative aspiration for autonomy in their formulations of military doctrine.

If the Navy seemed less apprehensive about their future than the Army, this was to some extent due to the fact that they had already carved out a partial responsibility for the deterrence of general war, and had acquired at least a subordinate role in the strategic bombing mission. While the Army had been bypassed in the distribution of strategic missions at Key West and Newport, the Navy had gradually obtained access to the atomic stockpile, the right to employ such weapons "to reduce and neutralize the airfields from which enemy aircraft may be sortying to attack the fleet," and an Air Force acknowledgement of their right to participate in any all-out air campaign. In return, the Navy recognized the Air Force's "dominant interest" in the atomic bomb. They also conceded that they were not to seek to build a Strategic Air Command of their own.[43]

Ultimately, the difficulties over roles and missions derived from the fact that the potential theaters and forms of warfare were proliferating at the very time when American military policy was being heavily weighted in the direction of the single functional mission of strategic deterrence. Strategic delivery systems would soon be available with sufficient range and destructive power that they could be launched from land, sea, or air

[43] Millis (ed.), *Forrestal Diaries*, pp. 392, 464.

with the same devastating effect. Service rivalries for the privi-
lege of performing that mission inevitably ensued, for to acquire the mission meant budgetary support for the means of its
implementation.[44] A partial consequence of the resulting animosities was the growing distaste for the interdependent relationships maintained for the planning and fighting of tactical or
limited encounters.

ARMY GRIEVANCES

During the mid-1950s many Army leaders began to consider
the costs of unification—that is, the creation of a separate Air
Force and the loss of all but a limited "organic aviation force"
—exorbitant. According to the Key West Agreement, the Air
Force was to furnish close combat and logistical air support to
the Army. This support was to include airlift and resupply of
airborne operations. Performance of this supporting role pre-
supposed the expenditure of funds for the requisite matériel.
The Air Force, however, had a number of claims on its resources. It assigned highest priorities to the Strategic Air Command and Continental Air Defense. As their concentration on
these roles steadily increased, the procurement of tactical assault
and transport aircraft correspondingly decreased.[45] The Army
was not, however, authorized to compensate for Air Force neglect. According to the Pace-Finletter Agreement they were ex-
pressly prohibited from developing or producing any aircraft
with a fixed wing load of more than 5,000 pounds.[46]

[44] For General Maxwell Taylor's commentary on the occasions for interservice rivalry, see his testimony in U.S. Congress, House, Committee on
Armed Services, *Reorganization of the Department of Defense, Hearings,*
85th Cong., 2nd Sess., 1958, p. 6330.

[45] When it was discovered by Congressman Daniel Flood that the Air
Force was diverting scarce funds from transports to luxury accommoda-
tions for Air Force VIPs in a group of DC-6s and Constellations, Army
resentment burst into rage. Douglass Cater and Arthur T. Hadley, "The
Army's Beefs Against the Air Force," *The Reporter,* XIV (June 14,
1956) , 16.

[46] The Pace-Finletter Agreement was a Memorandum of Understanding
between the Chiefs of Staff of the Army and Air Force and signed by their
respective Service Secretaries in November, 1952. It sought to define the
nature of the Army's "organic aviation" by limiting them to planes with

The interdependence created by the Key West and subsequent agreements was contingent for its satisfactory operation on a pattern of reciprocity of claims among the services. The Army's dilemma was that their growing irrelevance to the performance of Air Force strategic offensive and defensive missions left them no leverage with which to collect the Air Force promise to provide close combat support.

As important, too, as the Air Force's lackadaisical procurement efforts for subordinate missions, were the growing indications that the Tactical Air Force was becoming less and less suited for the type of combat support which Army leaders deemed essential in a future limited war. Evidence of this declining sensitivity to Army requirements was to be found in their past performance, present procurement, personnel training, and doctrinal preferences.

Air Force target selection in the Korean War had been highly unsatisfactory to many Army ground commanders.[47] The primary interest of the Air Force had been in keeping enemy airfields unserviceable.[48] This was of less immediate interest to the ground troops. Air Force development programs constantly sought improvements in the speed and range of their tactical craft. From the Army's vantage point, Air Force assault aircraft had extended their speed to the point where they were of diminishing utility for combat support and reconnaissance.[49]

---

a 5,000-pound empty weight, fixed wing load. Either Secretary retained the right to appeal to the Secretary of Defense in order to alter the accord. Senate Committee on Armed Services, *Airpower Hearings, 1956*, pp. 802–03.

[47] Regarding the adequacy of Air Force combat support during the Korean War the Army's position was far from unanimous. Despite persistent criticism, Gen. James Van Fleet, Commander of the Eighth Army, said in 1953 that, on the whole, air support had been quite satisfactory. Alfred Goldbert (ed.), *A History of the United States Air Force 1907–1957.* (New York, Van Nostrand Co., Inc., 1957), p. 118.

[48] For expositions of Air Force tactical air doctrines, considered anathema by the Army, see Brig. Gen. James Ferguson, *Air University Quarterly Review*, VII (Summer, 1954), 29–41; Brig. Gen. Henry P. Viccellio, "Composite Air Strike Force," *Air University Quarterly Review*, IX (Winter, 1956–1957), 27–38.

[49] This point was alluded to in U.S. Congress, Senate, Committee on Foreign Relations, *United States Foreign Policy: Compilation of Studies*

Moreover, as planes, airfields, and fuel storage sites became increasingly vulnerable to enemy air strikes—particularly in simulated tactical nuclear war situations—the Tactical Air Command (TACAIR) became more and more interested in refueling techniques so that planes could be deployed from the rear. This promised to increase the manifold difficulties of close coordination with field commanders.

At one time the Air Force could justly claim that their pilots were well-trained in the dynamics and requirements of both air and ground combat. Many of them, indeed, had been schooled at West Point. As the years passed, many veterans drifted out of the service, and the younger men who replaced them were trained almost exclusively on doctrines of strategic retaliation. This, perhaps, accounts for the Tactical Air Command's growing interest in participating in long-range strategic sorties against the enemy. Such tendencies were naturally anathema to the Army. One officer summed up the anxieties poignantly: "The Army has indeed been grievously hurt in the Unification Act. It has lost control of the ground battle, has become dependent for vital support upon an independent cavalry which is concerned primarily with its own separate objectives." [50]

The Air Force's limited procurement of transport aircraft for tactical and strategic airlift and supply also caused serious concern. When the Korean War broke out, an airlift capability for transporting only two rifle companies and one battery of artillery existed.[51] In 1956 the Military Air Transport Service (MATS) had less than half the planes required to meet Army needs to lift a single division.[52] Yet, in a time of emergency the Army would have to compete with NATO forces and TACAIR

(No. 8, *Developments in Military Technology and Their Impact on United States Strategy and Foreign Policy*), prepared by the Washington Center of Foreign Policy Research, Johns Hopkins University (Washington, U.S. Government Printing Office, 1961), p. 733.

[50] Col. W. B. Bunker, "Why the Army Needs Wings," *Army* (March, 1956), 19.

[51] Gavin, *War and Peace in the Space Age*, p. 122; Edward L. Katzenbach, Jr., "The Military Lessons of Suez," *The Reporter*, XV (November 29, 1956), 11.

[52] Senate Committee on Armed Services, *Airpower Hearings*, 1956, p. 849.

for the C-124s under the administrative control of MATS.

Some were even inclined to blame the aridity of Army tactical doctrine on their prolonged dependence on the Air Force. As one writer put it:

> Most grievous of all has been the effect upon Army thinking. The Army has come to accept the ground battle as bounded by the use of its own weapons systems. The tactical Air Force operations of reconnaissance and ground support, which are as integral to the fight as division artillery, have been lost to Army thinking and planning.[53]

Maxwell Taylor, Chief of Staff of the Army, summed up the accumulated grievances:

> Since 1947, the Army has been dependent upon the Air Force for tactical air support, tactical airlift, and for long-range air transport. Throughout this period the Army has been a dissatisfied customer, feeling that the Air Force has not fully discharged its obligations undertaken at the time of unification.[54]

ARMY EFFORTS TO ESCAPE DEPENDENCY

As their grievances were numerous, they were prepared to explore a variety of avenues of escape from the relationship of unsatisfactory dependency on the Air Force. Those Army leaders who were most concerned with increasing strategic and tactical airlift capabilities in response to peripheral war possibilities sought: (1) a revision of the Pace-Finletter limitations on Army support aircraft; (2) an increase in the magnitude of Army research and development expenditures in the field of assault craft and helicopters; and (3) a transfer of the tactical air support mission from the Air Force to the Navy and Marine Corps.

In their first objective they achieved limited success. In November, 1956, the Pace-Finletter Agreement was slightly liberalized to permit Army production and procurement of fixed wing and rotary wing aircraft with slightly heavier

[53] Bunker, "Why the Army Needs Wings," *Army* (March, 1956), 19.
[54] Taylor, *The Uncertain Trumpet*, p. 168.

weights.[55] Within the context of the Wilson Memorandum such a concession seemed slight compensation. Results were equally modest in the quest for increased research and development expenditures. A slightly accelerated program of funds and the continuing priority upon the strategic deterrence mission posed frustrations.

Proponents of a transfer of the air support mission pointed out the compatibility of Navy doctrine and their established competence in providing air support to marine amphibious operations. Their tradition of familiarity between pilots and the forces they were to support, and their reputation for designing planes in terms of a specific combat mission were also favorable points.[56] By suggesting a transfer to the Navy rather than attempting to usurp the mission themselves, they felt they could win valuable allies and simultaneously disarm anticipated Air Force charges of self-interested empire building. Yet these proposals were never vigorously pressed.

The most promising avenue to independence seemed to lie in a vigorous promotion of developmental efforts in the guided missile field. The reasoning behind this approach was later stated by Maxwell Taylor:

The Air Force, having something which the Army wanted, has been in a position to put a price tag upon cooperation and to insist upon acquiescence in Air Force views on such controversial issues as air ground support procedures, air resupply, and control of air space over the battlefield. As technical improvements in weapons and equipment offered the Army the possibility of escaping from dependence upon the Air Force, the latter has vigorously resisted these efforts and has succeeded in obtaining the support of the Secretary of Defense in imposing limitations on the size and weight of aircraft procured by the Army, on the ranges of Army missiles

[55] See the "Wilson Memorandum Clarifying Roles and Missions," reprinted in U.S. Congress, House, Committee on Government Operations, *Hearings, Organization and Management of Missile Programs,* 86th Cong., 1st Sess., 1959, p. 746. (Hereafter referred to as *Missile Program Hearings.*)

[56] Col. George C. Reinhardt, "Put TACAIR in Navy Blue," *Army Combat Forces Journal* (September, 1954), 21–25. Chief of Staff Ridgway had also expressed interest in relieving the Air Force of their less glamorous roles of assault transport and tactical support. Ridgway, *Soldier,* p. 314.

and on the radius of Army activities in advance of the front line of combat.[57]

Army leaders assumed that the pursuit of novel technology would appeal to those holding the military purse strings, and assist the Army in meeting the requirements of their new doctrine for tactical nuclear warfare. It would also enable them to exploit the talents of a major Army asset—the Huntsville Arsenal Missile Engineers. Incidentally, it provided an outlet for grievances against the Air Force.

The quest for consensus on such a departure was one which required the persuasive efforts of many leading Army officers. General John B. Medaris told his colleagues in an Ordnance Staff Meeting:

> You're fighting a losing game. If you put all your energy and effort into justifying these conventional weapons and ammunition even though I know we need them, I think you are going to get very little money of any kind. It is far easier to justify a budget with the modern items that are popular and I would strongly recommend that you increase the amount you show in the budget for the production of missiles, limiting yourself on the other items to the modest quantities that you know you can get by with. If you increase your demands for guided missiles, I think there is a fair chance you can get a decent budget. Why don't you accentuate the positive and go with what is popular since you cannot get the other stuff anyway? [58]

Salesmanship was called for within the Pentagon as well. There may well have been a relationship between the 1954 de-

---

[57] Taylor, *The Uncertain Trumpet,* pp. 168–69.

[58] General John B. Medaris, *Countdown for Decision* (New York, G. P. Putnam's Sons, 1960), p. 65. Beyond confirming James Schlesinger's judgment that "budgetary allotments have been based on the dominant enthusiasms of military planners," this statement indicates the pervasiveness of political calculations in the formulation of the budget. James R. Schlesinger, "Quantitative Analysis and National Security," *World Politics,* XV, No. 2 (January, 1963), 296. Medaris apparently calculated that the appropriate strategy for maximizing the Army's R&D budget was to adjust to the evident priorities of the Administration. If this adjustment came at the expense of the Army's established priorities, he was simply operating on the basis of Wildavsky's axiom that agencies will "seek to secure their other goals so long as this effort does not result in an overall decrease in income." Wildavsky, *The Politics of the Budgetary Process,* p. 20.

cision by the Chiefs of Staff that the Army be restricted to tactical ballistic missiles, and the increasing discussion in 1954 and 1955 in Army journals of the vast expansion in the tactical combat zone. General Gavin had previously discovered in exercises designed to test the requirements of European defense that "the area held by the infantry had to extend from a depth of about five to ten miles, which characterized World War II deployments, to about one hundred to one hundred fifty miles with reserves further back." [59] Gavin continued:

That suggested the need for the replacement of conventional artillery with missiles, if our firepower was to have adequate range . . . we would need missile ranges adequate to provide continuous fire of tremendous depth that could reach anything in the opposing Soviet Army. . . . A missile many hundreds of miles in range, with an accurate nuclear warhead, and one that was mobile and immediately responsive to the decisions of the ground commander was critically required.[60]

The logic of independence was clear. The Army would require the firepower to reach any weapons that could be employed against them. Missiles with ranges as deep as 1,500 miles could be justified in terms of the Soviet Army's abundant supply of medium-range ballistic missiles.

By deploying guided missiles from the rear of the battlefield area, the vulnerability of the Army's artillery could be reduced at the same time that logistic economies were being achieved. Moreover, superior integration of the air and ground combat arms could be claimed through the elimination of complicated interservice negotiations over target selection and the timing of air strikes.

Reinforcing the requirements of doctrine were the opportunities offered by guided missiles to escape the relationship of dependence, to restore the faith of the rank and file officers in the Army's future, and to break out of the cycle of diminishing budgets and apparently irrelevant missions. Hopes were buoyed by the plausibility of their case for operational control of long-range missiles as well.

After all, were guided missiles not simply a modern form of

---

[59] Gavin, *War and Peace in the Space Age*, p. 137.   [60] *Ibid.*, p. 138.

artillery? Was their Huntsville Arsenal Team not the most competent group of missile scientists and engineers in the country?
Was it not true that guided missiles were *ground*-launched and
did not require skills intrinsic to fliers? As one officer expressed
it: "Why should we throw away a hundred and fifty years of
artillery experience merely to keep the Air Force fat and
happy by handing them a weapon they are not suited either by
training or temperament to use?" [61]

Army hopes rested finally upon the Huntsville Arsenal and
the availability of von Braun's team for a major new project. By
late 1954 they had progressed to the point where the Redstone
tactical ballistic missile was virtually ready to be placed into
production. The primary in-house technical work on the Redstone had been directed toward the development of a reliable
and accurate inertial guidance system. The problems of accuracy and reliability were especially interesting to the German
scientists in the light of their unhappy experiences wth the V-2.
Army doctrine, which imposed stringent accuracy requirements, reinforced their concern.[62] If wars were to be kept
limited, such weapons would have to be capable of discrimi-
nately hitting only tactical targets. Accuracy was all the more
important since the warhead could then be relatively small,
thereby enhancing the possibilities of containing such conflicts.[63]

By early 1955, the results of a breakthrough in inertial guidance accuracies had been incorporated into the Redstone missile. Army missile engineers were in search of new and challeng-
ing opportunities.[64] Lt. General James Gavin, newly appointed
Assistant Chief for Research and Development, was anxious to

[61] Quoted by Harold H. Martin, "Showdown in the Pentagon," *Saturday
Evening Post,* CCXXX (November 9, 1957), 114.
[62] Senate Committee on Armed Services, *Airpower Hearings,* 1956, pp
1310–11.
[63] Charles Donnelly, *The U.S. Guided Missile Program,* p. 26. Com
mittee Print prepared for the Preparedness Investigatory Subcommittee
U.S. Senate Committee on Armed Services, 85th Cong., 2nd Sess., 1958.
[64] House Committee on Government Operations, *Missile Program Hear
ings,* 1959, p. 273.

pursue developmental efforts in rocket propulsion in order to permit range and payload increases in Army missiles of the future. He received little support from the Continental Army Command for such improvements, and they did not set forth new requirements for missiles of greatly increased range.[65] Nevertheless, convinced that a 150,000-pound-thrust engine was technically possible, Gavin toured the West Coast missile industry and discovered that Rocketdyne Corporation engineers were already dreaming of a power plant capable of a 500,000-pound-thrust.[66] On his own initiative, and without a specific requirement, efforts were begun to develop a larger basic engine for Army missiles.[67]

Another preliminary step was taken in late spring of 1955, when General John B. Medaris managed to win the support of the Industrial Division of the Ordnance Branch for the construction at Cape Canaveral of test stands which could take up to 500,000-pound-thrust blast-off.[68] Both of these steps were significant in that they were long lead time items which were important pacing factors for the progress of the missile programs. Neither was justifiable on the basis of existing Army requirements; both were the products of imaginative minds and administrative ingenuity.[69]

[65] Interview with General James M. Gavin, former Assistant Chief of Staff of the Army for Research and Development, August 22, 1963. A *pro forma* requirement for a tactical missile with up to 500-mile range was apparently on the books at the time, and it will be recalled that the initial programmed range of the Redstone was in this vicinity. Interview with Mr. Alvin Waggoner, former Civilian Executive Assistant to the Director of Guided Missiles, July 26, 1965.

[66] Interview with General James M. Gavin, August 22, 1963.

[67] General Gavin also personally authorized a $12 million expenditure for the construction of static test stands which could accommodate such large engines without the approval and apparently without the sympathetic understanding of the Secretary of Defense. Correspondence to the author, July 21, 1965.

[68] Interview with General John B. Medaris, former Commander of the Army Ordnance Missile Command, August 30, 1963.

[69] These actions of Gavin and Medaris appear to have been prudent hedges against an uncertain future rather than "camel's nose" or "coercive deficiency" gambits in the continuing scramble for scarce funds. Both tactics are designed to establish significant "sunk costs" which later can

As the Redstone moved into the production phase, Gavin recommended a proposal to Chief of Staff Ridgway for a $25 million commitment for the development of an intermediate-range ballistic missile.[70] General Ridgway was not sanguine about the likelihood of obtaining approval for such a project and suggested, alternatively, a more modest extension of the Redstone's range from 200 to 500 miles.[71] Further extensions in range might, of course, be contemplated in the future.

Money was doubtless a factor in his decision. He may also have been attempting to meet an existing requirement while averting a premature clash with the Air Force over the hitherto undefined limits of Army tactical missiles. The Joint Chiefs had earlier authorized the Army to develop surface-to-surface missiles for tactical use, without imposing explicit range restrictions. In this connection, Ridgway's preference for a more modest extension in missile capabilities may have grown out of his awareness that acceptance of a new project is more likely if it can be "sold" as a necessary modification of an existing program. As Herman Kahn once put it: "Barring a crisis or an exceptionally 'glamorous' idea, it is usually risky to phrase . . . [a] recommendation as an expansion of an existing program and disastrous to let it look like the initiation of a new program." [72]

The interest of the Huntsville engineers—and Gavin as well—was not limited to an extension in the range of Army striking power. A ballistic missile could as easily be employed to launch a scientific payload as a nuclear warhead. "Furthermore," as General Medaris aptly put it, "the interdependence of these two missions does not end with the use of common hardware; the human experience gained from one field is priceless in the

---

be used to justify further expenditures. See Wildavsky, *The Politics of the Budgetary Process*, p. 111.

[70] Gavin, *War and Peace in the Space Age*, pp. 153–54.

[71] House Committee on Government Operations, *Missile Program Hearings*, 1959, p. 375.

[72] Herman Kahn, *On Thermonuclear War* (Princeton, Princeton University Press, 1960), p. 339.

other." [73] The apparent ambition to gain access to future space missions was doubly inspired by the long-standing aspiration of von Braun to escape the confines of the world's atmosphere, and Gavin's recognition that the next military technological revolution would occur in outer space.[74] Army participation in this revolution would permit them to experiment with dramatic new methods of accomplishing their traditional roles in geodesy, survey, meteorology, intelligence gathering, and space defense.[75] With its "distinctive competence" in land warfare being threatened by technology and prevailing military doctrine, the Army, like a business organization confronted by a shrinking market for its primary products, felt driven to diversify. And as Charles J. V. Murphy commented, "the maneuverings of its planners, who include[d] some of the best minds in the military, to find more dramatic and useful employment for their honored institutions point[ed] up growing anomalies of the existing three-service establishment." [76]

TRIGGERING EVENTS

If the Huntsville team provided the means, and doctrinal revitalization brought the sensitivity to new requirements, and concrete grievances against the Air Force added the disposition

[73] House Committee on Government Operations, *Missile Program Hearings*, 1959, p. 253.

[74] House Committee on Government Operations, *Missile Program Hearings*, 1959, p. 253.

[75] *Ibid.*, It is essential to remember that the interests of the Army and the former Peenemunde rocket engineers were complementary rather than identical. Implicit in all of Dr. von Braun's efforts was the ambition first to put instruments and later men in space. He and his associates persistently sought to exploit and extend the state of the art for the purpose of building hardware which would implement this ambition. See, for example, his early musings on the nature of a national space program in "Baby Space Station," *Colliers* (June 27, 1953), 33. In this context their interest in the Jupiter proposal was self-evidently independent of any military requirements of the Army. See Dornberger, *V-2*, p. 27, for evidence of von Braun's early interest in space exploration.

[76] Charles J. V. Murphy, "Defense: The Revolution Gets Revolutionary," *Fortune*, LIII (May, 1956), 256.

to exploit new technology, three events in 1955 triggered new
Army space and missile proposals and prepared the atmosphere
for their adoption. The most important of these was the completion and distribution of the Killian Report.

The Technological Capabilities Panel was established in the
fall of 1954 under the chairmanship of Dr. James R. Killian.[77]
It was created in response to President Eisenhower's request
that a group of eminent American scientists reappraise the relative offensive and defensive capabilities of the Soviet Union and
the United States in the light of developments in thermonuclear warhead technology recently demonstrated in the second U.S. H-Bomb test at Eniwetok. Their report, dated February 14, 1955, was submitted to the National Security Council.
Since it included a number of urgent recommendations for bolstering American military capabilities, it was sent immediately
on to the Defense Department. There it was scrutinized carefully by the Service Departments which, in turn, stated additional requirements and submitted new requests for funds.[78]

The tone of the Report was one of ominous foreboding.
Among the most significant conclusions was the somber warning that the American lead in air atomic power was seriously
threatened.[79] Latest intelligence information suggested that the
Soviet Union had made spectacular achievements in both the

[77] The Technological Capabilities Panel was created at the direction of
the President by the National Security Council. See Senate Committee on
Armed Services, *Airpower Hearings*, 1956, pp. 554, 1086; Joseph and
Stewart Alsop, *The Reporter's Trade* (New York, Reynal, 1958), p. 276;
and Robert Cutler, *No Time for Rest* (Boston, Little, Brown and Company, 1965), p. 349.

[78] Senate Committee on Armed Services, *Airpower Hearings*, 1956, p.
554.

[79] Alsop, *The Reporter's Trade*, p. 277. It it not entirely clear whether
leading policy-makers concluded that a relative decline in America's air
atomic superiority would significantly diminish its capacity to deter provocative Soviet actions. For example, in August 1956 Secretary of the Air
Force, Donald Quarles, stated his conviction that nuclear war had become
unthinkable for both the United States and the Soviet Union and his
belief that this prospect was "not the result of the relative strength of the
two opposed forces. It is the absolute power in the hands of each." Quoted
in Huntington, *The Common Defense*, p. 101.

development of thermonuclear warhead technology and in missile testing. Extrapolating from these trends, it was feared that American superiority in the strategic balance would be jeopardized by the early 1960s unless extraordinary measures were taken to offset recent Russian advances.

Above all, the Killian Committee stressed the importance of matching Soviet long-range missile capabilities. In this connection, development of an operational intermediate-range ballistic missile disclosed a much greater likelihood of success than the ICBM, which many scientists doubted would be successfully deployed before 1962.[80] The lead time for the IRBM was considered to be shorter, since with more modest range requirements the accuracy parameters could be eased significantly. The IRBM's slower speed outside the atmosphere would also simplify the problems of reentry. Thus while no specific military requirement existed at the time for a missile of precisely 1,500-mile range, a consensus emerged within the circle of influential scientific advisers that a missile with this range could be developed, with a reasonable certainty of success, in time to meet the challenge of new Soviet missile capabilities in the late 1950s and early 1960s.[81] The initiation of projects directed toward early development of both a sea-based and a land-based IRBM was consequently recommended.[82]

The Killian Report strengthened the case for an IRBM capability. The Army's chances of providing it were enhanced in mid-summer by the report of a Department of Defense Technical Advisory Committee which had been created to determine the best method of organizing the efforts of services and suppliers to obtain an operational IRBM.[83] In the course of the

[80] Senate Committee on Armed Services, *Airpower Hearings*, 1956, p. 717.

[81] Interview, Alvin Waggoner, July 26, 1965.

[82] Medaris, *Countdown for Decision*, p. 67. See also Eisenhower, *Mandate for Change*, p. 557.

[83] This Committee was chaired by Deputy Secretary of Defense Reuben Robertson who was then giving most of his time and energy to the organizational and administrative problems of the accelerated missile development program.

52   INCENTIVES FOR INNOVATION

Committee's deliberations, the divergence between Army and Air Force approaches to an IRBM weapon system became manifestly clear. The Air Force's proposals started from the premise that "a lesser range missile would derive from the ICBM if the ICBM were carried to a conclusion." [84] By merely reorienting their component work slightly, they argued, they would be assured of successful development of an IRBM, since the components would have been overdesigned for the less demanding requirements of a shorter-range missile.

Von Braun and other Army engineers took vigorous exception to these Air Force concepts on the basis of upper atmosphere research they had previously conducted at White Sands. They contended that the Air Force design of a thin-skinned, nitrogen-inflated missile weighing little more than the Redstone (75,000 pounds) would not be capable of sustaining the shearing jet winds of the upper atmosphere. They insisted, rather, that the vehicle must have a "rigid, strong structure." [85] Other significant differences of technical approach were to be found in their preferred guidance systems and reentry heating solutions respectively.

From the standpoint of the Robertson Committee members, such divergent opinions as to the most appropriate technical approach to the new weapon system, coming as they did from highly respected members of the scientific and engineering community, reinforced their disposition to authorize a parallel approach to the land-based IRBM system. The urgency of the Killian Report's recommendations confirmed the prudence of such an approach. Thus the Robertson Committee concluded that the IRBM was not strictly a derivative of the ICBM.[86] In view of the new requirement, a separate program was essential.

This decision was congenial to both President Eisenhower

[84] Senate Committee on Armed Services, *Airpower Hearings,* 1956, p. 730.
[85] Correspondence to the author from General Gavin, July 21, 1965.
[86] Senate Committee on Armed Services, *Airpower Hearings,* 1956, p. 730.

and Secretary of Defense Wilson, since they apparently shared the conviction that the Huntsville team could not be excluded from the development program for long-range ballistic missiles without jeopardizing the success of that effort. The President was profoundly influenced, moreover, by the note of urgency in the Killian Report and convinced of the efficacy and significance of an IRBM program. He later expressed his conviction that "the political and psychological impact on the world of the early development of a reliable IRBM would be enormous, while its military value would, for the time being, be practically equal to that of the ICBM." [87]

The sense of urgency was heightened by continuing intelligence reports of Soviet success in firing medium-range ballistic missiles to distances of 900 miles.[88] By mid-1955, informed officials in the Pentagon could deduce that the Russians had liquid-fueled rockets with a thrust of 250,000 pounds, more than adequate for propelling powerful warheads to the major European capitals.[89] Reports such as these prompted the President to order the acceleration of the Atlas, to authorize the Titan backup project, and as of December, 1955, to request monthly progress reports from General Schriever and Secretary Wilson. He sanctioned competitive efforts to obtain an operational IRBM in the shortest possible time and called for intensified activities in the anti-ballistic missile defense field.[90]

Army hopes were further bolstered on July 1, when Wilber Brucker became Secretary of the Army. His energy, ambition, tenacity, and skill in advocacy—derived from a successful career in politics and law—were great assets to the Army during the ensuing years.

[87] Eisenhower, *Mandate for Change,* p. 457.
[88] *Aviation Week* (February 20, 1956), 26. Senator Symington was the first to discuss publicly the Russian medium-range ballistic missile flights. He claimed on a national television broadcast that the Defense Department and the National Security Council had acknowledged Soviet tests of 900 mile-range IRBMs as early as the fall of 1955.
[89] Albert Parry, "Why Should We have Been Surprised?," *The Reporter,* XVII (October 31, 1957), 14.
[90] *Aviation Week* (February 20, 1956), 26.

ARMY PROPOSALS

Prior to November 8, 1955, the Army had not programmed any funds for an IRBM.[91] Clearly this was not indicative of a lack of interest. Gavin's recommendation to Ridgway had been parried; other suggestions, however, quickly followed. Shortly after receiving the Killian Report, the Army submitted a "completely engineered proposal" to the Office of the Secretary of Defense.[92] On June 13, 1955, alternate proposals were submitted for a ballistic missile with a 1,000-mile range.[93] Both were described as tactical missiles which simply extended the range of the Redstone.

Two weeks later another proposal was offered to the Secretary's office. A formal presentation of a proposal for an Army IRBM was made to Secretary Wilson on September 22. Pending a decision by the Secretary, the Army was able to "bootleg" funds authorized for other areas and move ahead on the design. Indeed, by early autumn the engineers were rapidly completing a mock-up of the first model.[94]

Army interest in the IRBM was reinforced by the resentment and frustrations unleashed by the decision of the Stewart Committee, which met on September 9 and voted [7-2] to abandon Project Orbiter, the Army satellite proposal.[95] Not only did this strengthen the Army in the short run by releasing person-

[91] Senate Committee on Armed Services, *Airpower Hearings,* 1956, p. 1312.

[92] Senate Committee on Armed Services, *Satellite and Missile Program Hearings,* 1957–1958, p. 542.

[93] One proposal was for a single stage liquid-fueled rocket; the other was for two liquid-fueled engines in the first stage, with potential range extension through the addition of a second stage. House Committee on Government Operations, *Missile Program Hearings,* 1959, p. 374.

[94] *Ibid.,* pp. 271–272.

[95] The decision of the Stewart Committee was subsequently reviewed by the Department of Defense Policy Committee and was approved. House Committee on Science and Astronautics, *A Chronology of Missile and Astronautic Events,* 1961, p. 23. In addition to leaving the Huntsville Arsenal team without a major space project, the cancellation of Project Orbiter left them with a number of surplus Jupiter-C missiles which were later to be used to great advantage as reentry test vehicles. Senate Committee on Armed Services, *Satellite and Missile Program Hearings,* 1957, p. 545.

nel to work on the intermediate-range missile, it also encouraged Brucker to bolster the Army case for the Jupiter by seeking out Navy support.[96] The Navy expressed interest in a joint program for an IRBM, and meetings of their respective technical personnel were arranged. According to Brucker:

Out of the welter of discussions that occurred, during which the Army pointed out the success that it had attained and the Navy made known its desire for something which looked very reasonable for launching on shipboard, came a mutual desire to develop something that each could jointly and severally use.[97]

With the Army providing the technical competence and the Navy the military requirement, a marriage of convenience was quickly and easily consummated.[98]

AIR FORCE INTEREST IN THE IRBM

"I think the fact that the Army pressed on had a great deal to do with propelling the other service," Secretary of the Army Wilber Brucker told the Holifield Committee.[99] In a similar vein, the Commander of the Air Matériel Command, General

[96] Interview with Wilber Brucker, September 3, 1963.

[97] Senate Committee on Armed Services, *Airpower Hearings*, 1956, p. 1311.

[98] The Navy version of these events varies somewhat. Certainly the circumstances were such as to cast doubt on the permanence of the marriage. During the deliberations of the Robertson Committee, the Navy had made presentations favoring a solid-fuel approach to the sea-based IRBM. Contemplated advances in the specific impulse of solid fuels were not, however, sufficiently encouraging to support the feasibility of such proposals. Keith Rumbel and Charles Henderson, who were approaching a dramatic technical breakthrough in this field at the Atlantic Research Corporation, were working on a Navy contract at about this time. By adding large amounts of powdered aluminum to solid fuels they obtained astonishing increases in the specific impulse of the solid fuels. Perhaps optimism regarding the outcome of their research stimulated the alleged comment of one admiral: "We were shoved into the bed with the Army against our will. It was the wrong bed and everyone knew it." James Baar and William Howard, *Polaris!* (New York, Harcourt, Brace and Company, 1960), p. 34. What is clear is that while many of the Navy's most competent technical people held out for a solid-fuel approach, their proposals did not promise the early operational capability recommended in the Killian Report.

[99] House Committee on Government Operations, *Missile Program Hearings*, 1959, p. 274.

Clarence Irvine, mused before Representative George Mahon's Appropriation Sub-Committee, "There is nothing healthier for this country than inter-service rivalry, so called. I would say if anything helped the Air Force work like hell on THOR, it is the fact that we knew the Army was clawing at our backs." [100] It appears that such competition was as important in the initiation of the Thor project as in stimulating its rapid development.

During the late 1940s and early 1950s, Air Force interest in long-range surface-to-surface ballistic missiles, if persistent, had been quite sporadic. By 1953 a number of individual projects had been initiated and were reaching the stage where prototypes had to be constructed if further progress was to be made. Naturally this would entail significant increases in the level of development expenditures. At the same time their jet aircraft program was approaching a similar stage in the development cycle. But rather than being able to anticipate increases in defense spending, the outcome of the 1952 elections and the conclusion of the Korean War brought new pressures for economy. In this atmosphere of retrenchment the Air Force chose to defend its embryonic jet combat units by reprogramming funds away from their sundry missile projects.[101]

Simultaneously a Department of Defense Guided Missiles Study Group of the Armed Forces Policy Council began a comprehensive review of the entire missile field.[102] In the course of this review, extrapolations of the technical information yielded by the hydrogen bomb tests then being conducted in the Pacific came to the attention of the committee and profoundly influenced their subsequent recommendations. The promise of spec-

[100] U.S. Congress, House, Committee on Appropriations, *Hearings, The Ballistic Missile Program,* 85th Cong., 2nd Sess., 1957, p. 102.

[101] Gardner, *Airpower Historian,* V, p. 9.

[102] This was merely the latest in a series of such reviews. It was the result of a directive issued by Budget Bureau Director Joseph Dodge in the spring of 1953. In it he requested that all departments question all existing programs and take action "to eliminate unnecessary programs and to hold the remainder to minimum levels." Robert J. Donovan, *Eisenhower: The Inside Story* (New York, Harper & Bros., 1956), p. 55.

tacular improvements in the weight-to-yield ratio of nuclear warheads transformed the intercontinental ballistic missile from an improbable and uneconomical delivery vehicle into an exceedingly difficult technical accomplishment which, however, promised a revolutionary advance in the capacity to deliver nuclear payloads over vast distances.

Credit for converting the Air Force to a ballistic approach must in large measure go to Trevor Gardner. With the assistance of technical reports from both the RAND Corporation and the Strategic Missiles Evaluation Group, he successfully overcame resistance to a vastly accelerated program from scientific "nay sayers" and influential Air Force officers. Gardner had created the Strategic Missiles Evaluation Group and had shrewdly fashioned appointments to this committee with one eye on the personal influence individual members might have upon those important officials who did not share his enthusiasm for a crash program to develop an ICBM.[103] This panel of prestigious scientists, engineers, and business executives preoccupied itself with the administrative arrangements for an accelerated missile program, as well as with establishing the technical feasibility of developing an operational weapon system.

By mid-1954, Gardner had mobilized a substantial consensus behind the propositions that: (1) an ICBM was feasible technically and militarily essential; (2) that a broad industrial base would have to be fashioned virtually from scratch; (3) that a management-scientific-technical team of extraordinary competence had to be swiftly assembled; and (4) that normal procedures would have to be circumvented, eliminated, or temporarily set aside if the requisite sense of urgency was to infuse the Air Force's expanded program.[104] Gardner's selection of Major

[103] Interview with Mr. Trevor Gardner, May 8, 1963.

[104] With respect to the technical feasibility of the ICBM, the thermonuclear bomb tests in the Pacific led to a relaxation in the technical requirements in warhead weight, propellant thrust, guidance accuracy, and heat resistance capacity of the reentry vehicle. The loosening of these parameters allowed the Committee to conclude that successful development of an ICBM could be accomplished within 6 to 8 years. The Report

General Bernard A. Schriever to command the newly established Western Development Division of the Air Research and
Development Command reflected his conviction that this
young, technically sophisticated officer would be "unconven-
tional enough to find new methods of operation, to short-circuit
official red tape and circumvent bureaucratic meddling, and to
break through the barriers that stood in the way of the successful completion of the missile program." [105]

In the summer of 1955 when, in Gardner's estimation, the
Atlas program needed a further stimulus, he obtained, with a
powerful assist from Senator Henry Jackson and Senator Clin-
ton Anderson—leading members of the Joint Atomic Energy
Committee—a briefing before President Eisenhower. So impressed was the Chief Executive by the presentation made by
Gardner, General Bernard Schriever, and Dr. John von Neumann that he accorded to the Atlas project the highest national
priority research and development status. This substantially
ameliorated problems hitherto encountered in obtaining materials, recruiting personnel, and insuring industrial support.[106]

It is clear that Trevor Gardner was primarily concerned with
the development of an ICBM weapon system. While this was

---

of the Strategic Missiles Evaluation Group—variously known as the "Tea-
pot Committee" or the Von Neumann Committee—was transmitted to the
Air Force Secretary on February 10, 1953. The RAND Corporation Report, which contained a similar estimate of the feasibility of developing
an operational ICBM by 1960–1962 was submitted almost simultaneously.
RAND physicist Bruno Augenstein had been among the first to appreciate
the significance of the H-Bomb tests for ICBM development. Nor should
the role of the Joint Committee on Atomic Energy in promoting a vastly
accelerated missile development program be overlooked. Important members of that Committee consistently favored an increase in the level of
effort, and a centralization of control over the diffuse activities in the
missile development field. See Ernest Schwiebert, *History of the U.S. Air
Force Ballistic Missiles* (New York, Praeger, 1965), pp. 57–73. See also
House Committee on Government Operations, *Missile Program Hearings*,
1959, pp. 3–132.
    [105] *Ibid.*, p. 78. Schwiebert has written a comprehensive account of the
organizational structure and managerial techniques employed in the Air
Force program. See especially chaps. 5–8.
    [106] Interview, Mr. Trevor Gardner, May 8, 1963.

the dominant enthusiasm of the Air Force scientists and engineers in 1953, it should not obscure the fact that interest in a ballistic missile with more modest range parameters had been manifested by some of their research and development specialists since the 1940s. Indeed, at one time the IRBM had been considered as a transitional step to the ICBM. The appeal of a quantum jump in technology, and the prospect of significant Soviet progress toward an ICBM, caused the ultimate rejection of this timetable.[107] By 1956 a requirement for a tactical ballistic missile had, nevertheless, been stated for two or three years, and the requirement was listed on their research and development program roster.[108] No funds, however, had been devoted to it prior to 1956;[109] and by that time, in view of interest expressed by the Army, the Air Force had ceased referring to the IRBM as a tactical missile.

In January, 1955, the Air Force Scientific Advisory Committee gave serious consideration to the possibility of initiating a tactical ballistic missile project.[110] At one time the Air Research and Development Command had actively considered a ballistic approach to the development of a follow-on missile to the Tactical Air Command's Martin Matador, an unmanned jet aircraft with a solid propellant booster rocket. Design studies of a ballistic missile with a range of approximately 1,000 miles were invited as early as mid-1954. In some quarters such a missile was conceived of as an alternative to the Atlas and insurance against its possible failure.[111] Gardner, on the other hand, anxious to avert a dissipation of effort away from the ICBM program, and cognizant of the fact that a missile of intermediate range would serve British strategic needs, suggested that inves-

[107] General Donald Putt testified before the Symington Subcommittee that the Air Force initially thought of the IRBM as a "spin-off" from some of the early ICBM test vehicles. See Senate Committee on Armed Services, *Airpower Hearings*, 1956, p. 671.

[108] *Ibid.*, p. 552.   [109] *Ibid.*, p. 670.

[110] See Julian Hartt, *The Mighty Thor: Missile in Readiness* (New York, Duell, Sloan and Pearce, 1961), pp. 34–37.

[111] Schwiebert, *History of the U.S. Air Force Ballistic Missiles*, p. 113.

tigations be undertaken to determine whether the British were capable and willing to assume responsibility for its development. Subsequently, a study group organized by the Aircraft Industries Association concluded that the United Kingdom did not possess the resources to develop and produce such a missile within the time limit involved. Having just mobilized the requisite support for the Atlas project, however, Gardner was not anxious to see its priority diluted by an additional project. Moreover, while he was prepared to concede that the IRBM was a "vastly important device," he clearly did not acknowledge it as an urgent priority item.[112] Above all, he was sensitive to potential competition for scientists, engineers, money, resources, and testing facilities; and he was inclined to refer to the IRBM as a natural fallout from the ICBM—a bonus for which little special organization or financial effort was required at the moment.

It appears that General Schriever, the newly appointed Commander of the Western Development Division, shared Gardner's reservations. He advised against a Tactical Ballistic Missile program, since, in his view, "even the discussion of such a program was causing possible contractors to hold back from becoming involved in Atlas contracts in the hope that they would get contracts for the TBM." [113]

An additional reason for Air Force reservations about the IRBM may be surmised from the sheer number of projects directed toward development of strategic delivery systems. Within the framework of relatively fixed budgets, the project directors of existing programs and their industrial suppliers constituted built-in resistance to additional projects. In any event, additional projects were vulnerable to the charge of superfluity in

[112] Senate Committee on Armed Services, *Airpower Hearings*, 1956, p. 1114.

[113] Schwiebert, *History of the U.S. Air Force Ballistic Missiles*, p. 113. In order to insure that the ICBM programs retained their designated priority in obtaining the support of industry, Schriever persuaded General Thomas Power, then ARDC Commander, to transfer the TBM program to the Ballistic Missile Division and hence place it under his own jurisdiction. Hartt, *The Mighty Thor*, pp. 37-38.

view of the existing contracts with Convair, for the B-58 bomber; Boeing-North American, for the WS-110A chemical bomber; Convair-Lockheed, for the WS-125A nuclear bomber; Northrup, for the Snark pilotless plane; North American, for the Navaho intercontinental air-breathing missile; Convair, for the Atlas ICBM; and Martin, for the projected Titan backup ICBM project.[114] The elimination of less promising projects to make room for the new was not easy; costs already paid, and the political pressures of resistance created by the vested interests of suppliers, communities, and the responsible project agencies within the Air Force tended to frustrate such choices.

Finally, Air Force reservations toward the IRBM were presumably related to their growing disenchantment with overseas bases as launching platforms for SAC. In 1955, General LeMay responded to the growing vulnerability of medium-range B-47s by calling for the creation of a fleet of intercontinental bombers.[115] Support for an American-based SAC was reinforced by fears that in times of crisis, bases in areas of strongly organized minorities could be immobilized by sabotage. It was also feared that in an emergency some smaller allies, hoping desperately to

[114] Since the Titan was conceived as a two-staged rocket, BMD-STL personnel were instructed to determine whether or not an IRBM could be "realized from the second stage." Apparently these studies were an outgrowth of the impetus given an IRBM program by the conclusions of the Killian Report. By July, 1955, Air Force engineers had concluded that a derivative of the Titan second stage might realize a maximum 800-mile range. The National Security Council subsequently requested that Schriever determine the optimum method of achieving a 1,500-nautical-mile missile. Having anticipated this request, he had already instructed Commander Robert Truax of the Ballistic Missile Division and Dr. Aldolph K. Thiel of Space Technology Laboratories to give some preliminary thought to that problem. By late August, Truax, Thiel, Reuben Mettler, Major George Vanden Heuvel, and several others had completed a technical proposal for an IRBM with a range of 1,750 statute miles, a gross takeoff weight of 55 tons, and dimensions which would permit air transportability. Hartt, *The Mighty Thor*, pp. 39–43.

[115] During the Symington Committee Airpower Hearings, Donald Quarles conceded the vulnerability of the B-47 bases but claimed them nevertheless as a great asset in view of the difficulties of simultaneous attack and the significance of dispersal in complicating Soviet defense problems against retaliatory attacks. *Airpower Study*, p. 1542.

insure against their own involvement, might seek safety in hastily adopted neutralism, and attempt to prevent U.S. bombers from taking off. The formidable cost and logistic problems of supplying dispersed bomber or missile bases were adduced as additional reasons for concentrating on long-range delivery systems.[116]

Nevertheless, in the fall of 1955 proposals for an Air Force IRBM program emerged and were pressed vigorously before the Robertson Committee. Their sudden interest is not to be ascribed merely to selfish proprietary interests in the face of the Army's manifest interest. Anxieties over Soviet missile progress gave rise to apprehensions as to the defense of the retaliatory force. In this context, an IRBM could provide a useful complement to their other forces. It appeared to be more quickly obtainable, less vulnerable to air defenses than the bombers they replaced, and able to provide a significant complication in Soviet air defense and offensive planning.[117] Such considerations underlay the Killian Report, and the existence of this national requirement may provide much of the explanation of the genesis of the Thor proposal.

[116] For a detailed account of Air Force reservations about overseas bases, see Staff Monograph, "The Strategic Bomber," *Air University Quarterly Review*, VIII (Summer, 1955), esp. 131–32. The reluctance of Gardner and Schriever to overextend the technical commitment of their industrial and scientific base on a TBM project may have been buttressed by uncertainties in SAC regarding the deployment problems of such a missile system. While a ballistic TBM had been contemplated as a follow-on for the aerodynamic Matador and Mace, the extensions in range involved in developing an IRBM posed inescapable dilemmas for the command and control of systems with strategic capabilities. Would they come under the jurisdiction of the Theater Commander as a qualitative improvement of TACAIR or would the centralized command structure of SAC be sustained? At best it appears that SAC was restrained in its enthusiasm for systems of intermediate range, and was inclined to accept them merely as transitional systems to be employed only until operational ICBMs became available.

[117] U.S. Congress, House, Committee on Armed Services, Hearings, *Investigation of National Defense Missiles*, 85th Cong., 2nd Sess., 1957, p. 4762. (Hereafter referred to as *National Defense Missiles Hearings*.) General Thomas D. White testified that insofar as IRBMs were developed and

Yet Army interest, it seems fair to infer, had a considerable catalytic effect on the Air Force's interest in the IRBM. While posing an opportunity and challenge for the Army, the IRBM posed a potential threat to the Air Force. And having only recently obtained their independence, Air Force leaders were un usually sensitive to any threats to their newly won preeminence.

The threat was to be discerned in the implications of guided missiles for the execution of Air Force missions. The ICBM was the equivalent of their long-range bomber; the IRBM of their medium bomber. Shorter ranged tactical missiles could perform the missions of interceptors and combat support assault aircraft. A diminution in Air Force roles and missions might conceivably follow from a failure to achieve operational control over the new technology. Some expressed fears of the Air Force's reduction to a mere supporting arm employed for reconnaissance and transport.[118] The creation of a successful monopoly of the market, on the other hand, might enable them to cut into established Army functions in antiaircraft defense and the artillery field. Moreover, they, like the Army, felt impelled to diversify, since the farsighted among them recognized that the manned bomber was being ineluctably obsolesced, responsibilities for Continental Air Defense were cutting into SAC expenditures, and the Army was making a determined bid for expansion into the air defense field with missiles. In short, the balance of the established division of labors among the services was cast in doubt as the prospect of new technology promised to place a premium upon different skills and competences. Since the existing specification of roles and missions had been framed in exceedingly broad terms, it offered little guidance as to how guided missiles would be assimilated into the pattern of responsibilities.[119]

---

deployed, the necessity of centralized command and control required that the Air Force exercise jurisdiction over them.

[118] Martin, *Saturday Evening Post*, CCXXX, (November 9, 1957) p. 37.

[119] Regarding the stability of roles and missions agreements, Admiral Radford observed to the House Armed Services Committee that in response to new developments the Key West arrangements can be "changed

In any event, anticipating the President's decision to authorize, on a priority basis, the development of an IRMB, BMD-STL engineers had, as noted above, run preliminary studies of the design for an Air Force IRBM.[120] This explains the speed with which the Air Force was able to implement their responsibilities for the land-based IRBM project. It was authorized in November, 1955. On November 28, the Western Development Division was directed to proceed with the IRBM. On the same date contractors were notified for proposal briefings. Within ten days such proposals had been submitted and, by December 23, Secretary of the Air Force Donald Quarles approved the source selection of Douglas Aircraft over its competitors, North American Aircraft and Lockheed, as prime contractor for the Thor missile. Five days later the contract was signed, and within the month the airframe configuration for the missile was frozen.[121]

THE NAVY AND THE FLEET
BALLISTIC MISSILE FORCE

The Navy had been slow to generate interest in the potential of ballistic rockets. Work on solid fuel propellants had been sustained on a moderate scale since 1942, and wartime experience had aroused some enthusiasm for ship-launched missiles. Yet for a number of years, appreciation of the military potential of Navy fleet missiles was largely confined to a rather informal and

by agreement between the Army and the Air Force, but then somebody comes along and doesn't like the agreement, so they stir it up again." U.S. Congress, House, Committee on Armed Services, *Hearings, Reorganization of the Department of Defense,* 85th Cong., 2nd Sess., 1958, p. 6553. 6553.

[120] Schwiebert, *History of the U.S. Air Force Ballistic Missiles,* p. 114.

[121] Speed in fixing the design of the Thor was facilitated by borrowing most of the components and contractors from the Atlas program. Designed as a single-staged, liquid-propellant rocket powered by a gimbaled rocket engine and two gimbaled vernier engines, it could exploit the range differential to carry the same warhead weight as the Atlas-D. Thus their nose cones could employ identical design. The propulsion system was also borrowed from the Atlas booster, and the inertial guidance system being developed for the Atlas was simply reoriented to the Thor as were the electrical, hydraulic, and pneumatic systems. *Ibid.*

low-level alliance of junior officers and civilian scientists—among them Commander Robert C. Truax, Milton W. Rosen, and Captains Francis Boyle, Robert F. Freitag, Levering Smith, and Grayson Merrill.[122]

These officers and civilian officials attempted to elicit support for a major program of rocket and earth satellite development. They sought to demonstrate that ballistic rockets could be successfully launched from the deck of a ship, and tried to interest the Navy Staff in the importance of a ballistic missile program. A detailed proposal indicated how Navy experience with the Viking high-altitude research program could be exploited to develop a medium-range missile usable from land, ship, or submarine.[123] The latter suggestion, advanced by Freitag, Truax, Rosen, and Merrill, was vetoed by the Director of the Navy's guided missile program and the Chief of Naval Operations. This was but one manifestation of the general resistance encountered at the highest levels in the Navy until 1955.

Senator Jackson later hinted at the sources of resistance to suggestions for a fleet ballistic missile force. Of the Polaris program, he said:

I was interested in this program from the very outset, going back many, many years. I found that in trying to get the Navy to do something about it, I ran headlong into the competition within the Navy for requirements in connection with their day-to-day operational needs, whether it was anti-submarine warfare or limited

[122] For a summary of their activities in the early postwar years, see Vincent Davis, *The Politics of Innovation: Patterns in Navy Cases* (Denver, Social Science Foundation and Graduate School of International Studies Monograph Series in World Affairs, 1967), pp. 31–41.

[123] *Ibid.*, pp. 32–33. See also the letter from Dr. Homer E. Newell, Jr., Superintendent of Atmosphere and Astrophysics of the Naval Research Laboratories, to the Preparedness Investigation Subcommittee of the Senate Armed Services Committee in *Satellite and Missile Program Hearings,* 1957, p. 369. Captain Levering Smith did lead a project carried out at Inyokern, California, during this period in which the Navy experimented with the possibility of developing missiles capable of delivering the heavy atomic warheads of that day over relatively short range. The two-staged, solid-fueled Big Stoop missile was not a resounding success, although it did successfully negotiate a distance of about 20 miles on each of 3 flights in 1951. Baar and Howard, *Polaris*, p. 15.

war requirements; whatever it was . . . I was told that this strategic system would just eat away and erode their limited funds. . . . The result was that Polaris was not pushed hard until Sputnik came along.[124]

The budgetary consequences of a vigorous missile effort were obvious. Creating a sea-based IRBM force required either the expensive reoutfitting of surface ships, or the accelerated production of nuclear submarines.[125] Since funds for a fleet ballistic missile program were expected to come out of the regular ship construction budget, it would be directly competitive with dreams of a nuclear propelled task force and proposals for additional limited war-craft. As William Hessler put it: "Naval thinking puts top priority on the traditional roles and missions of the fleet—sea command above all—as against a new and purely strategic deterrent task." [126]

In addition, a contest between the Bureau of Aeronautics and the Bureau of Ordnance as to which would ultimately obtain control of the Navy's missile development program inhibited Navy efforts. In the Bureau of Ordnance especially, sentiment ran strongly to ramjet, air-breathing missiles of the Tritan and Regulus types and against the technically riskier but militarily more promising ballistic rockets.

Wilfred McNeil, long-time Comptroller of the Pentagon,

[124] U.S. Congress, Senate, Committee on Government Operations, *Hearings, Organizing for National Security*, I, 87th Cong., 1st Sess., 1961, pp. 1084–85.
[125] The first Polaris submarine, SS (N) 598, cost more than $100 million. Later models were expected to cost $90 million apiece. Specifications for the first nuclear-powered, missile-carrying submarines were submitted in late April, 1957. The first ship programmed, the "Ethan Allen," was to be commissioned in 1961. After Sputnik, however, the Polaris timetable was accelerated and submarine shipbuilding schedules were reprogrammed to permit the conversion of 5 attack submarines into fleet ballistic missile submarines. The first of these to be completed, the *George Washington*—formerly a nuclear attack submarine of the Skipjack class—was launched on June 9, 1959. See Ed Rees, *The Seas and the Subs* (New York, Duell, Sloan and Pearce, 1961), pp. 149, 163, 167.
[126] Hessler, "The Navy's Submersible," *The Reporter*, XVIII (June 12, 1958), 16.

suggested another cause of Navy resistance. Pointing to political factors that influenced the Navy's research and development orientation, he observed that the Navy "had been criticized for years for trying to get into the strategic business and there was a little bit of reluctance to expose themselves directly to what I would say would certainly be recognized as a strategic system." [127]

Finally, besides the inertia stemming from traditional priorities and budgetary concerns, there were widespread and quite plausible reservations about the technical feasibility of many of the proposals advanced. These were reinforced by memories of the tests conducted in 1949 to check the consequences of an accident with a liquid-fuel missile aboard ship. In that test the thermal shock of the liquid oxygen cracked steel plates and split the supporting I-beams of a mock-up steel warship. "One look at that mess," one officer recalled, "and a shudder ran through every ship in the Navy." [128]

By mid-1955 Navy leaders were no longer so openly opposed to the development of a fleet ballistic missile force. But there was surely no crusading spirit, no "missionary fervor" for such a force. An incipient interest was transformed into active advocacy by the Killian Committee's investigations into actual and prospective missile developments. The recommendation of this distinguished and independent Committee that the development of sea-based ballistic missiles was an urgent requirement provided essential support for the arguments being advanced by fleet ballistic missile force enthusiasts within the Navy. The Killian Committee papers were especially invaluable to Captain Freitag and Abraham Hyatt, the Director of BuAer's research division, in their efforts to persuade the Bureau of Aeronautics to accept a full commitment to an FBM research and development program.[129] In short, the Killian Committee

---

[127] Senate Committee on Government Operations, *Hearings, Organizing for National Security*, I, p. 1085.
[128] Baar and Howard, *Polaris*, p. 14.
[129] Davis, *The Politics of Innovation*, p. 35.

proved to be a crucial extraorganizational ally to the informal and low-level group of FBM advocates in the Navy, and assisted them greatly in evoking support from their superiors.

Opposition within the Navy was not to be easily overcome. Admiral Hyman Rickover, who fathered the Navy's nuclear submarine program, Admiral Robert Carney, serving at the time as Chief of Naval Operations, and Admiral "Savvy" Sides, director of guided missile developments within the CNO's staff, were still among those important officials maintaining reservations toward an ambitious FBM program. Their grounds for resistance ranged from different research and development priorities, as in Rickover's case, to a general reluctance to sacrifice current preparedness to risky projects promising novel capabilities in the indefinite future. The technical obstacles were particularly formidable. The efficacy of the entire FBM concept hinged upon dramatic breakthroughs that would permit accurate guidance, an adequate fire control system, a satisfactory navigational system, adequate thrust in the solid-fuel propellant, and major improvements in metals and other materials. Admiral Carney decided against a major FBM research and development project in the summer of 1955. Budget commitments or contractual obligations tending in the direction of an expanded emphasis in this area were explicitly precluded.

Nevertheless, the urgency inspired by the Killian Committee's Report, a growing confidence that the technical problems associated with an FBM program could be surmounted, and the maneuvering of the other services to obtain important responsibilities in the missiles and space fields occasioned renewed consideration of the desirability of an FBM program. The persuasive efforts of Freitag, Hyatt, Rear Admiral Russell, and Assistant Secretary of the Navy for Air James H. Smith were particularly instrumental in enlisting the support of the Secretary of the Navy and powerful civilian officials for such a program. Ultimately, the appointment of Admiral Arleigh A. Burke as Chief of Naval Operations in August, 1955, proved to be the decisive stage in the mobilization of high-level support in the Navy for a full-scale missile development effort.

The Navy's conversion to an FBM program was gradual and somewhat belated. By late 1955 decisions were already crystallizing in the Defense Department to parcel long-range missile development projects to the Army and Air Force. In early September, Captain Freitag initiated contacts with the Redstone Arsenal missile development team led by Werner von Braun to explore the possibilities of Army-Navy collaboration. A favorable response to these advances paved the way for the temporary alliance which was subsequently negotiated and which kept the door open for a future independent Navy program.[130]

Ironically, even as they were preparing to join the Army in quest of a sea-based system, the seeds of the Navy's future defection from the joint project were taking root. During the fall of 1955 technical breakthroughs on the specific impulse of solid fuels and an AEC announcement of drastic reductions in the weights of thermonuclear warheads opened up new and inviting possibilities for an independent program.[131]

DELIBERATE DUPLICATION

By the fall of 1955 all three major services had demonstrated an interest in the IRBM assignment. Although the Navy was prepared to join with the Huntsville Arsenal Team in quest of a sea-based ballistic missile, their support of Army ambitions in the strategic missile field was still somewhat equivocal. In October, 1955, the Joint Chiefs of Staff attempted to define responsibilities for operational control of guided missiles. A majority of the Chiefs apparently favored exclusive Air Force and Navy jurisdiction over the deployment and use of IRBMs, and only the most vehement protestations of Maxwell Taylor, the newly appointed Chief of Staff of the Army, induced Secretary of Defense Wilson to postpone a decision on the matter.

Meanwhile, Deputy Secretary of Defense Reuben Robertson had been studying alternative methods of organizing the anticipated expansion of ballistic missile efforts, and specifically the

[130] *Ibid.,* p. 39, n. 29.
[131] Charles J. V. Murphy, "U.S. Seapower: The New Mix," *Fortune,* LX (August, 1959), 78.

IRBM development program. A number of possibilities were discussed, including even the removal of responsibilities for developing strategic ballistic missile delivery systems from the services to an agency structured after the fashion of the Manhattan District Engineering Project of World War II.[132]

After extensive consultations, proposals for such a drastic reorganization were rejected, and developmental responsibilities were lodged with the services, although special procedures were devised to reduce red tape, hasten decision making, and facilitate the coordination of the various programs contemplated. This approach was consonant with Robertson's conviction that "the test of an organization is its capacity to respond to a crisis without modification." [133] It also would avert the dislocations and delays attendant upon any fundamental overhaul of a program which had already acquired considerable momentum within the Department of the Air Force. In addition, top Defense officials were anxious to exploit service thinking regarding technical specifications and tactical concepts for the novel weaponry, and to capitalize upon the urgency of effort which would be generated when the Secretary of Defense and his chief assistants were forced to spend a significant portion of their own time daily supervising, energizing, and disciplining the efforts of the services.

In view of the priority attached to the IRBM capability, the Robertson Committee was inclined to recommend a parallel approach to its development. The divergent technical approaches of Army and Air Force experts, expressed with vigor and plausibility; the natural inclination to hedge against the failure of either concept in the face of great technical uncertainties; the conviction that if one approach appeared clearly the more promising as the development phase moved along the other

[132] Robertson was reportedly a determined opponent of Navy involvement in the IRBM development program at this time. Nor was he convinced that the Army had a demonstrated requirement for IRBMs. On the other hand, he was prepared to exploit the Army's technical capabilities and would not foreclose the possibility of a Navy IRBM requirement. Davis, *The Politics of Innovation,* p. 38.

[133] Interview with Alvin Waggoner, July 26, 1965.

could be cancelled; and the expectation that a duplicative effort would in any event contribute to the broadening of the technological and industrial base of the United States missile and space effort all encouraged such a decision.[134]

On November 8, 1955, memoranda to the Secretary of the Air Force and jointly to the Army and Navy Secretaries notified them that an IRBM was to be developed at the "maximum speed permitted by technology." [135] The IRBM program, as determined by Secretary of Defense Wilson on the advice of the Robertson Committee, was to consist of "a land-based development by the Air Force (IRBM No.1) and a joint Army-Navy Program (IRBM No.2) having the dual objective of achieving an early shipboard capability and also providing a land-based alternate to the Air Force program." [136]

Although the programs were to enjoy equal priority, Army leaders were somewhat chagrined at the designation of their program as IRBM No.2.[137] That the primary Defense Department objective was the development of the sea-based Jupiter was perhaps suggested by Secretary Wilson's designation of the Secretary of the Navy as Chairman of the newly created Joint Army-Navy Ballistic Missiles Committee.[138]

Thus were parallel programs initiated. As Deputy Secretary

[134] *Ibid.* In view of the novelty of the systems being developed, the Secretary was doubtless exercising prudence in refusing to repose excessive confidence in the technical capabilities of either service. The Air Force team had yet to produce an operational ballistic missile, and the lack of significant progress in the ill-fated Snark and Navaho programs did not enhance their reputation as innovators. The Army team, on the other hand, was considered by some to be excessively conservative in its approach, and doubts were harbored in some quarters that they could improve much on the V-2. It seems quite likely that some scientists and soldiers may have subconsciously depreciated the qualities of the Huntsville team since they had been "the enemy." Robertson and Wilson ultimately decided that they could ill afford to overlook the competence of any group in the early phases of ballistic missile development.

[135] See Wilson's Memoranda to the Service Secretaries in House Committee on Government Operations, *Missile Program Hearings,* 1959, pp. 655–57.

[136] *Ibid.,* p. 655.   [137] Medaris, *Countdown for Decision,* p. 74.

[138] House Committee on Government Operations, *Missile Program Hearings,* 1959, p. 656.

of Defense Donald Quarles was later to explain to the House
Committee on Government Operations, this "was a perfectly
deliberate duplication on the part of the Secretary of Defense,
believing that by doing so, he would be sure to produce a sound
weapon system at the earliest possible date." [139] He may have
felt that ambiguity over roles and missions assignments might
contribute to the urgency with which the services would pursue
their respective developmental programs. It seems more likely
that he simply postponed a hard decision which did not seem to
require immediate resolution.[140] In any event, the decision was
deferred and the stage set for subsequent contention over the
right to deploy and use the weapons under development.

COMPETITIVE WEAPONS DEVELOPMENT
IN THE WILSON PENTAGON

Competition among the services for the right to develop and
deploy novel weapons was encouraged by the procedures of policy making in the Pentagon as well as by the substance of strategic doctrine. President Eisenhower was convinced that the
structure of defense organization was the prime source of interservice rivalries. In offering his plan for reorganization of the
Defense Department in 1958 he observed: ". . . while at
times human failure and misdirected zeal have been responsible
for duplications, inefficiencies and publicized disputes, the truth
is that most of the service rivalries that have troubled us in re-

[139] U.S. Congress, House Committee on Government Operations, *Organization and Management of Missile Programs,* 88th Cong., 1st Sess.,
1959, H.R. 1121, p. 150.
[140] In this respect his decision may aptly be described, in Warner
Schilling's phrase, as a "minimal decision," or a "course of action which
would close off the least number of future alternatives." Warner R. Schilling, "The H-Bomb Decision: How to Decide Without Actually Choosing," *Political Science Quarterly,* LXXVI (March, 1961), 37–38. The
Joint Chiefs of Staff did not reach a decision on the jurisdictional assignment of the IRBM at this time. Admiral Radford later explained to the
Senate Armed Services Committee, "I will come to the Chiefs later when
it is a question of operational use, that is, when a decision is required as
to which service will operate." Senate Committee on Armed Services, *Airpower Hearings,* 1956, p. 1458.

cent years have been made inevitable by the laws that govern our defense organization." [141] The pattern of interservice conflict over new weapons was surely influenced by the structure of defense organization. Actually, however, two parallel lines of conflict could be discerned within the Pentagon during the 1950s. Interservice rivalry was accompanied by strife between the military services and the civilian Secretary. Declining budgets and fierce competition for roles and missions, however, tended to accentuate the former while obscuring the latter.[142] Interservice competition was also shaped by the competence, style, and managerial techniques of the Secretary of Defense.

The 1953 organizational reforms in the Defense Department were designed to strengthen civilian control, improve strategic planning, and introduce businesslike procedures into the management of the vast post-Korea defense establishment. The reforms would also reinforce the hand of the Secretary of Defense relative to the Service Departments. Disenchanted with the results obtained from coordinating committees, and anxious to locate responsibility and authority for specific functional tasks in a single individual, Reorganization Plan No.6 had multiplied threefold the number of Assistant Secretaries in the Office of the Secretary of Defense. Such authority as these new Assistant Secretaries were to exert could only come at the expense of the Service Secretaries, and it was indeed hoped that interservice logrolling would diminish as coordinating officials were located directly in the office of the Secretary of Defense.[143] In reality, however, the services' loss was not necessarily the Secretary's gain. As John Ries has noted, "Power became diffused and harder to pinpoint. . . . It was extremely difficult, after 1953, . . . to determine the location of real power within the department." [144]

[141] See "The President's Reorganization Plan," *Air Force* (May, 1958), 103–08.

[142] John C. Ries, *The Management of Defense* (Baltimore, Johns Hopkins University Press, 1964), p. 167.

[143] Walter Millis, *Arms and the State* (New York, The Twentieth Century Fund, 1958), p. 381.

[144] Ries, *The Management of Defense,* p. 196.

To be sure, the Secretary possessed a secure base of power
through the prerogatives granted him in choosing and dis-
missing subordinates, influencing the formulation of the budget
and expenditures, and in his "general direction, authority, and
control" over all agencies in the military establishment.[145] Yet
Wilson, as well as his successor Neil McElroy, possessed a
uniquely civilian conception of his responsibilities. He had
been chosen by the President for his experience in the handling
of vast procurement, storage, transportation, distribution, and
other logistical functions, and was not expected to exert a guid-
ing hand in strategic matters.[146] "Leave the military stuff up to
the military," Wilson once observed with typical candor, "and
production up to us." [147] In contrast to a more recent incumbent, he envisaged his role in terms of *business management*
rather than *policy leadership*.[148]

Abundantly endowed with legal competences, the Secretary
also was to enjoy considerable "situational power" resting upon
a firm base of disagreements among the Service Departments.
Indeed, the occasion for the Secretary's assertion of power was
normally to be some stalemated issue which propelled him into
a mediating role in the resolution of conflict among subordinates. Unfortunately the 1953 reorganization of the Pentagon
had stopped considerably short of providing him with a personal staff, either military or civilian. Given Wilson's conception of the Secretary's role and denied the competence independently to evaluate the numerous disputes on substantive

145 *Ibid.,* p. 112.
146 Eisenhower, *Mandate for Change* (Garden City, Doubleday & Company, 1963), p. 86.
147 Samuel P. Huntington, *The Soldier and the State* (New York, Ran-
dom House, 1st Vintage Ed., 1964) , p. 443.
148 Secretary of Defense McNamara, by comparison, asserted a bold conception of his Office in his statement: "I see my position here as being a
leader, not a judge. I'm here to originate and stimulate new ideas and
programs, not just to referee arguments and harmonize interests. Using
deliberate analysis to force alternative programs to the surface and then
making explicit choices among them is fundamental." Cited in William
W. Kaufmann, *The McNamara Strategy* (New York, Harper & Row,
1964) , p. 171.

issues, the Secretary was reduced, in the view of Paul Y. Hammond, to "compromis[ing] service viewpoints at their many points of contact." [149]

There is little to suggest that Wilson welcomed jurisdictional conflicts as opportunities for self-assertiveness. By their very nature—involving as they did such matters as weapons capabilities and the strategic conceptions underlying their use—they fell outside the range of decisions with which he felt comfortable. Yet the Secretary could not evade the drastic decisions on jurisdictional conflicts, since the internal divisions within the Joint Chiefs of Staff and the combination of numerous short-tenured civilian assistants tended to propel all such disputes to the very top for resolution. Little wonder that procrastination and delay characterized the decision-making process.

Dubious of their own omniscience, particularly in questions involving research and development, and familiar with a world in which a measure of competition was a fundamental spur to productivity, the civilian leaders of the Wilson Pentagon were inclined to employ—or rather, to tolerate—a proliferation of projects and programs to make possible greater latitude in developments as well as to hedge against possible delays or failures in projects involving elements beyond the accepted "state of the art." [150] Confusion, controversy, and conflict were the by-products of such competition. But in the Wilson Pentagon these were accepted reluctantly as the price of technical progress.

Without a personal staff, and in the face of persistent cleavages within the Joint Chiefs of Staff, Wilson became increasingly dependent for military counsel upon the personal relationship he maintained with the Chairman of the JCS, Admiral Radford. As one study concludes: "the Chairman, not the JCS, became the spokesman for the military." [151] On jurisdictional matters, in particular, Wilson was inclined to defer to

[149] Paul Y. Hammond, *Organizing for Defense* (Princeton, Princeton University Press, 1961), p. 299.

[150] Interview with Wilfred McNeil, former Comptroller of the Department of Defense, August 26, 1963.

[151] Ries, *The Management of Defense,* p. 157.

his advice.[152] Radford conceded his influential role to members of the Symington Airpower Subcommittee and identified the source of his power. "I have often pointed out to the Chiefs," he claimed, "that the more they disagree, the more power they hand to the Chairman." [153]

Clearly, Army Chief of Staff, General Maxwell Taylor, was not inclined to accept the Chairman's views as impartial. Rather, he considered Radford, "an able and ruthless partisan, who did his utmost to impose his views upon the Chiefs." [154] The President, on the other hand, seems to have considered the Chairman's forceful role to have been the sole guarantee that military policy was not dominated by the special pleading of parochial partisans. He commended Radford as a man who possessed "breadth of understanding and devotion to [his] country rather than to a single Service." Certainly he welcomed the Chairman's assistance in imposing cuts on service estimates where they could be made "with little or no damage." [155]

The potential for authoritative decisions generally increased with the growing ascendancy of the Chairman in the JCS. Yet in the interest of interservice harmony he frequently acquiesced in a "live and let live" policy with regard to weapons development. As he later described the *modus operandi* of the JCS to the House Armed Services Committee: "Well, the way it works out, I imagine for the most part we have tended to make a decision which gave each service a chance to do something. And that in some cases has cost us a lot of money." [156]

The difficulties of rendering decisions in such matters were doubtless related to the momentum acquired by service programs before proprietary issues were resolved. In the Thor-Jupiter controversy, this was related to the urgency of the IRBM requirement and the conscious decision to exploit the technical resources of all three services. It also reflected, how-

152 Gavin, *War and Peace in the Space Age,* p. 168.
153 Senate Armed Services Committee, *Airpower Hearings,* 1956, p. 1457.
154 Taylor, *The Uncertain Trumpet,* p. 110.
155 See Eisenhower, *Mandate for Change,* p. 455.
156 House Committee on Armed Services, *Hearings, Reorganization of Department of Defense,* 85th Cong., 2nd Sess., 1958, p. 6554.

ever, the relation between budgetary procedures and weapons planning.

The crux of the problem was discerned as early as 1954 by Arthur Smithies, who noted that: "Planning and programming precede budgeting, and programs provide the basis on which budgets are prepared. Programs, however, are prepared in terms of military concepts and not in terms of dollars. When a program is completed, the cost in dollars is not known." [157] The Administration's conception of the budget, the analytic techniques employed in its formulation, and the form in which it was presented all tended to obfuscate rather than clarify the relationship between strategy and resource use.

Whereas Secretary McNamara later considered the budget as a "quantitative expression of the operating plans," [158] Mr. Brundage and Mr. Stans, who served as Directors of the Budget Bureau under President Eisenhower, were more inclined to equate sound budgeting with the "uniform distribution of dissatisfaction." [159] Concern was directed toward expenditure stabilization rather than to the relationship between weapons policy and the nature of future military conflicts. Such perspectives were buttressed institutionally by the great influence of the Director of the Budget Bureau within the National Security Council, and by the 1949 amendments to the National Security Act through which the Office of Comptroller of the Pentagon was created as a counterweight to the Joint Chiefs of Staff.

The discrepancy between the policy making and budget-making processes in weapons development was quite pronounced. The planning of weapon systems and tactical doctrine for their employment emanated from the services. Budgeting, on the other hand, began with the introduction of guidelines on spending developed out of discussions between the President,

[157] Arthur Smithies, *The Budgetary Process in the United States* (New York, 1955) , p. 241.

[158] Kaufmann, *The McNamara Strategy*, p. 169.

[159] U.S. Senate, Subcommittee on National Policy Machinery for the Committee on Government Operations, *Hearings, Organizing for National Security*, I, 87th Cong., 1st Sess., 1961, p. 1095.

key members of his Cabinet, and chief military and civilian advisers. The question as to whether such ceilings were imposed upon the military inspired a continuing political controversy. The question was largely academic, since the Chairman of the Joint Chiefs, Admiral Radford, accepted as self-evident the proposition that military planning should proceed out of stated assumptions as to the level of expenditure supportable by the economy.[160]

If the general level of defense spending represented a directed verdict of sorts, the allocation of those funds among the services was the subject of horizontal bargaining. In return for greater restraint by the services spokesmen in attacking the overall level of funds, the military received a relatively free hand in the expenditure of their own budgets. A process of mutual adjustment developed in which, as Samuel P. Huntington has noted, "the subordinate acquiesces in the authority of the superior to limit resources while the superior leaves to the subordinate a relatively free hand in how he uses them." [161]

Accompanying this relative freedom of the services to allocate their own portion of the defense budget there was a vacuum of leadership at the level of the Office of the Secretary of Defense, in the realm of weapons planning. The starting point for technological development was, therefore, a complex of rival projects backed by competitive services, rather than a comprehensive program embracing the complementary interests of all the services. Without self-assertive weapons planning in the Secre-

[160] See his statement to the Mahon Committee in U.S. House Committee on Appropriations, *Hearings, DoD Appropriations for 1955,* 83rd Cong., 2nd Sess., 1954, p. 83. The National Security Council as a corporate body appears to have had scant influence on either the allocation of the defense budget or advanced weapons planning despite the elaborate procedures which were developed by Dillon Anderson, and Robert Cutler for bringing matters before the Council. While those procedural arrangements may have postponed the intervention of the officials who could obtain decisions that would stick, it appears that they did not suffice to insure that vital decisions related to the selection of novel weapons, defense organization, or jurisdictional assignments having strategic implications would be made within the framework of the National Security Council.

[161] Huntington, *The Common Defense,* p. 151.

tary's Office, responsibility presumably devolved upon the JCS. The Chiefs, however, found it exceedingly difficult to divorce themselves from their responsibilities as the agents of powerful corporate groups embracing frequently divergent professional perspectives on war and strategy, reflecting different combat experiences, and possessing different and occasionally conflicting proprietary interests.[162] Nor were they, prior to 1958, endowed with a Joint Staff capable of transcending the perspectives of the individual services and of developing a unified military strategy.[163]

Inevitably the Comptroller of the Pentagon became a seminal figure in the resolution of interservice controversies, since his office was "about the only place in the Pentagon where all 3,000 programs come together." [164]

The character of the Comptroller's interventions was also illuminated by Wilfred McNeil, who explained:

[162] In so far as the JCS were involved in weapons planning, they seemed to live up to their reputation as a "trading post." The pervasiveness of bargaining in the Chiefs' deliberations was explained by General Thomas White to the Senate Committee on Armed Services. "Now, the Joint Chiefs of Staff," he said, "can split a paper, and past history shows to me that when that split goes to the Secretary . . . too often his decision is equivocal in the sense that there is a tendency . . . to make everybody happy and, as a result, the decision is a compromise. Therefore, the reaction on me personally as a member of the Joint Chiefs of Staff when such a case arises, the pressure on me to reach a unanimous decision is great because I believe that . . . among the three so-called military experts, I can get a better decision for the country . . . than I can by passing it up where I am quite sure somebody else who does not know as much as the three of us will make a compromise. So it is better to compromise in the first place." Senate Committee on Armed Services, *Space and Missile Hearings,* 1957–1958, p. 1564. It is not suggested that the existence of a single central authority in the Defense Department for the development of a comprehensive program for weapons development would have yielded a perfectly coordinated program. What is evident is that mutual adjustment among partisans does not inevitably yield perfectly coordinated efforts either. For a discussion of the processes of "partisan mutual adjustment" see Lindblom, *The Intelligence of Democracy, passim.*

[163] Hammond, *Organizing for Defense,* chap. 13.

[164] See the testimony of former Comptroller Wilfred NcNeil before the House Committee on Armed Services, *Hearings, Department of Defense Reorganization,* 1958, p. 6573.

. . . if the schedule for missiles prepared by one subdivision of the Department was not in line with the construction list, prepared in still another part of the building, I think you would be certainly lacking in any proper discharge of your responsibility if you didn't see that that was brought into balance. It shouldn't be our job to put it in balance. It should be our job to bring it up so that it could be put in balance.[165]

Certainly the Comptroller was anxious to preserve the line against excessive spending. Yet his lack of self-confidence in rendering technical judgments on the feasibility of advanced missile projects and his lack of legal authority to make program decisions, limited him to a relatively modest role in checking interservice competition for the IRBMs.

The proliferation of missile projects was encouraged by a number of other factors. Each service possessed its own intelligence network, whose evaluations of enemy capabilities and hunches regarding technical possibilities could energize its developmental efforts. The relatively modest costs of a more primitive technology had permitted the simultaneous procurement of a variety of new weapon systems adapted for only slightly different operational assignments. Budget Bureau representatives who participated in the deliberations of the Defense Department committees seeking to estimate the costs of the rival missile programs and the evaluations of their respective technical merits were relatively inexperienced in such matters at the time when the Thor and Jupiter programs were initiated. In addition, they, and Pentagon officials, were attempting to monitor the missile programs without the assistance of such procedures as the program definition phase, cost effectiveness tests, long-term cost estimating procedures for competing systems, and refined techniques of systems analysis.

This structure of policy making—with its diffusion of power, its confusion as to the precise locus of responsibility, its discrepancy between weapons planning and defense budgeting, and its somewhat tenuous cleavage between civilian and military responsibilities—reinforced rivalries animated by the implemen-

[165] *Ibid.*, p. 6572.

tation of the New Look doctrine. It provided incentives for the services to search widely and lobby vigorously for support in their quest for weapons, budgetary support, and roles and missions assignments. The system seemed to offer a premium to foot-in-the-door tactics designed to quietly initiate new programs at minimum expenditure and then to consistently expand budgetary support by exploiting complementarities among the various components in novel weapon systems.[166] The administrative style of the President, the shortcomings of the National Security Council and Joint Chiefs of Staff as agencies for coherent planning, and the perspectives of Secretary Wilson, Chairman Radford, and Comptroller McNeil all tended to postpone the resolution of jurisdictional decisions until the pressures arrayed against the cancellation of projects or against the determination of mission assignments were, in this case at least, well nigh irresistible.

[166] See Alain Enthoven and Henry Rowen, "Defense Planning and Organization," in *Public Finances: Needs, Sources, and Utilization* (Princeton, Princeton University Press, 1961), p. 383.

(3) THE QUEST FOR
OPERATIONAL CONTROL

During 1955 the services had campaigned for approval of their respective developmental projects; in 1956 their interests turned to the even more contentious issues of operational control over intermediate-range ballistic missiles. Throughout the year the ambiguity of Wilson's public and private statements, the style of management in the Pentagon, and the competitive ambitions of the services, abetted by their zealous industrial suppliers, sparked a vigorous competition for control over the IRBM.[1]

Guidelines for this jurisdictional assignment were ambiguous and outdated. Guided missiles had not even been mentioned in the Key West and Newport Agreements. The Joint Chiefs of Staff had never specifically restricted the range of Army surface-to-surface missiles, though it was presumed that they would develop and deploy only tactical ballistic rockets.[2] In 1949 Secre-

[1] Needless to say, neither the Army nor the Air Force was free to operate as a monolithic entity as each sought to fashion a strategy for obtaining operational control over the IRBM. No unanimity of either purpose or political tactics is to be anticipated in large multipurpose organizations like the military services. A careful reading of the Congressional testimony of leading officers and civilian officials of the services, as well as their later recollections of events recounted here, suggests that reasonably close coordination prevailed between the respective service secretaries, Chiefs of Staff, and technical organizations of the Army and Air Force with respect to service objectives in the Thor-Jupiter controversy. It is plausible to suppose that the degree of coordination is closely related to the intensity of this particular dispute.

[2] Senate Committee on Armed Services, *Airpower Hearing*, 1956, p. 1288.

tary of the Army, Gordon Gray, suggested that each service develop the weapons it needed, i.e., ground-launched to the Army, sea-based to the Navy, and air-launched to the Air Force.[3] Soon thereafter, General Omar Bradley, Chairman of the Joint Chiefs, determined that "guided missiles would be employed by each armed service in a manner and to the extent required to accomplish its assigned missions." [4] He made no attempt to set forth a dividing line between short- and long-ranged rockets. As previously mentioned, the initial programmed range for the Redstone had been 465 nautical miles. This had been adjusted downward as a result of more conservative AEC estimates as to the achievable weight-yield ratios for available nuclear warheads, and not as a result of explicit Defense Department restrictions.[5] In regulations issued March 16, 1954, the Army was authorized to "develop, procure, and man land-based surface-to-surface missiles for support of Army field operations." [6] Again, no explicit range limitations were included. Clearly, however, the development of missiles with sufficient range to strike targets in the Soviet Union if deployed by field armies on the European Continent raised not only proprietary questions but strategic issues as well. It proved difficult to persuade the Air Force, the Secretary of Defense, and the President that such a rocket could appropriately be designated "tactical."

Initially, Secretary Wilson was content to equivocate on the roles and missions problem. This was consonant with his deliberate decision to initiate parallel projects. Uncertainties of functional assignment might be exploited to reinforce the urgency with which the Army and Air Force sought to overcome the imponderables of missile technology. As he told a news conference in May, 1956, "I have been taking what I think

[3] Maj. Gen. H. N. Toftoy, "Army Missile Development," *Army Information Digest* (December, 1956) 30.

[4] *Ibid.*

[5] Senate Committee on Armed Services, *Satellite and Missile Program Hearings,* 1957–1958, p. 585.

[6] Department of Defense Directive 5100.1, March 16, 1954. See Senate Committee on Armed Services, 1958 *DoD Reorganization Act Hearings,* 1958, p. 438.

is a sound realistic position and that is, develop the missiles and then let's see how we ought to use them and who ought to be responsible for using them." [7]

Whether Wilson's utterances reflected studied ambiguity or persistent procrastination, the services were not given unlimited license, and the Chiefs of Staff and Service Secretaries were informed that success in their development programs would not "necessarily determine which service would have the roles and missions." [8] The logic of parallel development may have encouraged vagueness on the proprietary issue. The pressures of a limited budget and the extracurricular activities of Army and Air Force colonels, however, prevented the indefinite evasion of a decision on it.

The basic issue was whether or not the Army would be permitted to deploy the weapon it was in the process of developing. Air Force responsibilities in the strategic retaliatory mission had long been acknowledged. Army theories justifying their use of intermediate-range ballistic missiles in tactical nuclear war situations enjoyed no such broad support. [9]

THE POLITICAL RESOURCES OF THE ARMY

The task of mobilizing support for the Army's strategic views was not to be simple, as indicated by the promulgation of the New Look doctrine in the face of spirited resistance. Enjoying relatively less influence than the other services at the highest military and civilian levels of the Defense Department, the Army had few incentives to restrict their campaign for the Jupiter to the usual channels. On the contrary, there were obvious incentives to expand the arena of defense politics and ventilate the issues before a wider audience, even if this served to inflame the atmosphere of policy-making. [10] Their objective was to secure allies and activate clients. Since the former cannot

[7] New York Times, May 22, 1956, p. 14.   [8] Ibid.

[9] U.S. Congress, Senate, Committee on Appropriations, Hearings, Department of Defense Appropriations, 1958, 85th Cong., 2nd Sess., p. 42.

[10] So acrimonious did the exchange of "leaked" staff papers become in the spring of 1956 that Secretary Wilson felt obliged to hold a full dress press conference on May 21, "with the Chiefs of Staff and Service

be acquired, nor the latter retained for nothing, Army hopes of obtaining operational control of the Jupiter were contingent no less upon their political assets than upon the persuasiveness of their tactical doctrine.

The Army could anticipate support on some doctrinal issues from the Navy, from scientists formerly engaged on Project Vista, and from a growing number of civilian strategists. On budgetary issues they occasionally enjoyed the support of the "big defense spenders" and some industrial suppliers. Yet these somewhat diffuse sources of support were not easily mobilized on the proprietary issue of control of the land-based IRBM. The utility of missiles of such range and destructive potential for limited wars was not self-evident. The big defense spenders were less concerned about jurisdictional matters than the over-all magnitude of defense expenditures and the range of contingencies for which countermeasures were being developed. Many of the Army's prime contractors were neutralized on such an issue by their business relations with the rival service. Traditional Army Ordnance Corps arrangements for supplying weapons to the other services served to discredit claims that the Army must operate any new device they developed. Indeed, had they not agreed with the Navy jointly to produce a sea-based Jupiter?

The Army's doubtful prospects of a favorable decision on deployment and use also stimulated internal criticism of the Jupiter program. A long-range ballistic missile program was a luxury the Army could ill afford on their comparatively austere budget. It had to be financed to a large extent at the expense of conventional reequipment needs.[11] The Jupiter program was subsidized by the Department of Defense during the first year. The following year General Gavin was forced to absorb $25

Secretaries somewhat sheepishly disavowing the actions of their respective subordinates." "Reappraising United States Military Policy," *Business Week* (May 26, 1956), 26. See also *New York Times,* May 19, 1956, p. 1. Although the tender façade of unity was tenuously reestablished, it was unreasonable, under the circumstances, to expect that the political activities of the services could be easily suppressed.

[11] Senate Committee on Armed Services, *Satellite and Missile Program Hearings,* 1957–1958, p. 477.

million of its cost out of an otherwise very austere Army research and development program.[12] Such contributions to the financing of the Jupiter development program, he later observed to the Senate Special Preparedness Investigation Subcommittee, were "affected through such actions as the retardation of the anti-aircraft missile program, a stretchout of all surface-to-surface missile programs except Jupiter, and the adjustment downward of plans to replace obsolescent equipment."[13]

Those combat arms from whom sacrifices were demanded in order to finance the Jupiter program were predictably reserved in their enthusiasm for it. Intrabranch competition for scarce funds became even more intense as the unexpended funds left over from the Korean War dwindled to the vanishing point. Short on resources, the Army was long on requirements. Many shared the sentiments later expressed by one division commander: "For $5 billion worth of troop equipment, I'd trade Huntsville away in a minute."[14]

Despite their joint efforts on the sea-based Jupiter, the Army could expect no more than equivocal support from the Navy for their campaign to acquire operational responsibilities for the land-based IRBM. For several years, to be sure, Army-Navy relations had been free of troublesome disputes over roles and missions. There were hopes also that memories of the 1949 "revolt of the admirals" still rankled within the Navy, and that these could be rekindled to inflame their relations with the Air Force. The tenuousness of the Army-Navy alliance swiftly became apparent in 1956.

The primary task of the Huntsville Arsenal was to assist the Navy in developing a sea-based IRBM. Hopes for obtaining control of the land-based backup IRBM, however, lay in achieving an initial operational capability before the Air Force. At this point the proprietary interests of the Army converged with

[12] House Committee on Armed Services, *National Defense Missile Hearings,* 1958, p. 4351.
[13] Senate Committee on Armed Services, *Satellite and Missile Program Hearings,* 1957–1958, p. 1531.
[14] "Forces on the Ground," *Time,* LXXIII (May 11, 1959), 23.

the transcendent interest underlined in the Killian Report— that of acquiring a substantial missile capability at the earliest possible date—and dictated a substantial reliance upon components used in the Redstone rocket. Since the Redstone was a liquid-fueled missile, the Army was immediately confronted by problems with their Navy ally.[15]

The Army had the facilities, the competence, and the encouragement to switch to a solid-fuel approach. Jet Propulsion Laboratories, at the California Institute of Technology, had long been among the leaders in research on solid-fuel rocket propellants. Dr. Charles C. Lauritsen, an eminent physicist and a member of the Army Scientific Panel, recommended that the Army initiate studies of the "utility and the possibility of obtaining approval for a missile with a maximum range of 500 miles." [16] In view of his persistent skepticism as to the practicability of cryogenic propellants "for tactical employment where mobility and readiness are of importance," it is clear that he was recommending a reorientation of their efforts toward solid-fueled missiles with a genuine potential for field mobility.[17]

General Gavin, however, resisted such a reorientation if it meant yielding the Jupiter. He was naturally interested in the potential mobility afforded by solid-fuel rockets, but he was convinced of the efficacy of mounting the Jupiter on movable launching equipment. Moreover, he was anxious about evidence that the Soviet Union was acquiring a capability for putting satellites into space. He was concerned about America's technological prestige and, like von Braun, especially interested in those engine propellants which could launch payloads into orbit. Solid-fuel missiles did not promise such a potential at an early date.[18]

[15] It would be misleading to suggest a complete identification of Army and Huntsville Arsenal perspectives. In fact it appears that the von Braun team was so intrigued by the problems of shipboard launching that they occasionally neglected aspects of the land-based IRBM program which would have involved more modest advances on existing technology.

[16] Correspondence to the author, July 21, 1965.   [17] *Ibid.*

[18] Interview with General Gavin, August 22, 1963.

Among the Joint Chiefs of Staff, the Army dared to hope for the benevolent neutrality of the Navy; they anticipated vehement opposition from the Air Force. In the event of split decisions from the Joint Chiefs of Staff, Chairman Admiral Radford would assume the role of arbitrator. In view of his skepticism toward Army efforts to justify operational control of their own IRBM, a favorable decision was unlikely.

Nor were the Army's prospects significantly improved by broadening the base of politics to include "back stop" [19] organizations or industrial suppliers. Whereas the Navy and Air Force were consistently able to rely on the concentrated industrial support of the shipbuilding and airframe industries respectively, the Army had a much more diffuse group of suppliers. The Army Association was neither as well established as the Navy League nor as well financed as the Air Force Association.

Particularly significant was the opposition the Army encountered from the Aircraft Industries Association.[20] As manned bombers and fighter aircraft approached obsolescence, the airframe industry faced an uncertain and ominous future, unless they were successful in capturing a sizable segment of the military missile field in both its development and production aspects.[21] Unlike airplanes, missiles would be produced in limited

[19] For a discussion of the "back stop" organizations supporting the services, see Samuel P. Huntington, "Inter-service Competition and the Political Roles of the Armed Services," *American Political Science Review*, LV (March, 1961), 40–52.

[20] To be sure, the Army prime missile contractor, Chrysler Corporation, was free to join the AIA. Needless to say, they would not have been welcomed with open arms, and from the standpoint of the corporation, the $75,000 fee charged to members may have diminished their interest in membership.

[21] See Charles J. V. Murphy, "The Plane Makers Under Stress," *Fortune*, LXI (June, 1960), 134 ff.; Charles J. V. Murphy, "The Plane Makers Under Stress," II, *Fortune*, LXII (July, 1960). pp. 111 ff. An additional reason why Army suppliers may have been less vigorous in their political activities than their Air Force counterparts inhered in the fact that defense contracts were not nearly so vital to their prosperity. In 1958 the automotive industry had military sales ranging from 5%, as at General Motors, to 15% at Chrysler. The percentage of military sales for the Air Force-affiliated airframe industry, on the other hand, ranged from

numbers, would require relatively little airframe, and would be exceedingly expensive to develop. Thus the industry covetously eyed major responsibilities in the research, design, development, test, and assembly phases of future missiles programs.[22]

Huntsville Arsenal personnel provided central management capabilities, and they were responsible for the overall systems engineering and technical direction of advanced projects. Prototypes and experimental models were frequently produced in the arsenals in order that government engineers might acquire familiarity with the most difficult conceptual and engineering problems posed by novel projects. As a result, they were in a position to offer assistance to industries tooling up for quantity production. Their sustained competence in the frontier technologies provided them with the independence needed to evaluate both the technical proficiency and the cost efficiency of their contractors.

There were occasional representatives of the airframe industry who saw in the maintenance of such technical and managerial capabilities in the arsenals the potential for governmental interference in the preserve of "free enterprise." General Medaris and other Army officials at times seemed sensitive to such innuendos and attempted to counter them through their public statements. The arsenal system may have imposed an additional liability on their public relations efforts. Government employ-

---

67% at Beech Aircraft to 99.2% at Martin Company. See U.S. Senate, Document No. 94, *"Report to the President on Government Contracting for R&D,"* prepared by the Budget Bureau and referred to the Senate Committee on Government Operations, 87th Cong., 2nd Sess., 1962.

[22] The fact that Chrysler Corporation was to be the prime contractor for the airframe and assembly for the Jupiter surely reinforced the opposition of the Aircraft Industries Association to their program. Their selection was virtually inevitable in view of their familiarity with the production engineering for the Redstone tactical missile, many components of which were used in the Jupiter. The urgency of the Jupiter program and the desire for continuity with earlier programs counseled against the search for a new prime contractor. Nonetheless, since the airframe industry was already threatened by vigorous competition from several electronics firms for contracts in missile integration and assembly, one can imagine their apprehensions about the prospect of competition from the automotive industry as well.

ees were not as free to advertise their products as industrial suppliers of the Air Force. One of the remaining media for advertising was the calculated leak which Dr. von Braun candidly admitted was resorted to by Army partisans. "The Jupiter," he said, "involves several million dollars of the taxpayers' money. One hundred per cent security would mean no information for the public, no money for the Army, no Jupiter. . . . The Army has got to play the same game as the Air Force and the Navy." [23]

Finally, the Army could not look with confidence to the political parties for support in 1956. The New Look was in a sense a Republican strategy, and could hardly be repudiated in an election year; nor were the Democrats likely to find in the Army's quest for an IRBM an appealing springboard issue. In general, the Army was a most unattractive political ally. It was identified in the public mind with the "slug it out slowly wars" with Germany and Japan. Support for Army programs represented calls for higher draft rates and increased taxes, both of which resurrected memories of the trauma of Korea. And above all, the Democratic Party's preeminent defense critics— Senators Symington, Johnson, and Jackson—were all air power enthusiasts who simply entertained a greater tolerance than the Administration for the maintenance of balanced forces.[24]

AIR FORCE POLITICAL ASSETS

The Air Force had already been acknowledged by Wilson as legitimate user of the IRBM. Thus, it was to their advantage to prevent a diffusion of authority and control over the new weapon. At the outset their prospects appeared bright. It was

[23] Douglas Cater, "Government by Publicity," *The Reporter*, XX (March 19, 1959), 15.

[24] See Gordon Harris, "Wanted: More Politics in Defense," *Harper's Magazine*, CCXIII (September, 1956), 50–55. Professor Samuel Huntington pointed out the essential public relations dilemma of the Army when he wrote: "It is not simple to glamorize a foxhole." Indeed, part of the attraction of the Jupiter lay precisely in the Army's recognition that they had no equipment which could capture the popular imagination "in the same degree as the range of the atomic submarine, the speed of a jet or the size of a super carrier." Huntington, *The Common Defense*, p. 190.

widely assumed that either the Thor or the Jupiter project
would be eventually cancelled, and the Air Force missile had
been designated IRBM No.1. Their industrial allies were numerous and influential. That this support was substantial is
indicated by the fact that in 1955 the list of top defense contractors was topped by Boeing, North American, General Dynamics, and United Aircraft. All were, of course, airframe manufacturers; together they accounted for 19.3 per cent of the total
defense procurement expenditures. Seven of the top ten corporations, eleven of the top fifteen, and thirteen of the top twenty,
were aircraft firms. Chrysler, on the other hand, had been the
sixth largest defense supplier during the Korean build-up; by
1955, it had fallen to ninety-forth place.[25]

The only serious liability of the Air Force lay in the apprehension of some top officials that the Thor program would
drain energy, resources, and attention away from the Atlas
project, to which they assigned a more urgent priority.[26] General Bernard A. Schriever, however, later testified that the Thor
was financed with only a 10 per cent addition in the overall resources expended by the Air Force's Western Development
Division.[27] Diversion of technical personnel had, in his view, a
minimal impact on the progress of the Atlas missile.[28] To sum

[25] "Aircraft Electronics Rise to Top," *Business Week* (September 1,
1956), 33.
[26] Trevor Gardner, "Our Guided Missiles Crisis," *Look*, XX (May 15,
1956), 48.
[27] Senate Committee on Armed Services, *Airpower Hearings*, 1956, p.
1161. It is, of course, true that the Thor program had been underway
only a few months at the time of Schriever's testimony.
[28] This is not to say that the Air Force did not face budgetary dilemmas
of its own. Clearly they did. They were simultaneously heading down
two separate roads. On the one hand, they had to continue to procure
manned and unmanned airplanes for strategic and defensive purposes. On
the other hand, they were becoming deeply committed in the missile
field for tactical defense missiles, long-range IRBMs and ICBMs, the
Distant Early Warning Network, and the SAGE system of computer
control of air defense missile operations. Even for the generously endowed, such projects pressed upon existing resources. See Charles J. V.
Murphy, "Eisenhower's Most Critical Defense Budget," *Fortune*, LIV
(December, 1956), 246.

up, the Air Force had a mission, the favor of the Chairman of the Joint Chiefs of Staff, and numerous supporters within the government and without.

STRATEGIES OF CONTROL: ARMY

The pursuit of objectives in a political environment involves the "cultivation of an active clientele, the development of confidence among other governmental officials, and skill in following strategies that exploit one's opportunities to the maximum." [29] All of these elements were apparent in the Army strategy, which was based primarily on the assumption that should they win the developmental competition with the Air Force, they stood a fair chance of deploying the Jupiter themselves. Their strategy was directed toward (1) facilitating the development of the Jupiter with all deliberate speed; (2) deferring a decision on roles and missions as long as possible; and (3) designing a missile compatible with their tactical doctrine, able to exploit the unique skills of the artilleryman, and capable of maximizing the importance of established Army performance of supporting missions in logistics, geodesy, and survey.

To reinforce their contention that speed of development was of the utmost importance, Army commentators expressed alarm at the consequences of any unmatched Soviet capability in the IRBM field. This disposed them to credit what in retrospect appear to have been rather exaggerated estimates of Soviet progress in the missile race. In response to their own sense of urgency, they created a management structure which could significantly reduce the lead time for the development of new weapons.

In pursuance of Secretary of Defense Wilson's memorandum of November 3, 1955, which assigned the Army developmental responsibilities in the IRBM field, the Army Ballistic Missile Agency was created. Major General John B. Medaris—an officer with an engineering degree, extensive experience in Ordnance, and a reputation for getting things done—was appointed

[29] Aaron Wildavsky, *The Politics of the Budgetary Process* (Boston, Little, Brown and Co., 1964), pp. 64–65.

Commander of the new agency. He was delegated extensive authority for procurement contracting, and his problems of obtaining higher level reviews were simplified enormously through the establishment of a Joint Army-Navy Ballistic Missiles Committee (JAN-BMC), in which the respective service secretaries and their assistants for Research and Development, Applications Engineering, Installations and Logistics, and Financial Management could jointly consider, amend, reject, and approve the plans formulated at the operating level.[30] From the Army's standpoint the creation of this special agency not only reduced red tape, hastened decision making, and impressed outsiders, but served as well to distinguish the glamour weapons from other items in their development program.

Although some Army partisans considered the appointment of Navy Secretary Charles Thomas as Chairman of the JAN-BMC an additional reminder of their second-class citizenship, prudence counseled gracious acquiescence in that arrangement. They could ill afford a loss of Navy support. Army alliance policy consisted of an assiduous wooing of political and moral support from the Navy, coupled with occasional attempts to inflame relations among sailors and airmen.[31]

The Navy's strategic role was not to be challenged; nor were their technical efforts to be criticized. Even when they withdrew from the Jupiter project in December, 1956, General Medaris imputed to them nothing but the best of motives. He publicly acknowledged "the validity of the Navy's position with respect to the high desirability of a solid-propellant missile for submarine work." [32]

[30] Although the new organization began to take shape in early November, 1955, the order creating the Army Ballistic Missile Agency was not finally signed until February 1, 1956. For an account of the administrative rearrangements in the Department of the Army, see Medaris, *Countdown for Decision*, pp. 101–09.

[31] Army colonels even "leaked" to *New York Times* Reporter, Anthony Leviero, an Air Force staff paper which depreciated the contribution of Forrestal-Class carriers to the overall strategic mission. *New York Times*, May 20, 1956, p. 1.

[32] House Committee on Government Operations, *Missile Program Hearings*, 1959, p. 363.

As they hopefully solicited Navy support, they expediently borrowed from Navy doctrine. The Navy had established a requirement for sufficient striking power to neutralize submarine pens and naval storehouses which constituted a threat to their command of the sea; could the Army not justify a similar requirement with respect to enemy missile launching sites from which ground troops could be attacked? The Navy's demand "that it must 'own' lock, stock, and barrel, every weapon and piece of equipment and the operating crews if it is to accomplish the Navy mission," was quoted approvingly in the *Army Combat Forces Journal.* "It would seem," they editorialized, "that what is good for the U.S. Navy ought to be good for the U.S. Army—and the U.S. Air Force." [33]

Even descriptions of the atomic battlefield of the future, with dispersed units obtaining artillery support from long-range missile forces, were suggestive of the self-contained operations of surface ships and their reliance on carriers for long-range aerial support. Army leaders also used Tactical Air Command justifications for deploying their forces from "sites as near as possible to the dumps and depots where projectiles, food, fuel, and other supplies are stored." [34] This consideration not only justified extensions in the range of artillery support weapons, but reinforced the logic of centralized command and control of the combat support forces in the hands of one who could assure that supporting arms would be responsive to the needs of the battle area.

Army spokesmen naturally emphasized the tactical usefulness of an extended-range missile. They sought to identify the IRBM with traditional Army functions. Extensions in range of artillery support weapons was simply a response to deeper enemy tactical targets and the need to deploy from less vulnerable rear positions. The implications of the Jupiter as a strategic weapon, should it be deployed near the front, were conveniently disregarded. Army officials did, however, emphasize the fact that missiles of even strategic range were deployed and op-

33 *Army Combat Forces Journal* (October, 1956), 15.

34 Major N. A. Parsons, Jr., "THE IRBM: Artillery-Support Weapons," *Army* (March, 1956), 14.

erated by the Soviet Army as an extension of artillery rather than a sophisticated variant of the manned bomber.[35]

As he designed ground-launch equipment for the Jupiter, General Gavin, Assistant Chief of Staff for Research and Development, clearly thought in terms of a mobile field weapon. Such a concept was consonant with Army traditions, and it served to underscore their peculiar capabilities for handling such a weapon. As Air Force General Clarence Irvine commented: "Gavin is thinking in terms of equipment, quite properly, to chaperone an Army in the field, as an extension of artillery. And with this concept there is nothing wrong with what he proposes to do." [36]

Army partisans clearly hoped it would clinch the case for operational control, for they thought of themselves as the "one service fully equipped and competent to provide all the supporting elements necessary to missile warfare." [37] Their deployment concept, sharply differentiated from that of the Air Force, was serviceable for both deterrence strategy and their own tactical needs. As a mobile missile, it would enjoy immunity from surprise or preemptive attacks. Invulnerability could be achieved through dispersion and concealment, as well as mobility. Significantly, the Army alone could handle the weapon under field conditions. Their competence in camouflage and field defense, in logistic support of dispersed units, in the acquisition of target information from reconnaissance drones, in survey and geodesy, and in providing transportation to launching sites was vastly superior, they contended, to Air Force capabilities.[38]

The Jupiter might also provide them with a support system unaffected by weather, visibility, or enemy air defenses.[39] No

[35] Senate Committee on Armed Services, *Satellite and Missile Program Hearings,* 1957–1958, p. 490.

[36] *Ibid.,* p. 964.

[37] Claude Witze, "Army Expands Scope: Challenges U.S. Air Force," *Aviation Week* (November 5, 1956), 32.

[38] Senate Committee on Armed Services, *Satellite and Missile Program Hearings,* 1957–1958, p. 1509.

[39] Senate Committee on Armed Services, *Airpower Hearings,* 1956, p. 722.

new skills would be required to man the system; personnel already trained to launch other Army missiles could be easily adapted to the peculiarities of the IRBM.

The accuracy or validity of such claims is not our interest at this point. It is significant, however, to note that the Army was inhibited from pressing one of their most telling arguments too far. They were constrained from advocating the assignment of operational control over missiles on the basis of mobile versus fixed based characteristics of individual weapon systems.[40] Army leaders were not prepared to offer enthusiastic support to such a distinction since they had previously acquired important responsibilities in the air defense field, and the Nike missiles were fixed-based weapons. Such an argument would have been vulnerable, in any event, to the same devastating criticism that Army leaders had leveled at the Key West Agreement; namely, that it would relate roles and missions to the characteristics of weapons rather than the functional requirements of a coherent strategy.

It must, of course, be recalled that the Army was not pursuing a quest for exclusive jurisdiction over the IRBM. When they presented their case for operational deployment in 1956, they did so rather on the grounds that "each of the services that had use for it should be able to fire, regardless of who developed it." [41]

STRATEGIES OF CONTROL: AIR FORCE

The Air Force had no objection to Army development and use of short-range tactical missiles. The Army Jupiter program, however, not only appeared as an indication of growing interest in the strategic field, but threatened the classic mission of their medium-range bombers; namely "sealing off the battlefield by striking at enemy railheads, troop concentrations, and supply areas far behind the front." [42]

[40] Senator Flanders was among the supporters of such a distinction. See his comments in Senate Committee on Armed Services, *Satellite and Missile Program Hearings*, 1957–1958, pp. 2052–53.

[41] Testimony of Secretary Brucker, House Committee on Armed Services, *National Defense Missile Hearings*, 1958, p. 4218.

[42] Martin, *Saturday Evening Post*, CCXXX (November 9, 1957), 116.

Since Air Force rights to an IRBM had been established, their problem was to retain exclusive control over the new weapon. For this purpose an appropriate strategy called for an early decision on roles and missions, a gradual detachment of the Navy from support of the Jupiter land-based missile project, a vigorous development program, and an acknowledged capacity to produce enough missiles to cover all strategic needs. In these endeavors they achieved only partial success.

In October, 1955, prior to Wilson's decision for "deliberate duplication," the Air Force had pressed for a resolution of the troublesome roles and missions issue. Army dissent within the Joint Chiefs caused a split decision, and the Secretary of Defense chose to postpone judgment on the jurisdictional question. In February, 1956, Air Force recommendations for an early assignment of operational responsibility were again indefinitely deferred.[43]

Meanwhile, Air Force officials were most cordial toward the Navy. They expressed no criticism of the Navy's sea-based Jupiter concept, nor later of the Polaris. On matters of technical information exchange, they were paragons of cooperativeness. Toward the Army they adopted a policy of restraint and forebearance. General Twining counseled prudence to all commanders in the spring of 1956. He encouraged them to "emphasize the positive" in Air Force capabilities, but also to "strengthen the team as a whole, by acknowledging the competence of other members." [44] Confident that their position was unshakable, they were anxious to avoid unnecessary histrionics.

The reasons for their confidence were to be found in their managerial structure, developmental philosophy, strategic doctrine, and tactical assets in any interservice skirmishes which might develop. The Air Force research and development organization for guided missiles had been created to expedite the accelerated Atlas program, and was modified only slightly to

[43] U.S., Congress, House, Committee on Goverment Operations (Subcommittee on Information), *Hearings, Availability of Information from Federal Departments and Agencies*, 85th Cong., 1st Sess., 1957, p. 3074.

[44] "USAF Adopting New Approach to Interservice Rivalry: Ignore It," *Aviation Week* (June 11, 1956), 31.

accommodate the Thor project. The salient aspects of Air Force administrative arrangements for missile development and production can be briefly summarized.[45]

Program responsibility for the Air Force ballistic missiles was centered in the Western Development Division (WDD), a subdivision of the Air Research and Development Command (ARDC). Major General Schriever, the Commander of WDD, was simultaneously retained as Deputy Commander, ARDC, in order to hasten approvals at the Command level. Thus, authority and responsibility were concentrated in such a way as to permit fast reacting and responsible managerial control. Technical direction and systems engineering was provided by the Ramo-Wooldridge Corporation, working intimately with WDD headquarters in a staff relationship, though in a line capacity relative to the associate contractors for the various missile systems.[46]

Thus was the Air Force provided with a functional analogue of the in-house technical capabilities which the von Braun team provided for the Army. This was a critical resource, in view of the fact that vast sums of money had to be committed to high-risk programs based on technical expectations which had yet to be substantiated by test results.

Inasmuch as WDD was delegated complete responsibility for the Air Force first-generation missiles—from blackboard design to initial operational capability—close collaborative relations with the Air Material Command (AMC), the Strategic Air Command (SAC), and Air Research and Development Command (ARDC), were imperative.[47] Within the Western Development Division, therefore, a Ballistic Missile Division

[45] See Schwiebert, *History of the U.S. Air Force Ballistic Missiles, Passim;* Eugene M. Emme (ed.), *The History of Rocket Technology* (Detroit, Wayne State University Press, 1964), chap. 7, for more detailed description of those arrangements.

[46] House Committee on Government Operations, *Missile Program Hearings,* 1959, pp. 63–76.

[47] Decisions relating to the numbers of missiles to be procured, the location of their deployment, and other strategic choices were reserved for higher consideration and determination.

(BMD) was created to maintain continuous liaison with the Air Research Development Command; a Ballistic Missile Center (BMC) to handle coordination with the Air Material Command; and SAC-MIKE to assure intimate cooperation with the Strategic Air Command. From the standpoint of the Air Force the merit of these arrangements lay in the fact that "overall management control would reside within the Air Force, the use of associate contractors would provide the broad industrial base and permit the degree of control considered essential by the Air Material Command, which would administer the contracts, and the flexibility of organization and administration would attract the best brains of the nation to the project." [48]

The project managers of the Thor inherited not only a management structure but a burgeoning industrial base as well. The breadth of the Air Force's network of contractors and subcontractors is suggested by the fact that the Atlas, Titan, and Thor complexes included 18,000 scientists and technicians in universities and industry, 70,000 others in 22 industries, including 17 prime contractors and over 200 subcontractors, as well as innumerable smaller suppliers.[49] This broad industrial base constituted a significant political asset to the Air Force. Politically sensitive officers within the Air Force may have recognized it as a prudent hedge against economy drives. More important, the pattern of subcontracting was heavily influenced by then prevalent assumptions relating to industrial dispersion and civil defense. Considerations of regional equity and some logrolling

[48] Schwiebert, *History of the U.S. Air Force Ballistic Missiles,* p. 85. A further streamlining of review and approval procedures was adopted in response to recommendations of the Gillette Committee. Subsequently, overall programs were developed annually at the project management level. Those plans were then subject to review and approval at only two levels, the Air Force Ballistic Missiles Committee, chaired by the Secretary of the Air Force, and in a similar committee in the Office of the Secretary of Defense (OSD-BMC). See House Committee on Government Operations, *Missile Program Hearings,* 1959, pp. 639–64. Time-Consuming delays were reduced substantially, though by no means eliminated. See Gardner, *Look,* XX (May 15, 1959), 46.

[49] Senate Committee on Appropriations, *Hearings, Department of Defense Appropriations 1959,* 85th Cong., 2nd Sess., 1958, p. 900.

quite probably entered the picture. Yet in view of the sense of urgency which infused the missile programs, it seems most unlikely that such factors were allowed to intrude to the extent that major delays or inefficiencies might result.

In order to exploit these residual assets, the Thor had to be quickly translated from blackboard design into hardware. Rapid development was facilitated by the Air Force's philosophy of concurrency, which had been formulated in response to contemporary fears that the Soviet Union had solved the lead time problem more successfully than the United States. The objective of concurrency was to shorten the lead time on new weapons programs by developing an *operational base* and a *production base* even as research and development on a weapon system was proceeding.[50] The Thor was consciously designed as a maximum risk program with only three and a half years being provided for the transition from conception to operation. Rejecting the tried and true Air Force maxim, "fly before you buy," hard tooling for quantity production was installed, negotiations for base construction initiated, personnel for ground handling and launching trained, and storage and maintenance techniques studied even before Thor prototypes were successfully flight-tested.[51]

The significance of early tooling for quantity production was especially great. Such a step was taken by the Air Force on the assumption that there was sufficient information and understanding of ballistic rocketry "to warrant a program based on components designed and fabricated to operational standards." [52]

[50] It is noteworthy that the concurrency doctrine was elaborated as early as 1950 in a staff study, "Combat Ready Aircraft," prepared by (then) Col. B. A. Shriever. Emme, *History of Rocket Technology,* p. 148.

[51] Senate Committee on Armed Services, *Satellite and Missile Program Hearings,* 1957–1958, p. 843. All were pacing items with lead times ranging from 15 to 30 months. House Committee on Government Operations, *Missile Program Hearings,* 1959, p. 14.

[52] Senate Committee on Armed Services, *Satellite and Missile Program Hearings,* 1957–1958, p. 843. It seems likely that there was some contractor pressure for such a policy as for the concurrency principle in general. There is considerable evidence that contractors shared the conviction of the military services that the country had to obtain operational missiles at the earliest possible moment. More mundane motives doubtless rein-

Such a policy would obviously hasten the transition between development and production. The ancillary benefits of the policy were soon to become apparent in the context of interservice competition. Even if slightly behind in the development of the Thor, Air Force partisans could argue that such a lag could easily be offset in the rapidity of the transition to production. Moreover, when a choice between competing programs had to be made, "sunk costs" constituted persuasive grounds for the continuation of even marginal projects. Such wedging, or "camel's nose" tactics are frequently employed in budgetary struggles.[53] It is not suggested that the Air Force's interest in concurrency derived from tactical considerations alone. Rather it appears that there were beneficial side effects of a philosophy prompted by a concern to produce operational weapons in the shortest possible time period.

Of more serious concern to the Air Force was the growing interest displayed by the Army in rockets with strategic capabilities. Air Force doctrine, for quite cogent and plausible reasons, counseled against any dilution in the unified command and control arrangements governing the use of strategic delivery systems. The basic premise in Air Force thinking was that strategic airpower was "something that can be employed as a *single instrument* . . . all of it, or any part of it, can be directed, controlled, if need be, from a single source." [54]

The requirement of instantaneous, centralized control of

---

forced a genuine patriotism. The concurrency principle was certainly attractive to contractors engaged in both research and development work and production contracts. The former were normally contracted on a Cost Plus Fixed Fee basis, while production contracts were more often Fixed Price, Fixed Price Incentive, or Fixed Price Redetermination. The economic incentives thus encouraged contractors to prepare for production as early as possible, charging off some of the costs to the R&D phase. As Carl Kaysen has noted, "The more the solution of production problems and the acquisition of special tools and facilities can be charged off as costs on the CPFF basis, the less the contractor's risks under the fixed price portion of his contract." "Improving the Efficiency of Military Research and Development," *Public Policy*, XII (Cambridge, Harvard University Press, 1963) , p. 255.

[53] See Wildavsky, *The Politics of the Budgetary Process*, p. 111.

[54] Colonel Jerry D. Paige and Colonel Rayal H. Roussel, "What Is Air Power?" *Air University Quarterly Review*, VIII (Summer, 1955) , 5.

strategic weapons was based upon the speeds of delivery systems, the tempo of modern warfare, the capacity for a high rate of fire, the relative invulnerability of ballistic missiles once in the air, and the consequent necessity for split-second decisions—unhindered by committees, coordinating mechanisms, or negotiated agreements among service commanders. Central direction would provide insurance that all essential targets were covered and that inadvertent escalation would not occur.

Moreover, in view of the anticipated mix of manned bombers and ballistic missiles to be employed on strategic missions, planning and operations required extensive coordination and intimate cooperation. "There is nothing," one writer emphasized, "which should preclude the use of the existing command and control structure of the Strategic Air Command. The principle of central control of all strategic systems remains valid. I think it is absolutely necessary that all uses of large nuclear weapons, except in the missions of air defense and close support of the surface battle, be coordinated by a central agency." [55]

Assuming, however, the desirability of centralized control over the new means of strategic delivery—and the logic of this position was compelling—why should the Air Force be endowed with such responsibilities? Army officials had readily conceded that the characteristics of the bomber required certain peculiar Air Force skills for its effective operation. With respect to ballistic missiles, however, they drew analogies with artillery, and contended that Air Force officers were suited neither by temperament nor training to field them.

To Air Force leaders it seemed self-evident that the problems of missile deployment and use were related to strategic bombing. In their view, the similarity of mission rather than the characteristics of weapons should be the vital determinant. Considering the IRBM as a strategic weapon, they argued that their experience with quick reaction time weapons and with coordinated strikes from widely dispersed bases, their capabilities in

[55] Major Gen. Charles M. McCorkle, "Command and Control of Ballistic Missiles," in Lt. Col. Kenneth F. Gantz (ed.) *Air Force Report on the Ballistic Missile: Its Technology, Logistics, and Strategy.*

prehostilities reconnaissance, postattack damage assessment, and date processing conferred a clear advantage upon them as the operational agent for the Department of Defense over all strategic missiles.[56]

The persuasiveness of Air Force logic became all the more impressive when supplemented by their tactical advantages. Since Air Force doctrine was closely identified with the official military policy, attacks by the Army on Air Force doctrines may have been interpreted as attacks on the Administration itself.[57]

Finally, the Air Force held a trump card for the time when bargaining on roles and missions commenced in earnest. Throughout 1956 the Air Force and Army were engaged in a furious jurisdictional squabble over air defense missiles. The Air Force openly expressed its disregard for the Nike missiles and refused to emplace them around SAC bases. Instead, they installed the Talos, a Navy developed seeking missile of somewhat greater range. To make matters worse, they refused an Army request for a loan of B-52s to test its Nike B antijamming mechanism.[58] Positions hardened and animosities mounted. But with its Bomarc missile in the process of being developed, the Air Force could cheaply part with Talos as a bargaining ploy in return for exclusive control over both Thor and Jupiter.[59]

[56] Air Force philosophy was set forth clearly by Maj. Gen. Clarence Irvine, who explained to the Senate Special Preparedness Investigation Subcommittee that the objective of the Air Force on the Thor program was "to create another weapons system which would fit into the SAC war plan; and therefore, among other things we wanted fast reaction, the ability to shoot quickly, the same as in SAC we want an alert system to get the airplanes in the air quickly, while the people who fly them are still alive; and in the case of the missiles, while there is still a man there to push the button." Senate Committee on Armed Services, *Satellite and Missile Program Hearings*, 1957–1958, p. 964.

[57] While many commentators have alluded to the President's sensitivity to unsolicited military advice from his former colleagues, it appears that in this particular case President Eisenhower, while sympathetic with the general army desire to extend the range of its tactical firepower, felt that the Army was going beyond the bounds of its theater requirements.

[58] Cater and Hadley, *The Reporter*, XIV (March 19, 1959), 17.

[59] This is not meant to suggest that such a *quid pro quo* was intended by the Air Force or acceptable to the Army. But when the Secretary of Defense began searching for a formula for resolving the jurisdictional

NAVY DEFECTION FROM THE JUPITER PROGRAM

From the outset, Army-Navy collaboration on a sea-based IRBM was a tenuous marriage of convenience through which the Army borrowed a mission and the Navy acquired a role in the burgeoning missile field.[60] The advantages in this hastily consummated union were hardly symmetrical. The Navy, in effect, bought into the missile market at the Army's expense. Design plans for the Jupiter were delayed several months as compatibility with the Navy's requirements were built into the system.[61] But even with substantial modifications the Navy's reservations about the Jupiter missile could not be removed. The Jupiter did, of course, promise an earlier initial operational capability. This capability, however, appeared obtainable only if the Navy was prepared to burden itself with a costly, obsolescent, and hazardous missile system.

Since the Jupiter was a liquid-fueled missile, time and money dictated its deployment on surface craft, which could be converted and refitted faster than new submarines could be designed and built.[62] A submarine version of the Jupiter was, to be sure, considered, and the missile's size was ultimately based upon the requirements of submarine storage and launch space.[63]

---

struggle, the Air Force was fortunate in having some projects with which it could cheaply part.

[60] Interview with General John B. Medaris, August 28, 1963.

[61] House Committee on Armed Services, *National Defense Missile Hearings,* 1958, p. 4446. The Navy wanted a missile shortened from 65 to 55 feet in length and free of outside fins. Both of these design changes ultimately proved beneficial to the Army as well, since a shorter missile proved to be more maneuverable, and the elimination of fins led to the design of engine nozzles which swivelled to provide a more reliable means of assuring flight control. Baar and Howard, *Polaris,* pp. 57–58. Agreement was reached between the Army and Navy in February, 1956, on the following characteristics for the sea-based Jupiter: length: 58 feet; diameter: 105 inches; range: 1,500 nautical miles. Emme (ed.), *History of Rocket Technology,* p. 163.

[62] Baar and Howard, *Polaris,* p. 66.

[63] House Committee on Government Operations, *Missile Program Hearings,* 1959, p. 367. According to the testimony of Admiral Hayward, the Killian Committee had made no specific recommendation as between submarine-launched and ship-launched IRBMs. The state of the art favored the latter approach in 1955. *Ibid.,* p. 418.

Thus the Jupiter sea-based IRBM system represented for the Navy a compromise with the existing state of the art in rocket technology; it was far from their optimal weapon system.

The Navy had always been separate from the other services in its organization, its requirements, and its missions. For most of its life, the Navy received its sustenance from a separate Congressional Committee. In 1949 it had fought the battle for proprietary access to the nuclear stockpile without help from the Army. While the Air Force continued to be responsible on grounds of economy, for some targets of interest to the Navy, the latter had obtained recognition of its demands for partnership in the strategic retaliatory mission.[64] They were also taking steps to see that they did not have to rely on the Air Force for new weapon systems. Nor was such reliance upon the Army desired.

It was natural for the Navy to want its own missile program, and the unique problems of handling and maintenance of ballistic rockets on shipboard provided an easy rationalization for an independent approach. Their guidance problem was more difficult, for they could not use a base line for triangulation, as was standard for ground launch guidance systems. Only solid-fuel missiles could sufficiently minimize the dangers of fire aboard ship. They faced special structural problems as a result of the "strain imposed by catapult takeoffs and arrested landings." [65] Additional difficulties derived from the possibility of acid corrosion from the salt spray.

By early 1956 the opportunities for an independent Navy program were ripe. A growing appreciation of the special problems of nuclear deterrence increased the appeal of a solution through a marriage of missile and nuclear submarine technology. Exchanges between advocates of the Army and Air Force IRBM programs illuminated a number of the disadvantages of relying upon foreign-based missiles. The dilemmas of strategic vulnerability and political control were the most distressing. Submarine-based IRBMs, on the other hand, promised to avoid

[64] Senate Committee on Armed Services, *Airpower Hearings,* 1956, p. 1367.
[65] Donnelly, *U.S. Guided Missile Programs,* p. 70.

the diplomatic and military problems associated with the Jupiter or Thor systems. The mobility, concealment, and dispersion of such a sea-based system posed almost insurmountable obstacles to detection and attrition from the most sophisticated and resourceful adversary. In addition to complicating the defensive problems of the enemy, a fleet ballistic missile system would be far removed from American cities, industrial complexes, and land military installations. Counterforce attacks would thus be deflected away from the United States heartland.[66]

As felicitous as the diplomatic environment was the configuration of interservice politics. The Navy's fight for a strategic role had already been fought, and carrier planes were assigned to some enemy targets.[67] Even if Navy leaders were reluctant to reopen their 1949 feud with the Air Force, their position amid the strife of service contention in 1956 could not have been more fortunate. The major controversies had passed them by. As Admiral Radford reportedly observed, "You might say we had a small sweet voice singing lightly on one side and two anvil choruses going on the other." [68] They were innocent onlookers in both the Nike-Talos and Thor-Jupiter disputes. Even the cancellation of the Army's Project Orbiter satellite project in

[66] U.S. Congress, Joint Committee on Atomic Energy, *Report of the Underseas Warfare Advisory Panel to the Subcommittee on Military Applications of the Joint Committee on Atomic Energy.* 85th Cong., 2nd Sess., 1958, Joint Committee Print, p. 7. This argument was presented in terse and witty form by the contemporary ditty making the rounds in the Pentagon: "Move deterrence out to sea, Where real estate is free, And where it's far away from me." Cited in Ralph Lapp, *Kill and Overkill* (New York, Basic Books Inc., 1962), p. 75.

[67] The anticipated low yield and relative inaccuracy foreseen for the Polaris system may have left some Navy leaders reticent to reopen their 1949 feud with the Air Force. The Polaris could be justified as an efficient strategic weapon only if directed at civilian or industrial targets. Many naval officers were, however, still sensitive to the charge that this required a complete *volte-face* from the moralistic reservations they had expressed toward SAC strategy during the "revolt of the Admirals." For an account of that episode see Paul Y. Hammond, "Super-carriers and B-36 Bombers: Appropriations, Strategy and Politics," in Harold Stein (ed.), *American Civil-Military Decisions: A Book of Case Studies* (University City, Alabama, University of Alabama Press, 1963), pp. 465–567.

[68] Baar and Howard, *Polaris,* p. 40.

favor of the Navy sponsored Vanguard Project did not embroil the two services. Rather, it pitted civilian scientists and military technologists against one another as to the appropriate degree of military participation in a peaceful space program. Moreover, in the Polaris Program, the Navy was exploring a solid-fuel missile peculiarly appropriate for the defensive needs of the nation. Its mobility, simplicity, and reliability were of immense interest to both the Air Force and the Army, with both of whom technical information was widely shared.[69] Thus, between the Army and Air Force, the Navy could win the fruits of positive neutrality without displaying the demagoguery of a Nasser or Sukarno. The Army needed their support; the Air Force their neutrality.

Advancing technology paved the way for the Navy's defection from the Jupiter program. Navy leaders granted the highest priority to the development of a solid-propellant system, and Admiral Raborn did in fact request permission at the very first meeting of the Joint Army-Navy Ballistic Missile Committee to investigate solid fuels.[70] Even as work on the Jupiter was being initiated, plans were being laid for a follow on Jupiter-S, solid-fueled missile system.[71]

On the basis of dramatic increases in the specific impulse of solid fuel, demonstrated in experiments conducted by Keith Rumbel and Charles Henderson at Atlantic Research Corporation, and confirmed by Werner Kirchner of Aerojet-General Corporation, the Joint Army-Navy Ballistic Missile Committee approved on March 12, 1956, a Navy proposal for a solid-propellant program under its own cognizance. Less than a month later, on April 11, Lockheed was awarded a systems development contract, and Aerojet-General Corporation received

[69] House Committee on Government Operations, *Missile Program Hearings*, 1959, p. 422.

[70] Emme, *History of Rocket Technology*, p. 164.

[71] The Jupiter-S concept was to be based on a cluster of existing solid-fuel motors. Due to the inefficient fuels then available, the originally designed missile, had it been developed, might have weighed as much as 160,000 lbs. This would have posed virtually insurmountable problems of shipboard handling. See Baar and Howard, *Polaris*, p. 67. See also House Committee on Government Operations, *Missile Program Hearings*, 1959, p. 434.

a solid fuel rocket development contract for what eventually became the Polaris program. On April 14 the Secretary of Defense authorized the Navy to proceed with systems studies and component development for the project.[72]

Meanwhile, Naval Ordnance Test Station scientists, under the direction of Captain Levering Smith of the Navy's Special Projects Office Propulsion Branch, kept returning to Admiral Raborn with recommendations that the Jupiter-S concept be shelved in favor of a reoriented program aimed at the development of a small solid-propelled missile.[73] Smith and several of his colleagues were among the participants in a group established during the summer of 1956 by the National Academy of Sciences-National Research Council to study problems of underseas warfare. Chaired by Stark Draper, the group met at Woods Hole, Massachusetts, and made an exhaustive appraisal of the technical feasibility of a small solid-fuel fleet ballistic missile system.

Particularly significant was the contribution of Edward Teller who "gently criticized the Navy for thinking in terms of a ballistic missile which would be operational in 1963, but tying it to a 1956 nuclear technology." [74] Subsequent estimates of probable improvements in nuclear technology by 1963 reinforced Admiral Raborn's disposition to plan for a much smaller, lighter missile than the Jupiter.

During the spring of 1956 Garrison Norton joined the Navy Department as Assistant Secretary of Navy Air. He had been a member of the Killian Committee, and was thoroughly convinced of the urgency of the need for a submarine missile capability. Believing that the project was receiving insufficient attention within the Navy, he requested permission to spend 100 per cent of his time on the emerging Polaris program. During the early summer months he laid many of the initial plans for the submarine missile system. He was instrumental in altering the Navy Jupiter funding plan for the 1957 fiscal year. An increase from $93,180,000 to $113,210,000 was recommended

[72] Ibid., p. 367.   [73] Baar and Howard, Polaris, p. 69.
[74] Emme, History of Rocket Technology, p. 165.

and approved.[75] The cost breakdowns indicated a concentration upon solid-motor development, system design, testing, and supporting research and development.

Nor should the persistent efforts of Rear Admiral William F. "Red" Raborn be underestimated. Operating the Special Projects Office as an adjunct to the Bureau of Ordnance, he was endowed with a small and competent staff—and possessed of unfailing good luck. He was granted extraordinary managerial authority and fiscal freedom and allowed direct access to the Secretary of the Navy.

By late summer considerable progress had been made on the sea-based Jupiter. Perhaps the most appropriate commentary was offered by launch specialist Captain Dennett Ela, who wryly observed, "It won't be the safest thing afloat. We know that. But we're pretty damn sure it will work—and that's all that counts." [76] Yet in addition to the considerable remaining safety hazards, the size of the Jupiter missiles limited severely the number that were storable on shipboard, a factor which would necessitate a very costly program of refitting surface craft if a sizable deterrent force was to be created. In addition, the Jupiter-S follow on missile, while more manageable on shipboard, would be so large and unwieldy that submarines the size of cruisers would be required to carry them.

On the other hand, a smaller, solid-propellant missile still represented an exceedingly hazardous technical venture. The guidance system problems were far more exacting; flight control techniques had not been demonstrated or tested; control of propellant burning, which would determine the accuracy of ballistic flight, remained to be mastered; and developmental problems in solid-fuel missile design remained, whereas equivalent problems in liquid-fuel rocket designs were well along.[77]

Nevertheless, heartened by the positive report of the Woods Hole Study Group, which recommended an immediate high

[75] Senate Committee on Armed Services, *Satellite and Missile Program Hearings,* 1957–1958, p. 1753.

[76] Baar and Howard, *Polaris,* p. 65.

[77] Emme, *History of Rocket Technology,* p. 166.

priority program to develop a small solid-fuel missile, Admiral Raborn chose to press for cancellation of the Jupiter in favor of the Polaris concept. The Chief of Naval Operations and Secretary of the Navy acquiesced in Raborn's judgment. So, too, did Secretary of Defense Wilson.[78]

The final divorce of Army and Navy efforts did not come until after the publication, in November, 1956, of the Wilson memorandum defining roles and missions.[79] The movement toward independence was, however, unmistakable. Few expressed surprise when, on December 8, 1956, the Secretary of Defense authorized the Navy to delete Jupiter from its IRBM program.[80] The Joint Army-Navy Ballistic Missiles Committee was abolished, and the Navy allowed to proceed with the Polaris.[81]

A DECISION TO DECIDE

As the services worked furiously on their respective IRBM projects, and attempted to promote a favorable disposition of the jurisdictional questions raised by these developmental programs, the Secretary of Defense was attempting to harness interservice technical competition to the purposes of technical innovation without seriously compromising his freedom to sort out roles and missions assignments at a later date. In this respect

[78] In his efforts to persuade the Secretary of Defense of the potential of the Polaris program, Raborn particularly impressed Wilson with his arguments regarding the economies which could be obtained in ship construction. After the presentations Wilson is alleged to have remarked, "You've shown me a lot of sexy slides, young man. But that's the sexiest, that half-billion dollar saving." Baar and Howard, *Polaris*, p. 72.

[79] Once the decision to defect from the Jupiter program had been reached, Rear Admiral John E. Clark, Navy member of JANBMC, asked the Army if it wished to develop the Polaris. But the commitment by the von Braun team and the Army to liquid propellants was firm, and they chose to pursue the land-based Jupiter system. Emme, *History of Rocket Technology*, p. 166.

[80] Senate Committee on Armed Services, *Satellite and Missile Program Hearings*, 1957–1958, p. 300.

[81] Work on the sea-based Jupiter system had not proceeded far beyond the design stage by this time, so relatively little was lost other than time in shifting to a different concept. On the other hand, two test ships from that program, the Pass Island and the Observation Island, were later usefully employed in the Polaris test program for surface launchings.

the Thor-Jupiter episode proved instructive in the costs of buying time, deferring choice, and exercising the responsibilities of the Office of Secretary of Defense as an impartial judge rather than a policy leader. Responsibility for developing these promising new weapons tended to stimulate revisions in service doctrines and nourish hopes that each service would be allowed to deploy those weapons it managed to develop. Army partisans convinced themselves of the possibility of fielding the IRBM. They committed service prestige to the project and financed the expensive Jupiter program at considerable "opportunity costs" to themselves. The Ordnance Bureau was reorganized to expedite the project, and doctrine and deployment concepts compatible with their alleged requirements were developed. Such activities served to make the decision for project elimination an exceedingly difficult and unpleasant one.

Wilson's initial attitude toward novel missile projects was a technical variant of Mao Tse Tung's "Let one hundred flowers bloom." The corollary to the resulting proliferation of projects was a complicated machinery for coordination. Initially, centralized coordination was to be exercised in the Office of Secretary of Defense-Ballistic Missiles Committee, under Deputy Secretary of Defense Reuben Robertson. By February, 1956, however, Robertson was feeling the pressure of other neglected responsibilities. Congressional critics of the dispersed efforts in the long-range missile field clamored for greater concentration of authority over widespread activities. Fears of Soviet progress, the mounting costs of multiple programs, and public manifestations of bitter interservice feuds lent support to their cries. So, too, did the abrupt resignation of Trevor Gardner over his general dissatisfaction with the Pentagon's management of the missile programs and his specific objections to the Air Force Research and Development budget for the 1957 fiscal year.[82] Demands were raised in Congress and in the press for the appointment of a missile "czar" to aggressively force programs through the development stage and into production.

[82] "Gardner Quits, Starts USAF Research and Development Fight," *Aviation Week* (February 13, 1956), 28–29.

Daniel Katz has noted that in response to organizational conflict it is normal for initial efforts to be directed toward making the system work. Only in response to persisting inadequacies is a coordinator likely to be added, or more fundamental structural reforms contemplated.[83] As previously indicated, the creation of a Manhattan Project-type organization for the management of the missile programs had at one time been considered and dismissed. Concerned over the competition for scientific talent as well as for funds, President Eisenhower also considered placing all research and development projects directly under the jurisdiction of the Secretary of Defense. For the moment this proposal was not implemented.[84]

Some greater concentration of authority, however, was acknowledged as essential, and on February 1, 1956, Wilson indicated his intention of meeting the demands of Congressional critics, even though he publicly ridiculed the suggestion of a missile "czar" and "that kind of monkey business."[85] He announced the creation of a new Office of Special Assistant to the Secretary of Defense for Guided Missiles. The announcement came only hours after Senator Jackson ominously warned on the Senate floor that the Soviets would launch IRBMs before the year's end.[86] An additional incentive for such action was provided by the imminence of a major investigation of Ameri-

[83] "Approaches to Managing Conflict," in Robert L. Kahn and Elise Boulding (eds.) *Power and Conflict in Organizations* (New York, Basic Books, Inc., 1964), pp. 197–98.

[84] Sherman Adams, *Firsthand Report* (New York, Popular Library, 1962), p. 398.

[85] *New York Times,* February 2, 1956, p. 1.

[86] Senator Jackson had long been influential in American missile efforts, and he had consistently urged a considerable streamlining of administrative procedures in the Defense Department organization of those efforts. In a report issued by the Joint Committee on Atomic Energy in 1954 he apparently favored the appointment of a Presidential Assistant in charge of the Program. Senate Committee on Armed Services, *Satellite and Missile Program Hearings,* 1957–1958, p. 1653. The suggestion was not implemented and President Eisenhower was without a staff assistant with specific responsibilities for overseeing the programs until his appointment of Dr. James R. Killian as Presidential Scientific Adviser in the fall of 1957.

can Air Atomic Power by the Symington Subcommittee of the Senate Armed Services Committee.

Two months passed before Eger V. Murphree was appointed Special Assistant to the Secretary. The fact that a man of his scientific background and judicious temperament was chosen in preference to a hard-driving political animal like Trevor Gardner was certainly an earnest of Wilson's intentions. Among the qualities which attracted Wilson to Murphree were his knowledge of technology, proven administrative talent, experience in large organizations, and "talent in getting along with people." [87] Unlike K. T. Keller, who had assumed similar duties during the Korean War, his functions would be less those of establishing priorities, and rushing the most promising into production, than the quiet arts of diplomacy, mediation, and coordination. His power derived from the confidence of the Secretary; his duties were to be exercised from his position as Chairman of the OSD-BMC. It was clearly specified that Murphree's responsibilities would be in the area of facilitating administrative decisions and interchange of technical information. Decisions regarding jurisdiction were to remain with the JCS, where agreement in such matters had consistently proven elusive.

With the appointment of Murphree, service bickering temporarily subsided. But renewed outbursts over the Nike-Talos dispute, reverberations from the SAC-Carrier controversy, Army requests that it be allowed to train its own helicopter pilots, and above all, the continuing uncertainties about operational responsibilities for the IRBM provoked new incidents. Throughout, Wilson maintained a posture of "watchful waiting" on the Thor-Jupiter controversy. He either downgraded the entire issue by referring to the IRBM as "one minor weapon in the big international picture," or reiterated his conviction that roles and missions assignments should wait upon full development of the missiles. Controversies, he consoled himself, were more or less inevitable "in this future business, where we don't

---

[87] *Ibid.*, March 28, 1956, p. 1.

quite know yet how good the missiles are or what they might be able to do." [88]

There is evidence, however, which suggests that by the spring of 1956 the decision on operational roles was beginning to take shape. In response to continued leaks by Pentagon "Indians" in May and June, Wilson ordered the Army to "Separate out" in the submission of its plans, "those items necessary to the development and procurement, test, training, and check out and transport equipment required for the Research and Development program from those items required for tactical use." [89] In other words, as Secretary Brucker later recounted, "We were not to develop equipment that affected launching or ground equipment." [90]

Wilson was impressed by the Army's technical resources rather than their tactical doctrine. In this he was most probably influenced by President Eisenhower's reservations about the Army's requirement for a missile with a range of 1,500 miles. Asked later in a press conference about his opinion on the Army's need for a tactical missile of such range, the President replied, "Now just why or when or what reasons they assign any particular missile, any particular type to one service, is not always readily apparent, but I would say this just from a knowledge of the Army: Why would the Army want a 1500 mile missile itself, because the first requisite of using that kind of weapon is that you have very good observation to find out whether it is doing the job you thought it was. The only way that you could find out that would be with an Air Force that could penetrate at least 1500 miles into the enemy territory, and that puts you right square in the Air Force business." [91]

[88] *Ibid.*, March 7, 1956, p. 11.

[89] Senate Committee on Armed Services, *Satellite and Missile Program Hearings, 1957–1958*, p. 276.

[90] *Ibid.* While the Army did not directly violate this order, it adopted a subtle means of circumvention. Responsible for providing launch equipment for their own test firings at Cape Canaveral, they simply followed the "traditional practice" of using equipment for test firing that could also be employed for tactical field operations.

[91] *New York Times*, May 9, 1957, p. 15.

Army-Air Force competition for the Jupiter caused considerable consternation in the White House, and the President's
growing impatience with the intramural scuffling among the
services prevented an indefinite postponement of the jurisdictional decision.

Throughout the summer and early fall of 1956 the Army
high command became increasingly apprehensive that the liquidation of the Jupiter was imminent. This anxiety counseled
an attempt to buy insurance against the uncertain future of the
Redstone missile team by reopening the Vanguard-Orbiter
question. New proposals were offered by Secretary Brucker, but
in view of the delays anticipated in the Jupiter program schedule and out of fear of new jurisdictional squabbles, Army requests were politely but firmly refused.[92]

The Army also sought to publicize their considerable technical feats. On September 7, 1956, a Jupiter-C rocket hurtled
downrange some 3,300 miles in a test of the Jupiter reentry
vehicle. News of the accomplishment—to the manifest distress
of the Army—was suppressed in the interest of averting an upset in the so-called precarious balance between the services.
When the authoritative *Missiles and Rockets* released information of the feat in their November issue, they commented edi-
torially:

The new range and altitude marks represent convincing proof of
the Army's progress in its all-out drive to develop the Jupiter before the U.S. Air Force can get its competing Thor IRBM into
shape. Both services are working out IRBM versions with the
understanding that only one will be ordered into production.[93]

[92] Proposals for the resuscitation of Project Orbiter were made by the
Army in the spring of 1956. At the time Army R&D experts estimated that
a satellite effort would delay the Jupiter program by possibly three
months. Testimony of General Daley, House Committee on Armed
Services, *National Defense Missiles Hearings,* 1958, p. 4318. In refusing
the Army proposal the Department of Defense directed General Gavin
not to prepare any launch vehicles for satellites. Senate Committee on
Armed Services, *Satellite and Missile Program Hearings,* 1957–1958, p.
509.
[93] *Missiles and Rockets* (November, 1956), 33.

The shot not only underscored their capabilities for the cancelled Project Orbiter but emphasized their other ambitions. Brigadier General John P. Daley, Director of Special Weapons Office, had only recently told the Symington Air Power Subcommittee:

Now we are looking toward the intercontinental ballistic missile, confident that we can develop weapons to maintain the integrity and the independence of the land soldier.[94]

On September 11, the Army set forth two regulations asserting that missiles were an integral part of their weapon systems. This was considered to represent a formal bid for the right to employ a family of missiles "In a wide variation of ranges and yields." [95] Short-range missiles were required for assault and demolition; medium-range missiles were justified as a supplement and extension of conventional firepower; long-range IRBMs were required to support deep penetrations. A short time later, Secretary Brucker recommended further steps by the Army to reduce their ultimate reliance on the Air Force for close combat support and attack well behind the lines.[96]

During this period also, Chief of Staff Maxwell Taylor developed a novel concept for the use of new weapons. He referred to it as the national arsenal idea. In its outlines it bears remarkable similarity to notions later developed for the NATO alliance by French strategist Pierre Gallois.[97] The concept recommended itself as an oblique challenge to the Key West agreements. When Senator Symington challenged Taylor's support for both the Key West agreement and an Army IRBM, he reconciled the two by stating:

If you accept the fact that the Army exists to destroy hostile armies, then any missile which will destroy hostile ground forces should be available to the Army.

I would like to make the distinction, Senator, between availability

---

[94] Senate Committee on Armed Services, *Airpower Hearings,* 1956, p. 711.

[95] *New York Times,* September 12, 1956, p. 33.

[96] *Ibid.,* September 22, 1956, p. 6.

[97] Pierre Gallois, "New Teeth for NATO," *Foreign Affairs,* XXXIX (October, 1960), 61–81. The argument for a NATO "nuclear arsenal" to restore credibility to the American deterrent is set forth on pp. 74–78.

and exclusive possession. I personally do not feel these weapons
. . . should belong exclusively to any one service.

I view them as part of the National arsenal and any service that
can justify the use of one of these weapons at any given time for
its primary mission and can afford it, I think, should have access
to it.[98]

Although the concept was reiterated in General Taylor's
widely read book, *The Uncertain Trumpet,* apparently it was
not pressed vigorously within the Department of Defense. The
Army never made it a principal argument for control; and apparently it was never discussed seriously by the Armed Forces
Policy Council.[99]

THE WILSON ROLES AND MISSIONS MEMORANDUM

The Army-Air Force feud continued to smolder; costs continued to mount. It became increasingly evident that a decision
on roles and missions could be evaded no longer. In July, 1956,
Wilson had gathered the Chiefs of Staff at Quantico, Virginia,
to attempt a revision of the Key West and Newport Agreements. The roles and missions issues could not be resolved by
service representatives alone, and ultimately the Secretary of
Defense had to intervene to compel agreement where it could
not be freely negotiated.

A number of factors beyond growing intolerance for interservice wrangling forced the resolution of the proprietary issue.
In the first place, action could no longer be deferred on the development of ground launch equipment.[100] Development of
the missiles was proceeding to the point where the launch
equipment—a long lead time item—would become an important pacing factor. Previously, money for Army launch equipment had been withheld by Comptroller Wildred McNeil
pending a decision on roles and missions. Such a decision was
now imperative if development was not to be significantly delayed.

[98] Senate Committee on Armed Services, *Airpower Hearings,* 1956, pp
1287–88.
[99] Interview with Wilfred McNeil, August 26, 1963.
[100] Interview with General Medaris, August 30, 1963.

A second factor was the growing conviction, shared by President Eisenhower, that at the expense of their more appropriate functions the Army was crashing a field that legitimately belonged to another service. Besides, it had always been assumed that one of the missile programs would have to be eliminated. Possibly the decision on roles and missions was seen as an opportunity to subtly kill two birds with one stone. Certainly it was a widely shared and plausible assumption that the Army would not continue to expend energy, personnel, and funds on a project over which they no longer enjoyed jurisdiction.[101]

A third contributing factor was the defection of the Navy from the Jupiter program. Although no agreement could be elicited from the JCS at Quantico, it is quite apparent that the Army was isolated within the Joint Chiefs. In the autumn of 1956 Admiral Arleigh Burke, Chief of Naval Operations, sought to mediate the Army-Air Force dispute over airlift.[102] A compromise proposal attributed to him would have permitted a 25 per cent expansion in Army aviation, minor increases in the weight limitations of fixed wing Army aircraft from 5,000 to 8,000 pounds, and the maintenance of the present roles and missions of Army aviation, with the addition of limited Sky-Cavalry operations. In return, Army Air Research and Development would be transferred to the Air Force. To Army commentators, the proposal amounted to a mortgage on their future in return for slight immediate improvements. Burke's efforts were unavailing, yet they indicated that the Army could not count on Navy support in the Joint Chiefs of Staff. Evidently, in the October deliberations of the JCS, he supported the majority view to strip the Army of an IRBM role.[103]

Finally, Wilson's decision to issue a comprehensive statement on roles and missions in November, 1956, may have been encouraged not only by the need to straighten up such matters as a

[101] According to Alvin Waggoner, who served at the time as Secretary to the Ballistic Missiles Committee in the Secretary's Office, such was not Wilson's intent. Rather the priority of developing one IRBM remained as before, and the choice between the Thor and Jupiter remained to be made. Interview, July 26, 1965.

[102] *Army* (October, 1956), 15.

[103] Interview with General Gavin, August 22, 1963. It is not clear why

part of finalising plans for the budget for fiscal year 1958, but by his desire not to leave a series of unresolved disputes to his successor.[104] Already in the fall of that year there were reports of his early resignation. He had been distressed by the unfinished business he had inherited from former Secretary of Defense Robert Lovett, and perhaps his desire to be a decisive Secretary prompted him to act on the service conflict as a part of his "desk clearing."

Whatever the reasons for the precise timing of the Wilson Memorandum on roles and missions, its implications for the Army were unmistakable and disappointing. Although the Pace-Finletter Agreement was slightly modified, Army Aviation remained shackled by precise restrictions on the permitted weight of their craft. Contrary to the constantly reiterated convictions of practically all Army leaders, airlift was pronounced "adequate . . . in the light of currently approved strategic concepts." [105] Of greater significance for their ambitions, the Army was limited in its jurisdiction over tactical ballistic missiles to ranges not to exceed 200 miles. "Operational employment of the land-based intermediate range ballistic missile system" was to be "the sole responsibility of the United States Air Force." [106] To be sure, the Army acquired jurisdiction over the Talos missile and other point defense missile systems "with horizontal ranges out to 100 nautical miles," [107] but the Air Force was busily engaged in the development of the Bomarc, which was to replace the Talos in their plans.

In short, the Army sustained a heavy blow to their ambitions for modernization through missilery. The Air Force retained as low priority functions missions which the Army considered ab-

---

the Army should have expected Navy support on the roles and missions decision. Air Force Chief of Staff Nathan Twining later testified that as early as October, 1955, "The majority felt that the Army had no valid requirement for an IRBM capability and should get out of the business." House Committee on Armed Services, *National Defense Missiles Hearings,* 1958, p. 4064.

104 Interview with Wilfred McNeil, August 26, 1963.

105 House Committee on Government Operations, *Missile Program Hearings,* 1959, p. 747.

106 *Ibid.,* p. 748.   107 *Ibid.*

solutely vital, e.g., troop carrying and tactical air support. Army contentions on airlift had been ignored. Army research and development in aviation was restricted to "development and determination of specific requirements peculiar to Army needs." [108] Above all, they found themselves pouring money and effort into a missile which they were not to be allowed to control. After June 30, 1957, the Jupiter Project would be funded by the Air Force. Since they were the user, and one missile was to be eliminated, the chances for the Jupiter looked very remote indeed.

Despite, however, the apparent finality with which the Army's aspirations had been thwarted, optimists discovered two sources of hope. In the first place, there was a certain tentativeness about the range restriction. "The U.S. Army will not plan *at this time* for the operational employment of the intermediate range ballistic missile or for any other missiles with ranges beyond 200 miles." [109] Even more significantly, they were not foreclosed from undertaking "limited feasibility studies in this area." [110] Inasmuch as studies had already been made of a mid-range tactical ballistic missile of 500 mile range, hopes of circumventing the arbitrary restriction were buoyed.

ARMY REACTION TO THE WILSON MEMORANDUM

Within the Army, reactions to the Wilson Memorandum varied. Somewhat paradoxically, those whose interests and ambitions were most immediately involved responded with least emotion. Generals Medaris and Gavin, and Secretary Brucker—however virulent their private resentments—preserved a public calm and reacted with cool calculation.[111] They all apparently felt that intemperate outbursts might provoke the Secretary of Defense to rash reprisals, and they were concerned lest the Jupiter program itself be immediately liquidated.[112]

Some assumed that the roles and missions assignments would

---

[108] *Ibid.,* p. 298.   [109] *Ibid.,* p. 298. Italics added.   [110] *Ibid.*
[111] Medaris, *Countdown for Decision,* p. 126.
[112] At the project level the technical personnel apparently responded to the negative decision on deployment with a heightened desire to

control the determination between the competing projects in favor of the Thor; consequently, they counseled the Jupiter's early elimination. Among those urging such a course was General Austin W. Betts, Military Executive Assistant to the Director of Guided Missiles.[113] To head off such a decision, the Army leaders anxiously asserted (1) that their confidence in the Army's chances of obtaining operational control had never been high; (2) that roles and missions assignments had no bearing on the choice of weapons in any event, since the Army Ordnance Corps had a long tradition as a supplier of other services; and (3) that the Jupiter project had been undertaken as a national priority rather than solely a response to the Army's internal requirements.

Their first objective was to remind the Secretary of Defense and his Director of Guided Missiles that the initial basis of competition was to provide insurance that one IRBM would be available in the shortest possible time. Since at the present juncture in their respective development programs, their missile was technically in advance of the Air Force's Thor, they urged that any judgment on their competitive merits should be deferred until there was a possibility of choosing on the basis of a completed test schedule.

The self-restraint of Generals Medaris and Gavin, and Secretary Brucker was related to a second objective as well. If Army hopes were tied to their exploitation of the new technology of electronics and ballistic rocketry and the challenge of outer space, their fate was in a sense contingent upon their retention of the services of the German scientists and technicians at Redstone Arsenal. It was to be anticipated, in view of the Wilson Memorandum, that the integrity of that team would be threatened by lucrative offers from industry and from rumored attempts by the Air Force to have the missile team disbanded.

---

demonstrate their superiority in missile development to the Air Force. Interview with Alvin Waggoner, July 26, 1965.

[113] Interview with General Austin W. Betts, August 28, 1963. His views were not, however, shared by Eger Murphree or by Alvin Waggoner. Interview with Waggoner, July 26, 1965.

THE QUEST FOR OPERATIONAL CONTROL

Such blandishments could be resisted only if new and stimulating opportunities were provided for them. Initially this meant the preservation of the Jupiter program and various follow-up projects; subsequently, responsibilities in the satellite and space field would have to be secured.

Resentments were further mitigated by the realization that Army shortcomings had encouraged the Wilson decision. Gavin later conceded that "generally speaking," it was a "reasonable memorandum when reviewed in the light of the existing circumstances." [114] He, like General Medaris, was inclined to assign much of the onus for the adverse result to Continental Army Command. CONARC had never stated a requirement for a missile with a range of 1,500 miles. Indeed, in the summer of 1956 General Gavin eagerly sought assignment to CONARC as a result of his apprehensions that their tactical and strategic concepts were unimaginative, and their requirements dated. As he explained it to the Johnson Committee: "I thought by getting in there I could give momentum to what I have been working on in G-3, Deputy Chief of Plans, to Chief of Research and Development, I could get this momentum right into it, to give it full expression." [115]

General Medaris was likewise convinced that the Army had not persuasively stated its case, and that under similar circumstances he very likely would have reached the same conclusion as Wilson. Indeed, he felt that outside the narrow circle of General Gavin, Chief of Staff Taylor, and a small circle of professional missile experts in the Army, the potentialities of the new weaponry were little understood in the service.[116]

Finally, as previously indicated, permission to make feasibility studies of missiles with ranges exceeding 200 miles softened the impact of Wilson's directive slightly.[117] Such studies were

[114] U.S., Congress, House, Committee on Appropriations, *Hearings, Department of Defense Appropriations 1958*, 85th Cong., 1st Sess., 1957, p. 502.
[115] Senate Committee on Armed Services, *Satellite and Missile Program Hearings, 1957–1958*, p. 1447.
[116] Interview with General Medaris, August 30, 1963.
[117] Senate Committee on Armed Services, *Satellite and Missile Program Hearings, 1957–1958*, p. 1505.

immediately resumed. After Gavin was discouraged from an early attempt at the IRBM by Ridgway in April, 1955, he had initiated plans for an extension of the Redstone's range up to 500 miles. This program was dropped in October, 1955, when the Killian Report lent urgency to proposals for an IRBM program. Now the Army again embraced the mid-range missile and rapidly developed two different approaches to it. Technical breakthroughs made by the Redstone team permitted a considerable extension in that missile's range. Later they hoped to develop a solid-propellant missile of light weight, extended range, and enhanced mobility.[118]

As Gavin pointed out, "The residual effect of this is, we feel, that if we can demonstrate a capability and a need to the Secretary of Defense's satisfaction beyond 200 miles, he may be responsive to that and authorize the planned use of such missiles." [119]

Secretary Brucker's concerns were somewhat broader in scope. Above all, he was anxious to preserve the Army's in-house technical team intact and keep them in business in the aftermath of Wilson's Memorandum. On November 27 he restated to the Secretary the Army's case for an alternative satellite program as insurance for the Vanguard project. He proposed a six vehicle, $18 million program to launch a satellite by June, 1957. As proof of the Army's credentials, he cited the 3,300 mile shot of September 7, which would have gone into orbit had they not weighted the nose cone with sandbags.[120]

Budgetary concerns were foremost in his thoughts. If the Army was not to be permitted to field the IRBM, they had to cease committing their scarce resources to it. Yet spokesmen for the Air Force—the user—indicated that they had no funds to support a backup project to their own Thor, in which they had the greatest confidence. Ultimately, Brucker was successful in persuading Wilson to finance further developmental expenses

[118] *Ibid.,* p. 477.
[119] House Committee on Appropriations, *DoD Appropriations Hearings 1958,* 1957, p. 502.
[120] *Ibid.,* pp. 285–86.

for the Jupiter, from a Department of Defense emergency fund, if tests indicated the desirability of its continuance.

On December 7, 1956, Brucker formally recommended that the Jupiter be continued through 1957, in order that further testing would reveal the relative merits of the competing missiles.[121] Such authorization was the more essential, since the following day the Navy severed its connection with the Jupiter project. On December 20, the Army undertook a complete revision of the Jupiter program, projecting it through the 1961 fiscal year. Their report, which included funding requirements, was submitted through the director of Guided Missiles to the Secretary of Defense. Assured of funds through July 1, Brucker waited impatiently until April 2, 1957, when he finally received notification from the newly appointed Director of Guided Missiles, William Holaday, that the OSD-BMC had approved its revised program with an authorization of funds to carry it through November 30, 1957.[122]

THE NICKERSON INCIDENT

Cool heads did not prevail in every quarter. In the weeks following the publication of the Wilson Memorandum, Colonel John C. Nickerson, a key administrative aide and Congressional liaison man for the Army Ballistic Missile Agency, wrote, apparently on his own initiative, a series of memoranda criticizing Wilson's decision. He not only asserted the superiority of the Jupiter but insisted upon the Army's right and need to deploy it.[123] The "Nickerson Incident" threatened to destroy the impact of the moderate response of the Army leadership. General Medaris was even fearful that the Jupiter project itself might fall victim to the backlash anticipated against the zealous colonel's indiscretions.

[121] House Committee on Government Operations, *Missile Program Hearings,* 1959, p. 300.

[122] *Ibid.*

[123] He characterized the Wilson Memorandum as a "sweeping denial to the Army of important means for the prosecution of modern war by air power advocates not professionally qualified to make this denial, who do not understand the necessity for a modern Army." *New York Times,* June 29, 1957, p. 7.

Although compared by some to Billy Mitchell as a martyr for principle, the comparison seems scarcely apt. To be sure, Nickerson, like Mitchell, was a visionary who recognized well ahead of the public or his colleagues the value of an exotic and powerful air weapon. Here, however, the similarities end. Mitchell revolted against his military superiors to initiate a flamboyant public campaign on behalf of a weapon neglected by the military hierarchy. Nickerson, on the other hand, will be remembered as an officer who stood not upon principle in a matter of strategic importance but rather as a partisan in a major jurisdictional dispute. Moreover, his views were substantially shared by his service superiors, though they were far more circumspect in presenting their case. Long-range ballistic missiles were acknowledged by the managers of the Pentagon establishment as an essential for our future defense. The various projects enjoyed the highest national priority. They were being accelerated. The issue in dispute was, therefore, not *whether* or not a promising new weapon would be developed, but rather *who* would be allowed to operate it. And, indeed, this issue was not really in doubt, for Wilson had resolved the roles and missions question, and his directive was formally accepted by Army leaders.

Actually the incident has its roots in a document prepared by General Medaris and a small staff to be presented to Deputy Secretary of Defense Reuben Robertson in late November, 1956, in order to head off pressures for the precipitate elimination of the Jupiter project.[124] The product of their labors—the so-called Dagger Report—was a "no holds barred" comparison of the services' efforts in the missile field. It sought to document Army superiority in missile development capability, and it proclaimed the logic of the Army case for their deployment of the weapon system.

In the aftermath of the Wilson Memorandum—evidently without explicit encouragement from his superiors—Nickerson attempted to develop public pressure for a reversal of the roles and missions assignment on the IRBM. In pursuit of this objec-

124 Medaris, *Countdown for Decision,* p. 124.

tive he formulated a document entitled "Considerations on the Wilson Memorandum," based upon classified information compiled for Medaris' report. This paper was to be circulated among influential members of Congress, the Washington press corps, and important industrial supporters. Erik Bergaust, editor of the trade magazine *Rockets and Missiles,* was also the recipient of a copy.[125] Such a strategy was adopted by Nickerson as a more promising alternative than circulating a staff paper through the usual channels, a time-consuming and frequently inconsequential process. It seemed compatible with his own temperament as well. Major General J. H. Hinrichs had characterized Nickerson in a 1955 efficiency report as "a freewheeler and an operator rather than a team player." [126]

The paper itself was a frontal assault on all those in authority over the missile programs. It contained innuendos of deviousness by the Defense Secretary in favor of the Thor program, implying favoritism on behalf of the Air Force missile, whose guidance system was developed by AC Spark Plug, a division of General Motors.[127] Admiral Radford was attacked for his alleged prejudices against the Army. Donald Quarles was vilified as an ambitious man seeking the position of Secretary of Defense by currying the support of the most powerful service. The propaganda and political support of the airframe industry on behalf of the Air Force missile program was assailed, and Nickerson warned of the dangers of placing confidence in that industry in the missiles and space field. He also deplored the concentration of that industry in the southwest. "The Southeastern United States," he asserted, "is strategically a sound location for a missile program." [128]

His strategy aborted when the document came to the attention of Defense Department and Army officials. Attention

125 For Bergaust's account of the Nickerson episode, see Erik Bergaust, *Reaching for the Stars* (New York, Doubleday & Co., Inc., 1960), pp. 209–24.

126 *New York Times,* June 29, 1957, p. 7.

127 Drew Pearson and Jack Anderson, *America: Second Class Power?* (New York, Simon and Schuster, 1958) , pp. 153–54.

128 *Ibid.,* p. 154.

thereafter focused upon the colonel rather than his cause, and court-martial proceedings were instituted against him. The excitement occasioned by the incident was actually heightened by the widespread initial impression that General Medaris had explicitly or tacitly encouraged Nickerson's attack on official policy. Moreover, Nickerson's substantial influence in the initiation of the Jupiter project lent added drama to the affair. He had served as liaison man between Huntsville, the Pentagon, and Congress on the Jupiter program's behalf. The Redstone scientists celebrated him as an operator, skilled in the ways of bureaucratic politics. Von Braun memorialized him as a "kind of quarterback, telling us what to do, which move to make, and what meeting to attend to present our case. I think that there would have been no Jupiter had it not been for him. It was Colonel Nickerson who enabled us to sell the Jupiter program to the Department of Defense." [129]

As the court-martial proceedings were initiated in June, 1957, Nickerson faced a maximum sentence of thirty years imprisonment or dismissal from the Army. In addition to insubordination, he was charged with having compromised privileged security information. Before the trial, Colonel Nickerson offered to plead guilty if the more serious charges were dropped. Eventually he received only an official reprimand, suspension from his rank for a year, and a forfeiture of $100 a month in pay for 15 months.[130]

In a sense, the court-martial proceedings were transformed into a "show trial" designed to provide a platform for the Army's presentation of their case for a vigorous IRBM program. Even after the verdict was decided, the trial was continued in order to hear of the "extenuating circumstances" in the case. This enabled Army officers and scientists and technicians to tell their story under the full glare of nationwide publicity. Many of the witnesses sought to support Nickerson's contention that the Department's decision to give the use of the IRBM to the Air Force flew "in the face of the facts that the Army can de-

[129] *Ibid.,* p. 161.   [130] *New York Times,* June 29, 1957, p. 7.

velop it better, use it better, needs it worse, and are more interested in it." [131]

The consequences of the Nickerson Incident are exceedingly difficult to gauge. Certainly it contributed to the growing impression that service quarrels were becoming intolerable and to the resolve of Wilson and Eisenhower to eliminate such rivalries. Of more immediate significance to the Army, the episode may have helped shatter General Medaris' hopes to obtain Air Force support for the production and deployment of the Jupiter.[132] He apparently believed that the Strategic Air Command, as the chief consumer of strategic weapon systems, was more interested in the quality of novel systems than in which service had produced them. Hopeful that he could convince SAC officials that the Jupiter was the superior IRBM and that it could be procured earlier than the Thor, he saw the Nickerson Incident as the equivalent of a major crisis in the cold war, occasioning a hardening of service lines. Potential intercommand rivalries within the Air Force were sublimated by the appearance of a transcendent common threat. Further maneuvers calculated to exploit internal divisions were to prove futile.

[131] *Ibid.,* June 28, 1957, p. 10.
[132] Interview with General Medaris, August 30, 1963.

(4) THE DILEMMAS OF COLLABORATIVE COMPETITION

Deliberate duplication of IRBM approaches had been adopted to hedge against technical uncertainty; it did not imply acknowledgment of the Army's asserted requirement for the weapon. Hence, it did not necessarily follow that the roles and missions decision prejudged the selection of the Thor over the Jupiter. The nature of Army-Air Force rivalry was, however, fundamentally altered. This was especially true when, after December 8, the Army no longer was in the position of developing a missile for the Navy, but was competing with the Air Force in the development of a weapon which that service alone would deploy.

But just as roles and missions decisions did not foreclose the elimination of the Thor, neither did the continuance of both projects through the development phase imply dual production. On the contrary, it continued to be the premise of the competition that at some point one or the other missile system would achieve demonstrable superiority and thereby render the technical decision obvious.

This is not to say that strong pressures were not exerted on behalf of an immediate choice. As previously indicated, General Betts, Murphree's military adviser, recommended the immediate selection of the Thor on the grounds of economy—recognizing that as the Air Force was to deploy the weapon, the choice of the Army missile over their own was extremely remote. Others were persuaded that an early decision was desirable in order to avoid the accumulation of substantial "sunk costs" as the programs entered the prototype and testing phase. Finally, the continued interservice strife led some to favor the liquidation of the Jupiter in order to finally crush any Army notions of a long-range strategic mission.

Murphree, however, was not persuaded by such arguments; [1] nor, apparently, was Wilson. The priority for an IRBM still obtained, and the source of its development seemed irrelevant. The desire for technical insurance was no less pressing in December, 1956, than in November, 1955, for neither missile had entered its testing phase; and the competence of the Air Force-Douglas-Ramo-Wooldridge team in the development and production of long-range rockets was still an unproven quantity. It appears that the President had no preference between the two missiles, but directed the Secretary of Defense to choose one or the other within six months. The urgency of rapid development was actually increasing as a result of continuing reports of Soviet testing of medium-range missiles with sufficient range to render the American SAC bases in Europe extremely vulnerable. Finally, a major technical appraisal of the competing missile programs, conducted by panels under the chairmanship of Dr. Clark Millikan, yielded a noncommittal report approving the technical feasibility of both the Thor and the Jupiter. The panel did not hazard a judgment as to which represented the most promising approach.[2]

Though the inclination to temporize was strong, no one took serious issue with the strong policy statement of Secretary Wilson at his February, 1957, press conference: "It's going to go one way or the other on down the road. There is only going to be one of them made, not two of them." [3] Such assurances were reiterated to inquiring newsmen on April 18, May 2, and June 13.[4] They were frequently interpreted as subtle cues that the

[1] Interview with General Gavin, August 22, 1963.

[2] Medaris, *Countdown for Decision*, p. 133.

[3] House Committee on Government Operations, *Missile Program Hearings*, 1959, p. 280.

[4] U.S. Congress, House, Committee on Government Operations, *Organization and Management of Missile Programs*, 86th Cong., 1st Sess., 1959, Report No. 1121, p. 114.

Jupiter would be cancelled. At one point Wilson was quoted by the Washington press as having announced its cancellation. His statement was subsequently clarified by Deputy Secretary Reuben Robertson to mean that *one* of the missiles would be cancelled. Yet his explanation did not alleviate the anxieties of Huntsville scientists.

Pressures for a decision mounted as the Thor and Jupiter entered the testing phase. Meanwhile the uncertainties of choice compounded the dilemmas of cooperative competition between Huntsville and the Air Force-Douglas team.

FRICTIONS OF COMPETITION

In their various commentaries on military development and procurement programs, Congressmen apply two rather distinct models of competitive market situations. One is the pure competition model. The production units are presumably privately owned. Whatever their size, collusion in matters of product development, financial arrangements, or price setting is considered taboo. Information on such matters is not shared as a general rule. Inhibitions on the diffusion of knowledge relating to new technology are not merely tolerated; they are absolutely sanctioned by patent law and trade secrets practices. Such restrictions are permitted on the assumption that the economy obtains long-range benefits through the creation of incentives by which individuals or firms are conceded temporary monopolies in the application of new inventions. Duplicative efforts in product innovation are accepted not as "waste" but as the necessary price of progress. Centralization in the making of economic decisions is eschewed lest initiative and inventiveness be choked by constraints upon competition.

Another model is generally applied to the relations between productive units in the quasi-public sphere of defense procurement. Here, firms heavily subsidized by the government and in a modified competitive environment develop weaponry for the nation at the taxpayer's expense. Duplication of effort with tax revenues appears wasteful. Diffusion of decision making appears confusing and costly to Congressmen.[5] Refusals to share tech-

---

[5] Charles Hitch, "The Character of Research and Development in a

nical information among the services or their suppliers are viewed as a luxury not to be afforded—a vehicle for empire building at the public's expense. The emphasis is upon the development of more efficient and concentrated authority for decision making, and the elimination of rivalry, secretiveness, and duplication.

Evidences of these latter phenomena were occasionally dismissed with allusions to the market economy. Secretary McElroy, for example, declared, "I think you could really make a case that the inter-service rivalry has speeded up the development of the Thor and Jupiter, because, as you well know, in our competitive economy, a competitive spirit, if it does not run amuck, does something to stimulate people to strive toward a result more than if they do not have that competitive spirit driving them." [6]

Such allusions did not, however, persuade all the Pentagon's critics. The concern of the House Committee on Government Operations was expressed in their report, *Organization and Management of Missile Programs:*

The real question is whether the benefits of inter-service competition in missile building outweigh the burdens. The record is persuasive that the burdens are greater than the benefits—so great, in fact, that drastic action is needed to remove the destructive effects of inter-service rivalry. The matters are too serious to be dismissed lightly by homilies about healthy competition.[7]

Actually, confusion inevitably arose when Congressmen expected to have the benefits of all possible worlds. Such a world would enable the government—in the area of defense development and production—to capitalize upon the incentives of industrial firms assuming technical and financial risks in order to maximize profits. At the same time, provision would be made

Competitive Economy," RAND-Paper-1297 (Santa Monica, California, The Rand Corporation, May, 1958) .

[6] House Committee on Appropriations, *Ballistic Missile Program Hearings,* 1957, p. 58.

[7] House Committee on Government Operations, *Organization and Management of Missile Programs,* 1959, pp. 101–02.

for the sharing of technical information, in order that a service would not be deterred by its own oversights from developing new technologies discovered by others. That such hopes were slightly contradictory was not acknowledged.

The arrangements for contracting in the Thor-Jupiter case were somewhat deficient if one cherished hopes for the benefits of both competition and cooperation. The improbability of cooperation was built into the competitive situation. While the Army had just been denied its request to deploy the Army Ballistic Missiles Agency's Jupiter system, some officers still nourished ambitions of overturning that decision. The contractors for the Thor were closely tied in with the legitimate user of the IRBM system, the Air Force. Justly proud of the in-house technical capability which the fortunes of war had provided them, the Army was nevertheless dependent upon a major industrial affiliate of the Air Force for the development and production of engines for its missiles.

The result was competition of great intensity. Indeed, at the project level, liaison officers performed the functions of intelligence agents of rival sovereignties. According to General Medaris, Colonel Glenn Crane, the Army Ballistic Missiles Agency's representative at the Air Force's Western Development Division in Inglewood, California, did "an outstanding job of ferreting out every piece of paper that he could get hold of, *legally or illegally* . . ." which could assist them in their attempt to preempt the Air Force in the development of workable IRBM systems.[8]

Nor was this competition structured in such a way as to produce optimal technical results. The Thor and Jupiter projects did not represent sharply differentiated technical approaches. Evidence of this is to be found in the comparisons of the products by major participants. Frequently they were referred to as being as similar as the Chevrolet and Ford. Both were built around power plants developed by North American Air-

[8] Medaris, *Countdown for Decision,* p. 149. Italics added. General Medaris also compared Colonel Crane's role to the "position of an ambassador to an unfriendly nation." *Ibid.,* p. 104.

craft Corporation; the configurations of the engines were quite similar. The two employed similar warhead designs. Both were to be equipped with inertial guidance systems. The most notable difference was to be found in their respective approaches to the problem of reentry. The Air Force initially preferred a copper heat sink method of absorbing the terrific heats of the atmosphere during reentry. The Army chose an ablation approach. In short, the yield from this technological competition could have been enhanced by a greater effort to encourage alternate technical approaches to the fundamental problems of an IRBM system: propulsion, guidance, reentry, and warhead.[9]

As a consequence, competition was diverted from the quality of new techniques to the competence of competing technical teams. Clearly this complicated difficulties in the area of information sharing. Such difficulties may become more easily understandable through concrete examples of discord experienced between the rival contractors of the Thor and Jupiter missiles. Frictions emerged with regard to the sharing of industrial suppliers, technical information, and concepts of operational deployment.

[9] It must, of course, be recalled that the emphasis throughout was upon the earliest possible development of operational missiles, rather than the objective of optimizing the technological yield of the parallel approach. Similarity of engine design resulted from the simple fact that the Rocketdyne S-3D engine was the only one which could be developed within the time limits of the IRBM program. One-half of an Atlas booster engine, it was capable of generating 150,000 lbs. of thrust, and used liquid oxygen as an oxidizer and kerosene as fuel. In both missiles, pitch and yaw movements were facilitated by mounting the main engine on gimbals. Since the two missiles were being designed to perform identical missions, the AEC argued persuasively that they be equipped with identical warheads. Although the Atlas was to employ a radio-inertial guidance system, the Thor relied upon an all-inertial system for guidance. Their systems were similar, though by no means identical, to the delta-minimum inertial guidance system developed by Army engineers for the Redstone and modified for the Jupiter missile. Yet despite these evident similarities, the decision to support a parallel effort was certainly favorably influenced by a recognition of salient differences in Army and Air Force technical approaches to the problems of reentry and divergences in the design of their respective guidance, heating, and other component systems.

ENGINE PROCUREMENT CONFLICT

In the immediate postwar years, North American Aircraft Corporation was virtually alone in its interest in advanced research into rocket propulsion systems. Consequently, they accumulated considerable experience and were able to attract impressive scientific and engineering personnel to carry out extensive developmental projects when American interest in long-range missiles finally stirred in the early 1950s.[10] Initially, the Army rocket programs had been dependent upon General Electric Corporation as a supplier of engine components for the Hermes Project.[11] When, however, that company failed to develop a strong commercial interest in the rocket propulsion field, the Army could only turn to North American's Rocketdyne Division in their search for a power plant sufficient to propel a nuclear warhead over distances of 1,000 miles. North American was, of course, deeply involved in Air Force efforts in ballistic rocketry, and they were associate contractors for their ICBM and IRBM programs.

As the Thor-Jupiter competition began to take shape, Army representatives were apprehensive lest the service become dependent for an essential component upon a contractor under the surveillance of their rival, the Air Force. They consequently proposed that North American devote one of their facilities solely to the fabrication of rocket engines required by the Army. This proposal was rejected by the Defense Department in favor of an alternative Air Force proposal to turn over funds to North American for the construction of an additional facility from which the Army would get a designated portion.[12]

Above all, the Army was anxious to obtain assurances from the Defense Department that it would be allowed to procure engines directly from North American rather than having to

10 See Herbert Solow, "North American: A Corporation Deeply Committed," *Fortune*, LXV (June, 1962), 145.
11 See Walter Guzzardi, Jr., "G. E. Astride Two Worlds," *Fortune*, LXV (June, 1962), 127.
12 House Committee on Government Operations, *Organization and Management of Missile Programs*, 1959, p. 103.

channel requests through its competitor.[13] Initially, General Medaris agreed to work on the basis of a Military Interdepartmental Procurement Request (MIRP) to the Air Force. He also directed requests to the Office of the Secretary of Defense Ballistic Missiles Committee to allow the Army to develop an alternate contractor for high-thrust engines for the long-range missile programs. Twice such requests were rejected, although the Assistant Secretary of Defense for Research and Development reviewed with a special panel the requirements for long-range liquid engine developments.[14] The Army Ballistic Missiles Agency actually sought to promote interest in the engine development field among executives of Reaction Motors Incorporated and General Electric Corporation. General Medaris has argued that such initiatives were undertaken as a means of causing apprehension among corporate directors of North American in order to detach them from their Air Force patrons, rather than as a serious effort to introduce new contractors into the propulsion field.[15]

In his Research and Development plans for 1957, Medaris indicated his intention to negotiate directly with North American. General Schriever demurred on the grounds that the general interest would best be served by avoiding confusion in contractor relations with the services. He offered assurances that the Army would be represented on joint technical committees of Western Development Division and Army Ordnance Missile Command, which would process engine requirements.[16]

Probably no such assurances could have allayed Army anxieties about such an arrangement, for they had no means to exact

---

[13] Interview with General Medaris, August 30, 1963.   [14] Ibid.

[15] Ibid. They were not considered mere tactical ploys by civilian leaders in the Secretary's Office. Alvin Waggoner, Civilian Assistant to the Director of Guided Missiles, personally rejected the Army proposal for a new engine source on the grounds that the numbers of engines to be produced would not be sufficient to warrant the addition of another supplier. The demonstrated competence of North American Aircraft and Aerojet-General in the engine development field insured an adequate industrial base. Interview, Mr. Alvin Waggoner, July 26, 1965.

[16] House Committee on Government Operations, *Missile Program Hearings*, 1959, p. 379.

reciprocity from the Air Force in honoring their stated intentions. They simply were not prepared to tolerate dependence on the good faith of their chief rival. North American was sufficiently alarmed by the prospect of industrial competitors that they were amenable to direct procurement from the Army, and such direct relations were initiated by General Medaris in 1957.[17] General Schriever then had to cancel contracts with North American for the equivalent number of engines which Medaris now ordered directly.

When the question of the production quantity of engines came up, Medaris extended Army autonomy in the matter of engine procurement by applying the principle of direct relations to Chrysler Corporation, the main production contractor for the Jupiter missile. His professed aim in instructing them to by-pass the Air Force—which had "plant cognizance"—was to keep the lines of accountability absolutely clear for their prime contractor.[18]

While this may have appealed to public administrators, it was not necessarily normal procedure. Indeed, General Schriever contended that it had been standard for the Air Force to buy from the subsystem contractors and furnish items as Government-Furnished Property to the prime contractors without any alteration in the degree "to which the Government can hold the prime missile contractor responsible for the over-all reliability of the missile." [19] He reminded them that the Air Force had cognizance of the engine builder's plant, that "it was established Department of Defense policy and procedure in the field of aeronautical equipment for the service having plant cognizance to do the procurement," that since the government was specifying the subsystem to be used it had to assume responsibility for the reliability of the subsystem, and that the degree to which the government could hold the prime contractor responsible for the entire reliability of the missile had nothing to do with the method of precurement.[20]

<hr/>

[17] House Committee on Government Operations, *Organization and Management of Missile Programs*, 1959, pp. 103–04.
[18] *Ibid.*   [19] *Ibid.*, p. 104.   [20] *Ibid.*

Medaris stood on principles of sound business practice and Army policy. He further researched the directives relating to plant cognizance and discovered that the document establishing procedures in such matters had no reference to large liquid-fueled missiles; that the procedures were not designed to apply to research and development projects, as Jupiter was then defined; that exemptions were possible where compliance would delay production; and that precedents existed for direct procurement from plants under Air Force or Navy cognizance.[21]

The Army *fait accompli* was accepted reluctantly by the Air Force. Ultimately, General Schriever even submitted to their requests to be allowed their own inspection of the plant. He contended that this was unnecessary in view of the Air Force's cooperative attitude toward the Army, as demonstrated by the delivery of the initial engines produced by North American to the Army and Air Force on a one-for-one basis, even though originally all seven had been earmarked for the latter. Needless to say, the Army partisans were not prepared to consider this a benevolent gesture of magnanimous generosity. Rather, they suggested, the Thor and Jupiter programs were initiated by the Secretary of Defense on the basis of equality; hence, General Schriever was under an obligation to treat the programs equally. Munificence, they argued, had nothing to do with his action.

COMPETITION AND COLLABORATION
IN TECHNICAL DESIGN

In hearings conducted by the Holifield Subcommittee on Government Operations and the Senate Preparedness Investigating Subcommittee, differences of opinion between the Army and Air Force over technical prescriptions for turbopump failures and the appropriate approach to the reentry problem were apparent. The concern of Congressmen was focused upon failures of communication which might conceivably have contributed to waste or unnecessary duplication.

Differences of opinion of a technical nature regarding the

21 *Ibid.*

Thor and Jupiter engine components became a possibility after the Jupiter engine production became a separate project at Rocketdyne. Though the basic design was very similar, the configurations gradually began to take on differences as "the Thor engine proceeded to a more advanced configuration . . . [while the] Jupiter continued to use the earlier experimentally configured engines with some modification." [22] Consequently, once the flight test programs were initiated, there was room for honest disagreement as to the source of difficulties.

Such disagreements were not long in emerging. The first hint of difficulty with the turbopump came in mid-1957, during preliminary flight test ratings. During such tests on the Thor, indications of "marginal turbopump design" appeared "in the form of bearing walking." [23] Rocketdyne was immediately directed by the Air Force and Space Technology Laboratories to investigate "means of preventing recurrence." [24] [25]

In October, November, and December, 1957, unsuccessful firings of the Thor and Jupiter missiles occasioned concern about engine design. No consensus emerged, however, with respect to the source of the failure or the appropriate technical remedy. Indeed, whereas the Army identified the first failure attributable to turbopump difficulties to an October flight of the Thor, the Air Force denied that prior to 1958 any "failures had occurred on the Thor which could be identified with the Jupiter-type failures." [26] They countered that the first indications of problems with the turbopump emerged in Jupiter failures in November and December, 1957.

After the latter abortive tests, the Army Ballistic Missile Agency was clearly alarmed. Consonant with their test philosophy of thorough analysis and correction of any problems before

[22] House Committee on Government Operations, *Missile Program Hearings,* 1959, pp. 380–81.

[23] *Ibid.,* p. 381.   [24] *Ibid.*

[25] These test failures were the more unsettling, coming as they did upon the heels of the Soviet Union's successful launching of Sputnik I, which tended to focus public attention upon the progress of the American Space and Missile program.

[26] *Ibid.*

continuation of tests, they suspended further testing and ran extensive evaluations of the existing torbopump. This philosophy was characteristic of the thoroughness of the German scientists and engineers at the Redstone Arsenal and a consequence of their limited financial resources. It was also a shrewd tactic designed to preserve the image of experience and competence enjoyed by the Army missile team against the public relations effects of an extended series of failures.

Though Army experts apparently first assigned the causes of malfunction to "altitude effects and induced oil frothing," they instrumented their December test, and the results confirmed suspicions of a turbopump design deficiency.[27] Simulated tests at Redstone enabled them to "pinpoint the difficulty as 'bearing walking,' making the chance of successful engine flight tests extremely marginal." [28]

The evidence suggests that there was no dearth of joint attempts to discuss, diagnose, and prescribe for the apparent technical difficulties. According to General Medaris, "Repeated attempts were made to interest AFBMA in this mutual problem in an effort to gain their support so as to hasten its solution." [29] General Schriever's comprehensive memorandum to Secretary of the Air Force Douglas on the subject reveals information of a meeting held at Huntsville on February 24, 1958, in an effort to pool technical knowledge of experts from the Army Ballistic Missiles Agency, Rocketdyne, Air Force Western Development Division, and Ramo-Wooldridge.[30] That communication at this gathering may have left something to be desired is suggested by the contrary recollections of Army and Air Force representatives as to the results. Schriever recalled a "consensus of opinion that the failures were caused by inadequate lubrication resulting from either altitude conditions or flight stresses induc-

[27] House Committee on Government Operations, *Organization and Management of Missile Programs*, 1959, p. 106.

[28] *Ibid.*

[29] U.S., Congress, Senate, Committee on Aeronautical and Space Sciences, *Hearings, Investigation of Governmental Organization for Space Activities,* 85th Cong., 1st Sess., 1959, p. 271.

[30] House Committee on Government Operations, *Missile Program Hearings,* 1959, p. 381.

ing abnormal bearing loads." [31] This was sharply at variance with the Army contention that the Air Force spokesmen alone refused to recognize the existence of a bearing deficiency.[32]

Meanwhile, the Army had suspended flight tests, run exhaustive simulated tests to overcome the turbopump deficiency, and induced Rocketdyne to employ a new bearing retainer in the Jupiter engine. In March, 1958, they began retrofitting all Jupiter engines at Rocketdyne with this device. Subsequently, they were enabled to resume testing with only slight delays. Their reputation for technical proficiency was intact, and the "economic motif" of their test philosophy redeemed.

The Air Force remained unconvinced that their difficulties were necessarily identical to those of the Army. Since the engine mounting installations on the two missiles were dissimilar, and other differences were known, the Army diagnosis was not automatically valid for them. Not until the abortive test flights of the Atlas and Thor missiles on April 1, 1958, did the Western Development Division become alarmed about design deficiencies in the turbopump. A number of other technical "fixes" were introduced, among them increased gear case pressurization and a redesigning of "the connecting shaft between the turbine and the pump gear train to make it stronger and less sensitive to loads imposed through the exhaust-duct connection." [33] Rocketdyne had been at work on a new bearing for the Thor since the spring of 1958, but that was introduced into production models only in October, 1958. Flight tests were not suspended in the interim; nor were Thor missiles, already off the production line, retrofitted with the improved bearing during the summer.

Those decisions were consistent with the Air Force test philosophy, their financial affluence, and their tactical needs in the Thor-Jupiter competition. Endowed with relatively greater resources, they were able to engage in extensive testing on the

[31] *Ibid.*

[32] House Committee on Government Operations, *Organization and Management of Missile Programs,* 1959, p. 106.

[33] Such a duct weakness had previously been corrected by the Army after a Jupiter flight failure in March, 1957. *Ibid.,* p. 107.

assumption that tests yielded valuable information even if they were not entirely successful. General Schriever justified the continuation of flight testing during the summer on the grounds that important information regarding "verification of performance of the inertial guidance system; verification of design of operational launch equipment; verification of satisfactory performance of the missile nose cone separation mechanism, and demonstration of the maximum range capability of the missile system," [34] was obtained. Moreover, having been in the business of developing missiles systems a somewhat shorter time than the Huntsville team, there were positive advantages in carrying out a multitude of tests in order to maximize experience, build up a backlog of knowledge about their missile, and handle as much hardware as possible.

As it finally emerged the Air Force testing approach was evolutionary, "moving gradually from the simple to the complex until the operational missile was realized. Beginning with a mental picture of the completed missile, it would then be stripped of its components, one by one until the simplest possible vehicle capable of leaving the ground was obtained." [35] If this approach maximized publicity accompanying successful launchings, it was an incidental by-product of a test philosophy designed to increase Air Force experience in handling missiles, and to identify and resolve interface problems as component development was progressing. Nor was the continuation of tests despite the malfunctioning bearing without its risks. As Rube Mettler put it, "Politically, it's absolute dynamite to lose a missile at this time. Each one lost means at least two trips to Washington for key BMD and STL people. The Army would make hay and the public would not understand." [36] Yet he and other leading officials acquiesced enthusiastically in the decision to continue testing, in view of the important information to be obtained and the pressing deployment schedules to be met. Another STL engineer, Dolph Thiel, expressed the opinion of

[34] House Committee on Government Operations, *Missile Program Hearings,* 1959, p. 382.
[35] Schwiebert, *History of Air Force Ballistic Missiles,* p. 107.
[36] Hartt, *The Mighty Thor,* p. 163.

project managers when he said, "If we can get a final fix on the guidance system in June instead of October and get some nose-cone flights out in June and July instead of September and October, we are well ahead even if it costs us one or two of these birds." [37]

Furthermore, if Secretary of Defense Wilson had called upon the Army missile team in the first place only as insurance against the uncertainty of the outcome of Douglas' first major effort in the long-range missile field, they had to demonstrate in the shortest possible time that they could overcome all the technical problems involved. Besides, the concern with earliest possible deployment of an IRBM in Britain precluded, in the Air Force view, any delay in the testing program.[38]

In retrospect, it appears that while service pride may perhaps have contributed to the reluctance of the Air Force to accept Army prescriptions for overcoming turbopump design difficulties, interservice competition did not prevent a sharing of information, a pooling of technical knowledge, or the ability of their mutual contractor, Rocketdyne Corporation, to apply to the Thor and Jupiter respectively the remedies deemed essential as a result of prolonged consultations with the contracting service. The turbopump episode reveals not unwillingness to share information but the inability of either service to persuade the other that its diagnosis of difficulties was correct. Such a failure can, however, be explained with reference to strong personalities at Huntsville and Inglewood, the varied backgrounds of the technical teams, and the slightly different engine configurations for the Thor and Jupiter, without exclusive reference to service rivalries.

DIFFERENCES ON REENTRY CONCEPTS

Prominence was also assigned to different approaches to the reentry problem. The technical problem involved was that of providing protection for the warhead against the fantastic heat

[37] *Ibid.*, p. 169.
[38] It does appear that continuance of the flight test program during the period of turbopump difficulty "permitted verification of the compatibility of the airframe, engine, and control system; verification of guidance subsystem performance; verification of the missile nose-cone

generated by reentry into the atmosphere. While several ·technical methods of solving the problem were theoretically justifiable, there was no self-conscious effort to design alternate approaches with a view to making results available for application to a variety of different missile projects.

The most promising approaches in 1955 were those of *heat sink*—that is, coating the nose cone with metallic substances with extremely high capacity for absorbing heat, and *ablation*—whereby "minute layers of the nose cone material are successively eroded or melted when aerodynamic heating is encountered in the reentry." [39] The Air Force chose the heat sink approach on the basis of the judgment of several technical panels of eminent scientists. It was considered the most promising solution to the significantly more difficult problem of the reentry heating encountered in their ICBM programs. While contracts with AVCO Corporation and General Electric included directives to investigate a variety of approaches to the problem, including ablation, it appears that their major efforts were oriented toward the heat sink method. The Air Force did not order a division of labor between competing contractors. [40] They pursued no systematic investigation of all promising approaches.

The Army, on the other hand, was more interested in the ablation technique, with which Cornell University scientists had long been preoccupied, and on which the Army had been carrying out investigations since 1953. [41]

Army criticisms of the Air Force centered upon (1) their

separation process; and demonstration of the full-range potential of the missile system." Emme, *History of Rocket Technology*, p. 153.

[39] House Committee on Government Operations, *Organization and Management of Missile Programs*, 1959, p. 108.

[40] House Committee on Government Operations, *Missile Program Hearings*, 1959, pp. 382–84.

[41] House Committee on Government Operations, *Organization and Management of Missile Programs*, 1959, p. 108; Senate Committee on Armed Services, *Satellite and Missile Program Hearings*, 1957–1958, p. 1724. Admiral Bennett averred that the cheap payoff on the Army Jupiter nose cone program was due to the extended basic research directed by Dr. Cantrowitz of Cornell University on Shock-tubes, research which had been subsidized since 1946 by the Navy.

failure to support competing concepts of reentry between their two nose cone contractors; (2) their failure to demonstrate significant interest in ablation until a full Jupiter nose cone had been successfully tested; and (3) the comparative costs of the two programs.

While the Air Force may have overlooked the potential of the ablation method, and did not specifically encourage their contractors to study it, such a parallel approach did in fact emerge as a consequence of Army efforts. Clearly, in this instance, an important technological opportunity may have gone unrecognized or unexploited for an indefinite period but for the decision for deliberate duplication on the IRBM. The proliferation of projects allowed a greater diversity of technical investigation and experimentation. Where the Air Force had conducted investigations of interest to the Army, there is no evidence that the results of such experiments were withheld. Reports of contractors of Wright Air Development Center relating to the "properties of metallic materials, ceramics, and other coating under various test conditions" were made available to the Redstone Arsenal scientists from December, 1955, on an "automatic distribution basis." [42]

The Army research was of great value to the Air Force programs, and the ablation technique was ultimately applied to the ICBM programs. The heat sink principle was retained for the Thor because their own "nose cone development was well along and provided more than adequate assurance for IRBM purposes." [43] Reluctance to accept the successful innovation of a competitor may have also entered into the picture. That, however, cannot be deduced from the evidence at hand.

[42] House Committee on Government Operations, *Missile Program Hearings,* 1959, p. 383. Later, in 1956, the Army contracted, with Air Force approval, with the Battelle Memorial Institute which was carrying out studies on coatings for the Air Force. Other technical reports from AVCO Corporation and General Electric Co. were loaned or given to the Army Ballistic Missile Agency. Army spokesmen, however, asserted that little relating to the ablation method was included in the technical reports of the Air Force contractors. House Committee on Government Operations, *Organization and Management of Missile Programs,* 1959, p. 109.

[43] House Committee on Government Operations, *Missile Program Hearings,* 1959, p. 383.

As far as the comparative costs of the two programs were concerned, confusion was inevitable, due to the fact that ICBM research and development was to be applied to the IRBM program. According to Schriever the "cumulative initial operational capability nose cone costs through fiscal year 1959," [44] were $22.5 million. This purportedly included procurement of "substantial numbers" of nose cones, the development of ground support equipment, and the obtaining of "a number of complete sets" of such equipment.[45] The costs of research and development of the nose cone was set at $45.8 million by General Schriever.[46] The basis of the figure is not clear. General Medaris claimed that Army expenditures on nose cone research and development were $22 million.[47] Reports in the press intimated that Air Force costs were in excess of Army costs by a factor of ten. The credibility of such reports was supported by William Holaday's estimate that Air Force outlays to ICBM and IRBM nose cone contractors were "in the neighborhood of $200 million." [48]

While Army research efforts in the reentry field may have been both cheaper and more successful than Air Force programs, it by no means follows that interservice rivalry produced wasteful duplication in this instance. Rather, in the absence of such competition, a promising approach might well have been neglected. The additional cost of that alternative appears within reason, and service competitiveness does not seem to have prevented its adoption by the project directors of other Air Force programs.

CONFLICT OVER OPERATIONAL CONCEPT

A more substantial conflict appeared with respect to the operational concept for the IRBM and the resulting design parameters of the ground handling equipment. Although the Air Force had been named the user of the missile, Army parti-

[44] *Ibid.,* p. 384.   [45] *Ibid.*   [46] *Ibid.*

[47] House Committee on Government Operations, *Organization and Management of Missile Programs,* 1959, p. 109.

[48] House Committee on Government Operations, *Missile Program Hearings,* 1959, p. 510.

sans were outspokenly critical of operational concepts preferred by the Air Force. Above all they were convinced of the essentiality of mobility or movability for the IRBM. The significance of mobility for survival was, they contended, the unalterable lesson of World War II. Certainly the experience of the German V-2 scientists and engineers confirmed this perspective.[49] Army officials were also sensitive to political considerations. By creating movable weapon systems that could be easily moved into or out of unstable regions, crises could be met without long-term commitments. But while political insight and doctrinal preference influenced their position, so, too, did their proprietary interests. Some officers still nurtured hopes of seeing the Wilson Memorandum revised. General Taylor later explained Air Force distaste for mobile concepts as follows:

Although the Jupiter was specifically designed for field mobility, in November 1958, the Air Staff directed the Army to remove this feature completely as if it were something unholy. The reason for this attitude is hard to determine. Perhaps it is also the fact that a mobile missile needs Army-type troops to move, emplace, protect, and fire it. Such troops include transportation units for mobility on the road and site construction, signal troops for field communications, infantry for close defense, and ordnance units for repair and maintenance. All these would be needed if the Jupiter were used in its mobile configuration. Thus, a decision to organize mobile ballistic missile units would in logic have led to transferring the operational use of the weapon back to the Army—where it should have been all the time.[50]

In designing ground handling equipment the Air Force proceeded from quite a different philosophy. Secretary of the Air Force, James Douglas, later explained Air Force instincts:

Their first inclination was to say, 'Here is another airbase problem. We will create launchers.' At that time there was more interest in a short reaction time than there was in hardening or protecting the missile system.[51]

[49] Gavin, *War and Peace in the Space Age,* pp. 76–77.
[50] Taylor, *The Uncertain Trumpet,* p. 141.
[51] House Committee on Government Operations, *Missile Program Hearings,* 1959, p. 32.

As in the Army's case, more than habit or doctrine was involved. Fixed-base ground launch equipment was thought easier to place into production quickly.[52] Since the IRBM was supposed to be an interim capability, speed of development was considered a legitimate concern. Moreover, from early 1957 on, it became apparent that Britain would very likely be the first country to deploy IRBM squadrons. Air Force sources contended that the Royal Air Force had expressed little interest in a mobile or movable missile system; rather, they preferred "hardened" bases.[53] General Clarence Irvine made it quite clear that his preference for the Air Force concept was related to the greater ease and lessened cost of handling operational and logistics problems posed by fixed bases.[54] With typical Air Force aplomb he argued for that route which promised the greatest firepower per unit of cost. That this route involved neglect for the survivability of the missile force did not seem to trouble him.

Nevertheless, the Army case for mobility was not apparently without its effect on its rival. Irvine asserted to the Johnson Subcommittee that the Air Force actually had five plans for operational deployment, "which go from a completely mobile solution, to where we would have a large number of fixed sites, some unoccupied, maybe some we would not use at all in time of peace, that we could move to. We are in a position," he continued, "to put this stuff on trucks and drive it around the country if that seems like a good idea." [55]

Actually there was a great deal of confusion created over the use of the term mobility. Not only did Air Force and Army understanding of that term differ, but Army representatives

[52] Senate Committee on Armed Services, *Satellite and Missile Program Hearings*, 1957–1958, p. 1629.

[53] *Ibid.*, p. 1643. If Air Force spokesmen sought to create the impression that the projected Thor sites would be "hardened," they were fostering delusions. "Fixed" bases and "hardened" bases are not synonymous.

[54] House Committee on Armed Services, *National Defense Missiles Hearings*, 1958, p. 4839.

[55] Senate Committee on Armed Services, *Satellite and Missile Program Hearings*, 1957–1958, p. 962.

used it with different connotations. General Gavin, for example, claimed that the Jupiter had been designed "to be as mobile as any piece of equipment in the present day field army. It was designed for movement on highways to launching areas through all kinds of weather. Its configuration was influenced by the design to enable it to be stored in highway or rain tunnels." [56] Medaris also considered it to be as mobile as an eight-inch gun.[57] Other members of the official Army family were more cautious. Von Braun conceded that the Jupiter was movable rather than mobile. The significant distinction was that fixed sites were unnecessary. "No concrete need be poured. No permanent real estate need be leased. It can be set up overnight." [58] It was thus movable in the sense that "you can pull out of one launching site in the evening and be ready to fire from another one the next morning." [59]

Air Force officials harbored doubts about the feasibility of such concepts. General Irvine, for example, suggested that "some people ought to take a look at some World War II pictures of what you could do to a bunch of trucks on the road with a bunch of fighters, and the Russians have lots of fighters." [60] In reply to General Gavin's contention that their Jupiter and ancillary equipment could be moved to prearranged sites in two to four hours, he declared:

The laws of nature are the same for everybody; whether it is an Army truck or an Air Force truck, it sinks in the sand just the

[56] Gavin, *War and Peace in the Space Age,* p. 145.

[57] Senate Committee on Armed Services, *Satellite and Missile Program Hearings,* 1957–1958, p. 2041.

[58] U.S., Congress, Senate, Joint Meeting of the Preparedness Investigating Subcommittee of the Committee on Armed Services and the Committee on Astronautical and Space Sciences, *Hearings, Missile and Space Activities,* 86th Cong., 1st Sess., 1959, p. 260.

[59] *Ibid.* It is evident that mobility was further limited by the requirement that geodetic and gravometric surveys precede the launching of missiles since the results of both were essential to assure accuracy. House Committee on Armed Services, *National Defense Missiles Hearings,* 1958, p. 4820.

[60] Senate Committee on Armed Services, *Satellite and Missile Program Hearings,* 1957–1958, p. 962.

same. If you set up a hundred-thousand pound missile, we have the idea that maybe you ought to lay out a little piece of concrete about twenty feet square to put it on.[61]

Their different approaches reflected different conceptions of future contingencies, as well as past combat experiences. What was clear was that the Air Force view was more persuasive in the Office of the Secretary of Defense. Deputy Secretary Quarles elucidated the Department view to the Johnson Committee:

If you assume that we are fighting a war over a period of months in which we are maneuvering our missiles around and they are trying to destroy them, you might very well come out with von Braun's conclusion about his V-2s, that the mobile ones would survive and the fixed ones would not.

But what we are talking about instead is maintaining an instant retaliatory position with these missiles and one that can respond to tactical warning within fifteen minutes and actually launch the missiles in such a time.

Now to do that, you need arrangements associated with the missile's very rapid fueling and tanking up with liquid oxygen and conditioning the electronics equipment and warhead equipment and all the rest, which means that you must have arrangements, I won't call them fixed; they are not fixed; they are movable, as you say, but in any concept that it is mobile and you will get into action in any such length of time is just not realistic with these liquid oxygen systems.[62]

But aside from the semantic confusion over mobility versus movability, the crux of the Army-Air Force antipathies lay in the difficulty experienced by the Army Ballistic Missile Agency in acquiring guidance from the Air Force as to the nature of the ground handling equipment specifications for the IRBM the Air Force was to deploy. In view of the long lead time involved in the design and fabrication of such equipment, complete

61 *Ibid.*, p. 963.

62 *Ibid.*, p. 2053. Quarles added, "an installation that is not ready to respond within the tactical warning time might be a useless installation no matter how mobile it is." Senator Flanders called Quarles' attention to the danger of preventive warfare implicit in his expectation of being able to respond to "tactical warning."

candor' in information exchanges regarding Air Force concepts was essential to the Army's competitive position.

Prior to November 26, 1956, both services implemented their conceptions of concurrency by proceeding to develop concepts for the operational deployment and handling of their respective IRBM missiles. Once the Jupiter had been assigned to the Air Force, however, the Army faced the dilemma of having to acquire information on Air Force ground launch equipment concepts for the Air Force Ballistic Missiles Division, where, as Medaris noted, "the project directors for the Thor missile were. It was rather apparent," he added, "that they would just as leave we crawled back under the rug someplace." [63]

Procedures had been devised for the exchange of precisely such information. Contacts between the Army Ballistic Missiles Agency and the Air Force Ballistic Missiles Division had been initiated as early as mid-1956. Although General Medaris and General Schriever both claimed to have initiated requests for such contacts, they agreed that the first such meeting was held at Huntsville, Alabama on June 12, 1956, "for the purpose of avoiding duplication of effort in the design of ground support equipment." [64] It was later agreed to hold further meetings at regular intervals, commencing in September or October, 1956. This meeting was postponed, first until November and then indefinitely, at the Air Force's request. Although General Schriever maintained that numerous exchanges of technical information followed the initial meeting, such information exchange apparently did not take place on a planned, regularized basis.[65]

[63] House Committee on Government Operations, *Missile Program Hearings*, 1959, p. 280.

[64] House Committee on Government Operations, *Organization and Management of Missile Programs*, 1959, p. 113.

[65] *Ibid.* A report prepared by the Comptroller General concluded that some of the costs of parallel development might have been averted in terms of engineering and technical manpower utilization through more effective communication of technical information. The mechanics of information exchange were adequate—consisting of technical liaison and procedures for the distribution of published technical reports. But on the average it took the Air Force Ballistic Missile Division 65 days to

Liaison officers from the Army Ballistic Missile Agency did attend a November meeting of Thor project personnel, at which Air Force contractors presented proposals for ground handling equipment. A report of this briefing session was sent to Medaris; but while Schriever considered the report "in effect the complete operational concept and requirements" [66] for the Air Force IRBM, ABMA officials understood it to be merely the "contractor's interpretation of requirements." [67]

In mid-December the Army began its frustrating efforts to get more precise guidance from the Air Force on their deployment requirements. A request for such information was initially directed to the vice-commander of the Air Force Ballistic Missiles Division. When it was turned down on the grounds that authority for such a grant of information resided only at higher levels, the request was consequently referred to Chief of Staff Thomas D. White who directed them back to the Ballistic Missiles Division. Again they were refused until Air Force personnel in Inglewood were reminded of General White's order. Air Force officials continued to equivocate until General Medaris personally visited Ballistic Missile Division Headquarters on March 20, 1957, in order to impress upon General Schriever "the urgent need by ABMA of the complete, official operational concepts and requirements of the IRBM." [68] On April 12 he received from Schriever what he considered "abbreviated requirements" insufficient to "provide real guidance for the development or even for the design of the ground equipment that would be necessary to support it." [69]

General Schriever visited Redstone Arsenal for the first time in June, 1957, for a briefing of the Jupiter system. Redstone Arsenal engineers presented a deployment plan for the Jupiter which Schriever considered less complete than that of their own

---

furnish technical documents and reports specifically requested by Army liaison officers. In other words such exchanges were normally accompanied by significant delays. See Comptroller General, *Initial Report on Review of the Ballistic Missile Program of the Department of the Air Force* (Washington, 1960), pp. 46–48.

[66] *Ibid.*   [67] *Ibid.*   [68] *Ibid.*, p. 114.

[69] House Committee on Government Operations, *Missile Program Hearings*, 1959, p. 280.

November, 1956, contractor presentation. Finally on July 30, 1957, the Air Force Ballistic Missile Division provided Medaris and von Braun with the Thor operational plan. In the light of this information the Army technical team reviewed their own plans and prepared a new proposal, which was forwarded to General Schriever with hopes that it would be confirmed as guidance to them. The reply to this request of August 10 came only on August 27. The Army Ballistic Missile Agency was advised that staff planning could proceed on the basis of the policy guidance letter of August 10, but that action on a definitive development plan would be suspended, pending the outcome of the Holaday *ad hoc* committee's deliberations into the question as to whether one of the IRBM programs could be eliminated. That committee had been constituted only three days after the Army request had been sent to the Air Force Ballistic Missiles Division.

Only after the inconclusive outcome of the *ad hoc* committee's deliberations were major technical interchanges undertaken. In October, Army personnel visited the Air Force's Inglewood, California, installation to look at their ground support equipment. On November 25 a full scale review was initiated. Finally in January, 1958, a final engineering design review was held at Huntsville, and the Air Force accepted Army designs.[70] Previously, on October 15, due to the conclusions of the Holaday *ad hoc* committee, restrictions on Army development of ground handling equipment were removed, and Medaris was directed to develop a complete Jupiter weapons system including tactical support equipment.[71]

INDUSTRY AND THE THOR-JUPITER CONTROVERSY

Industrial contractors for the services were far from passive spectators in the Thor-Jupiter project competition. Indeed, the controversy was more than merely an internecine quarrel between the two services, and the stakes went beyond the assignment of operational responsibility for the IRBM to one or the other service. It involved a fundamental difference of approach to the pattern of weapons procurement, alternative methods of

[70] *Ibid.*, p. 282.   [71] *Ibid.*, p. 284.

organizing for weapons innovation, and a healthy dose of industrial rivalry. General Gavin was among those who attributed considerable influence in interservice disputes to the combative role of their industrial suppliers. As he later declared:

Industry can make extravagant claims for their products and convince Congress of the accuracy of these claims, even though they are not valid. If a service will go along with industry it means an increased budget and money to spend, sometimes on things not directly associated with the industry-supported product. It is difficult for a service to resist such pressures since by going along they can rationalize their position in terms of the overall good that can be accomplished with more money. The amount of money that is spent on nationwide advertising, by industry, for hardware that is obsolete, is sizable, and the pressure that industry can place through lobbies in terms of employment, payrolls and effect upon constituents is impressive to Congress. Finally, when such forces come into play in the committee system that presently characterizes the decision-making processes of the Department of Defense, they can become very harmful.[72]

Army partisans were inclined to believe that what was publicly chastized as interservice rivalry was "in most cases . . . fundamentally industrial rivalry." [73] They were less forthright in admitting their rivalry with Space Technology Laboratories, the technical directors of the Air Force programs. Clearly it is difficult to dissociate enmities, but it appears that part of the reason for excluding Dr. Simon Ramo from a group of Air Force personnel planning to visit Huntsville in 1958 was General Medaris' refusal to "buy the idea of having our system evaluated by the man who invented a different one." [74]

The multibillion dollar aviation industry which emerged from World War II was far more dependent on sales to the Defense Department than any other industrial supplier. This complicated the formulation of a rational military policy during the early postwar years. It further complicated the adjustment of deterrent capabilities in the early 1950s as missiles appeared ini-

[72] Gavin, *War and Peace in the Space Age,* pp. 255.   [73] *Ibid.,* p. 257.
[74] House Committee on Government Operations, *Missile Program Hearings,* 1959, pp. 280–81.

tially to be complex, scientifically sophisticated, costly to develop, and characterized by a requirement for relatively small numbers. Nevertheless, in 1954 in the face of the anticipated obsolescence of manned bombers, the Air Force and its industrial associates accepted the missile era as inevitable and made a major effort to capture the new market. At that time, the industry was in the unhappy state of a producer falling upon evil days, with but a single buyer—the Government—and facing competition from new sources—the Army, the Navy, and their industrial affiliates. The instinct to crush the competitor was compelling, and in the highly politicized atmosphere of defense supply, political methods were among those employed. If the Air Force was interested in excluding the Army from missile and space missions, the airframe industry was equally desirous of eliminating competition from the automobile industry and liquidating the competition emanating at that time from the Redstone Arsenal missile engineering team. They also wished to discredit the concept of weapons development implicit in the Army's arsenal system.[75]

ARSENAL PHILOSOPHY VS.
WEAPONS SYSTEM CONTRACTOR METHOD

Their experiences in World War II led the Air Force to recognize the significance of maintaining high technical compe-

---

[75] Ironically, when the Army first became interested in the development of ballistic missiles, they sought to enlist the support of the airframe industry on their Redstone program in 1951. Rebuffed, they looked elsewhere and, purely by chance, struck up a felicitous working relationship with the Chrysler Corporation. Chrysler had, of course, long been a major Army supplier, and had come to respect the work of the von Braun team in metallurgy to the extent that K. T. Keller, Special Assistant for Guided Missiles under Secretary of Defense Marshall, sent a team of Chrysler experts to study their techniques. Somewhat later, General Toftoy, the commanding officer of the Redstone Arsenal, discussed the possibility of Chrysler becoming interested in the potentially lucrative field of military missiles with a former Army officer, K. T. Tritchel, who had since become an executive with the Chrysler Corporation. Subsequently, Chrysler became the prime contractor on both the Redstone and Jupiter projects. Interview with Mr. Thomas Morrow, Vice President of the Defense Operations Division, Chrysler Corporation, September 3, 1963.

tence in aeronautical engineering in peacetime. Project Rand was conceived of by General H. H. Arnold as a means of sustaining precisely such a capability. Established initially as a subsidiary of the Douglas Aircraft Company, it constituted an alternative to starting from scratch to build an in-house technical capability within the Air Force, a possibility most officials viewed skeptically in the face of mass defection from the military services following the war. Without such an in-house capability there was necessity as well, perhaps, as virtue in what General Schriever termed the Air Force philosophy of "going to industry and having industry develop and produce for us." [76] As Karl Kaysen later explained, the Air Force policy of relying upon industry for weapons development followed from "recruitment problems, manpower limitations, and its own internal priorities." [77]

Some Air Force officers contended that the arsenal system was characterized by; (1) lack of imagination; (2) long lead times between development and production; and (3) inefficient exploitation of technical concepts and techniques by the civilian economy, as well as inefficient use of industrial facilities.[78] Less restrained critics in the Airframe Industries Association thought it sufficient to point to what they described as the "socialistic" aspects of the arsenal system. Their charges were peculiarly ironic in view of the dependence of the airframe industry upon government contracts.

Relations with suppliers were heavily influenced by the Air Force's dearth of technically oriented personnel,[79] their de-

[76] Senate Committee on Aeronautical and Space Sciences, *Government Organization for Space Activities Hearings,* 1959, p. 25.

[77] Kaysen, *Public Policy,* XII, p. 240. Unlike the Army they had neither the technicians, groups skilled in development testing, nor personnel and facilities for production. The airframe companies, on the other hand, on whom the Air Force had principally depended had become habituated to long production runs on new airplanes and had not developed strong research and development departments.

[78] Hall, *Air University Quarterly Review,* X (Fall, 1958), 36.

[79] General Schriever praised the Air Force management system as one which "greatly improves and increases the Air Force capability from a technical standpoint to evaluate and analyze what is being done in the

pendence on the airframe industry, and their conviction that intimate relations with industry did promote a significant shortening of the long period of weapons gestation.

Actually, several patterns of military industrial relations had developed in response to the complexity and urgency of particular projects. Preeminent among these patterns was the weapon system contractor method. It combined simplicity of administration with clear-cut accountability in the technical realm. The Air Force would simply contract directly with a prime weapon system contractor for the finished product. Responsibility for project design, engineering, subcontracting, technical integration, interface problems, and end item performance rested with the contractor.[80] This arrangement appealed to those concerned with maximizing business efficiency and minimizing governmental intrusion into the industrial process. It also seemed to offer contractors scope and incentives for inventiveness within the limits of what would be technically acceptable as a final product. The Bomarc and the B-58 were examples of weapons systems developed on the basis of such contractual arrangements.

Alternatively, the Air Force occasionally contracted directly with the manufacturers of subsystems, equipment, or components. Such equipment then entered the service inventory and could be provided to prime contractors as "government furnished equipment." Clearly such a procedure would not be adequate on futuristic concepts and equipment such as predominated in the ballistic missile programs.

Finally, there could be direct contracting with a prime weapon systems contractor and with one or several associate contractors responsible for major components or subsystems. The associates were "primes" to the extent that they contracted and negotiated directly with the Air Force; yet they developed

---

program because we don't have the in-house capability to do this. These large companies have us pretty much over a barrel." Senate Committee on Aeronautical and Space Sciences, *Government Organization for Space Activities Hearings,* 1959, p. 443.

[80] House Committee on Government Operations, *Organization and Management of Missile Programs,* 1959, p. 53

equipment along lines or specifications suggested by the prime contractor and approved by the Air Force. A variation on this method was devised for the Atlas, Titan, Thor, and Minuteman projects. The Air Force chose to work through more than a single prime contractor. The existing state of the art suggested the need to induce wide interest and strenuous efforts to create a broad industrial base for missile development. Five prime contractors were engaged on the Atlas program, four on Thor, eight on Titan, and five on the Minuteman. Industrial and technical skills in the fields of guidance, propulsion, nose cones, and payloads were rapidly and substantially increased.[81]

Insofar as technical direction and systems engineering were to be maintained over these industrial contractors, the Air Force relied upon Space Technology Laboratories, a private corporation with unique technical capabilities which occupied an intermediate position between the Air Force and its contractors. In short, the Air Force retained formal overall control; Space Technology Laboratories exercised technical direction; associate contractors assumed responsibility for the development and fabrication of specific components; and the Air Force retained the services of the Convair, Douglas, Martin, and Boeing corporations respectively to provide not only airframe, but test and assembly services as well. Consistently critical of the Army's arsenal system, the Air Force strove imaginatively to develop a variety of alternative methods of contractor service relations to produce weapons with speed and economy.

If World War II left the Air Force with an overextended Airframe industry ally, it confirmed the Army's fears of the "feast famine" cycle of American defense preparedness. The arsenal system seemed essential to Army leaders as the only hope of keeping pace with advancing military technology in peacetime. It also appeared to them to provide distinct advantages as a management technique for the design and development of

---

[81] Duplication of subcontractors also encouraged the rapid accumulation of knowledge and skill in the fields of aerodynamics, combustion, computers, electronics, gas dynamics, gyrostatics, heat transfer, metallurgy, propulsion, servomechanisms, telemetry, and thermodynamics as well as many other fields.

novel weapon systems.[82] The civil service status of the arsenal personnel provided, they claimed, the basis for genuine *objectivity* in assessing the performance of end items—objectivity which industrial contractors, dependent upon sales of their products for their very existence, could not muster. The *stability* insured by government employment enabled them to assert a long-range view. They averted overcommitment to a single program, formulated more realistic estimates of costs, lead time, and performance, and were able to develop the talents of an integrated team of experts in a wide variety of fields. The *expertise* of their technical staff permitted government contract officers to check up on the performance of their suppliers and assess the technical validity of concepts advanced by industrial contractors. Moreover, their experience in developing prototypes could serve as a yardstick in determining negotiated prices.[83]

Army partisans denied that the arsenal system was inflexible and rigid. On the contrary, as much or as little in-house production was possible as was compatible with the objective of keeping the technical team on the fringes of research and development work,[84] or assuring the most rapid development of a specific item.[85] On the Jupiter Program, where the pressures of

[82] The Army was not, to be sure, exclusively committed to the arsenal concept of weapons development. As early as 1945, for instance, they had delegated virtually complete responsibility and authority for the development of the Nike weapon system to their prime contractor, Western Electric.

[83] One of the standard criticisms of the arsenal system suggested that the transition from development to production was accompanied by intolerable delays. General Medaris mitigated the effect of this by associating Chrysler production engineers with the work at the Redstone Arsenal in the research and development stage. A pilot production line was installed at a cost of $9 million, or approximately 1% of the total program costs. Not only did this facilitate rapid conversion to production, but it gave Army development engineers "an intimate familiarity with the Jupiter Missile's special production problems." Scherer, *The Weapons Acquisition Process: Economic Incentives* (Cambridge: Harvard University Press, 1964), p. 395.

[84] House Committee on Government Operations, *Missile Program Hearings,* 1959, p. 260.

[85] House Committee on Government Operations, *Organization and Management of Missile Programs,* 1959, p. 50.

time were intense, and the research in the nose cone and guidance areas were basic and advanced, the Huntsville team took the missile from the drawing board to construction of a prototype model. On the later Pershing Missile, Huntsville exercised only technical direction and development work on the guidance system.

General Medaris was certainly sensitive to the public relations stigma of the Army's identification with the arsenal system. He directed considerable effort toward overcoming the pejorative overtones in the term, *arsenal;* eventually he even began to refer to the arsenals as research and engineering centers. Above all, he was interested in countering Air Force efforts to portray interservices differences in terms of a government vs. industry rivalry. As he explained in April, 1957:

These enterprises require the capabilities and experience of a completely integrated group, working in one place, so that you get the benefit of daily interaction between people whose abilities and problems are well known to each other. There you have maximum efficiency. That is what we require. It's not a question of industry vs. government.[86]

SPACE TECHNOLOGY LABORATORIES
AND THE AIR FORCE

Although the Air Force was able to mobilize significant industrial support for their philosophy of development and their managerial techniques, their relationship with the Space Technology Laboratories rendered them increasingly vulnerable to the criticism that they were sponsoring the growth of their own variant of the arsenal system. Air Force management of ballistic missile programs had been hastily improvised in the summer of 1954. Lacking in-house technical capabilities, they cast about for an organization, industrial or academic, which could provide such services to them. None of the airframe companies appeared to contain sufficient scientific competence, or the ability to mobilize it. Neither Massachusetts Institute of Tech-

[86] *Missiles and Rockets* (April, 1957), 33.

nology nor California Institute of Technology was prepared to assume responsibility for a program of such magnitude. Little consideration was apparently given to the possibility of obtaining the services of the Army arsenal team.[87]

The Air Force sought broad scientific competence, on the one hand, and objectivity in tendering advice on the other. Disinterested competence was, however, at a premium. They were assisted by the fortuitous circumstances of the recent defection of two brilliant scientist-engineers from Hughes Aircraft, where they had recently been instrumental in the design of air defense missiles. After leaving Hughes Aircraft Company, Simon Ramo and Dean Wooldridge provided technical staff assistance to the Strategic Missiles Evaluation Group, a committee created by Special Assistant Trevor Gardner to examine the technical feasibility of an ICBM. Having demonstrated their own scientific and engineering competence and radiating confidence that they had the capacity to build up swiftly a flexible and sophisticated technical team, the Air Force determined to rely on the newly formed Ramo-Wooldridge Corporation for technical assistance.

Their problem was in devising an organizational pattern which assured the desired technical sophistication and objectivity. Would they, in short, occupy the position of a technical staff to the Air Force's Western Development Division, leaving ultimate systems responsibility in the hands of the prime contractor? Alternatively, might they be transformed into a line organization with responsibility for systems engineering and technical direction over a group of associate contractors, while remaining in a staff capacity relationship with the Western Development Division?[88] Though Ramo-Wooldridge appar-

[87] General Curtis LeMay requested the consultative services of Dr. von Braun from General Toftoy, commanding officer of the Huntsville Arsenal, in 1951. Since von Braun was engaged at the time on the Redstone missile project, the request was denied. No further requests of this sort were received according to Toftoy. Correspondence from General Toftoy, August 8, 1963.

[88] House Committee on Government Operations, *Organization and Management of Missile Programs*, 1959, p. 76.

ently preferred the former, the latter option was chosen. Ultimately they were given responsibility for maintaining direction over the work of a group of associate contractors, one of whom retained the lead role as integrating contractor with the responsibility for assembling subsystems and components and for performing systems testing.

Thus, Ramo-Wooldridge occupied an intermediate position between the Air Force and the industrial contractors. Having obtained their technical services, the Air Force sought to insure their *objectivity*. Two devices were employed in this quest. The Ballistic Missiles Division work was isolated from the rest of Ramo-Wooldridge's corporate activities. A separate Guided Missiles Research Division, later reconstituted as Space Technology Laboratories, was established. This division of Ramo-Wooldridge decided:

> How big the missile should be, what warhead it carries, what accuracy it can be expected to have, how to get that optimum accuracy by the proper interaction between the rocket engines that produce the thrust and the gyros that hold direction. The systems engineering organization decides how many tests one must call for to get the information required and, hence, how many test facilities are needed to provide these data on a timely basis.[89]

They also provided staff assistance to the Air Force Ballistic Missiles Division to assess the importance and technical feasibility of advanced missiles systems.[90] Finally, they assisted in the evaluation of intelligence data and the training of officers in technical matters. Early Air Force missiles were programmed, and some nontechnical or housekeeping services of an administrative variety were provided.[91]

Secondly, the Air Force imposed a hardware ban on the company, which was even extended to Thompson Products, Inc.,

[89] House Committee on Government Operations, *Missile Program Hearings*, 1959, p. 204.
[90] House Committee on Government Operations, *Organization and Management of Missile Programs*, 1959, p. 85.
[91] U.S., Congress, House, Committee on Government Operations, *Air Force Ballistic Missile Management* (Formation of Aerospace Corporation), 87th Cong., 1st Sess., 1961, Report No. 324, p. 12.

their major financial backer and major stockholder.[92] As Secretary of the Air Force James Douglas said, "We certainly would be in an impossible situation to assert we had clear, objective, disinterested advice if our technical advisers could in another part of their organization sell missile hardware to the Air Force."[93] Confidential information would have conferred a clearly inequitable competitive advantage. It would also have effectively foreclosed candid information exchanges with contractors, without which their tasks of systems integration and direction would have been impossible.

While a temporarily satisfactory solution of the problem, the hardware ban was not sufficient to inspire confidence in industry of the disinterestedness of Ramo-Wooldridge. Thompson Products, Inc., meanwhile, had considered their ties with Ramo-Wooldridge a vehicle for their entry into the defense field. Unhappily for them, that affiliation turned out to be a millstone around their necks, for they were precluded from acquiring substantial production contracts. And as executives at Thompson became increasingly restive, industry became equally dissatisfied with the Air Force-Space Technology Laboratories relationship, due to the latter's access to privileged data, their proximity to the source of Air Force decision making, and their initial efforts to circumvent the hardware ban. In short, if the Army proved increasingly flexible in their approach to industry, some aspects of the Air Force-STL relationship bore a striking resemblance to the salient characteristics of the arsenal system.

A PROFIT AND LOSS STATEMENT
ON PROJECT COMPETITION

The Thor-Jupiter competition was keen; exchanges of information were rarely spontaneous, nor were they always marked by candor. Occasionally, when information was transmitted, it was not accepted at face value; when accompanied by evalua-

[92] It was deemed essential to include them in the ban as a consequence of the interlocking directorate which grew up between the companies and the sizable intercorporate sales of equipment. *Ibid.*, p. 5–6.

[93] House Committee on Government Operations, *Missile Program Hearings*, 1959, p. 54.

tion and prescription, these were at times discounted or ignored. Yet, if this was the price of duplication, it was no more wasteful than comparable examples in the private sector of the economy. Nor is it necessarily to be ascribed to service rivalry any more than the natural competitiveness of rival industries or project teams of proud and self-confident engineers.

Other costs inhered in the terms of competition. While the threat of concellation was presumed to spur both the Thor and Jupiter teams to a maximum effort, it is not clear that this was the consequence of the induced uncertainties. Contrary evidence was provided by the contention of engineers at Huntsville that

The primary bottleneck throughout the entire Jupiter program can hardly be called a bottleneck. It is more in the nature of an impediment, it has been that of uncertainty, it has been the fact that the program was under constant examination for possible cancellation. We had lifetimes given to us that varied from five months at the beginning to as low as forty-five days that we were looking forward to as the lifetime of the project possibly, and this has a very profound psychological effect naturally.[94]

Furthermore, by structuring the competition in terms of the most rapid development of operational missiles, the incentives were arranged to favor lead time minimization at the possible expense of promising design innovations, which would have been dislocative and costly in terms of both time and money once a commitment to a basic configuration had been made. This was probably acknowledged as the price of meeting the requirement of deploying operational units at the earliest possible date.

More serious may have been the neglect of more conventional Army matériel requirements as a consequence of their preoccupation with the Jupiter and the failure of the Defense Department to absorb the entire cost of the project. In addition,

[94] Cited in Frederic Scherer, *The Weapons Acquisition Process: Economic Incentives,* p. 43. See also Medaris, *Countdown for Decision,* pp. 125, 150, and 178–79. House Committee on Government Operations, *Missile Program Hearings,* 1959, p. 550.

the time and energy of a good many colonels was doubtless expended in the effort to justify an Army mission in the IRBM field. Finally, Army morale may have suffered when their quest for an IRBM assignment came to naught.

But while Congressmen tended to emphasize the excessive costs of duplication, its benefits were not negligible. It insured the early availability of both IRBM weapon systems and space booster vehicles. It provided civilians in the OSD with a means of checking the estimates and claims of the services. In this respect competition proved the equivalent of litigation in judicial decision making. The adversaries were provided with strong incentives to state their own case in the most persuasive manner conceivable to them and at the same time to pick at vulnerable spots in the armor of their rivals. Interservice discord contained a certain potential, then, for assisting the OSD in disciplining technical programs.

In short, competition provided the incentives to hasten the solution of technical problems and the elaboration of tactical doctrine. The state of the technological art was thus advanced even as the pros and cons of alternative deployment concepts were illuminated through partisan advocacy. The Army program may have paid for itself simply by insuring against the possible neglect of the ablation approach to the solution of the reentry problem. Their emphasis upon mobility also stimulated awareness of the need to secure deterrent forces against preemptive attacks at a time when the need to insure the invulnerability of American strategic retaliatory forces was insufficiently recognized as a practical problem.

With the advantage of hindsight it appears that the charge of wasteful duplication is less substantial than the failure to structure the competition to exploit alternative technical approaches to the development of components and the solution of interface problems. By focusing attention on the performance of rival suppliers of a similar product the intensity of competition was heightened, and the difficulties of rendering a timely decision among them were increased.

(5) A DECISION
NOT TO DECIDE

Throughout 1957 the pressures for a decision on the elimination of one of the rival IRBM programs steadily mounted. Although General Gavin suggested after the November, 1956, memorandum that an either/or approach to the Thor-Jupiter controversy was short-sighted, since both would be needed in the space program, all other principals seemed agreed that only one of the two would be placed into production. On this point Wilson, Quarles, Medaris, and Schriever were at one. A decision gradually began to appear overdue. The initiation of the testing phase, the pressures of budget deliberations for the 1958 fiscal year, and the persistent interservice sniping all prompted some resolution of the competition.

Additionally, the proliferation of projects in the missile and space field threatened to get out of control unless firm decisions were forthcoming. On May 31, 1957, Eger V. Murphree was replaced by William Holaday as Special Assistant to the Secretary of Defense for Guided Missiles. Several weeks earlier the jurisdiction of the Special Assistant had been extended to enable him to more easily coordinate projects and programs throughout the missile and space field. The earth satellite program was brought under the purview of the Ballistic Missiles Committee, and Holaday was given the authority to coordinate all of the guided missile programs, which now included such nonpriority items as the Navaho, Redstone, Snark, Triton, and the anti-ballistic missile program. With the expansion of responsibilities came new expectations of decisiveness.

Yet stronger powers did not ease Holaday's Thor-Jupiter dilemma. Rather, they served to alert the Army that some decision might be in the offing. To this extent their efforts to prevent cancellation of the Jupiter program were redoubled. Army anxieties increased throughout the year as changes in personnel portended ill for their long-range missile efforts. Curtis LeMay, one of the few high-ranking Air Force officers who had not attended West Point, was advanced to Vice Chief of Staff of the Air Force. At the same time Lyman Lemnitzer, who was not identified with Army missile and space aspirations, was promoted to Vice Chief of the Army. Donald Quarles, the Secretary of the Air Force, was made Deputy Secretary of Defense. All three moves suggested a downgrading of the Army missile program.

Meanwhile, Holaday's predicament was becoming acute. The competing products were only beginning to enter the test phase. Rather than being able to choose one of the competitors simply on the basis of superior technical performance, he was confronted with a choice between the Jupiter, with its more limited immediate production capacity but with a more impressive test record, and the Thor with its more impressive production facilities yet only marginal test performance. This was a choice, as Holaday put it, between "potatoes" and "peaches." [1]

Flight testing began in the spring of 1957. The first two Jupiter missiles malfunctioned, although the second yielded useful telemetry data after a flight of about a 100 miles. The third firing, on May 31, was a complete success over a full 1,500-mile course. The fourth, held on August 15, reportedly fell within 400 yards of the intended target over a range of 1,200 miles. On August 7, 1957, a Jupiter C test vehicle successfully negotiated a 1,200-mile course with a scale model, ablation-type nose cone which was recovered by the Navy the following day. The re-entry problem had been solved! [2]

[1] House Committee on Appropriations, *Ballistic Missile Program Hearings,* 1957, p. 35.
[2] House Committee on Science and Astronautics, *A Chronology of Missile and Astronautic Events,* 1961, p. 160.

The Thor, on the other hand, suffered a series of initial set-backs in its flight testing. Certainly it is confusing to speak of failures in missile testing, since identification of the source of malfunctions is a principal means of assuring technical progress. Nevertheless, there is some justification in measuring success of performance on the basis of the results of similar tests under-taken by rival technical teams. On this basis the Thor was out-performed by the Jupiter. Thor tests launched on January 25, April 19, and unspecified dates in May and August all ended abortively, either by premature explosion or through detonation by the Canaveral Range Safety Officer.[3] Throughout the sum-mer of 1957 a choice between the Thor and Jupiter was made the more difficult by expectations aroused by partisans of both programs that forthcoming tests would render the decision ob-vious. As Comptroller McNeil later reported, both sides were claiming, "In two months we will have proved ours." In the face of considerable uncertainty, it seemed prudent to watch and wait.[4]

The President had already expressed his desire for a selection of one of the programs. The prospect of expensive production tooling costs for two missiles loomed on the horizon. The Army had received notice in the spring of 1957 that funds might be provided for the Jupiter program only through November 30, by which time a choice between the competing projects would presumably be made.[5] In August, consciousness of mounting defense expenditures led to approval by the National Security Council of a Defense Department recommendation that the bal-listic missile programs be reoriented slightly, that an *ad hoc* committee consisting of General Medaris, General Schriever, and William Holaday (chairman) be created to investigate the

[3] *Ibid.,* p. 161.

[4] House Committee on Armed Services, *Reorganization of the Depart-ment of Defense Hearings,* 1958, p. 6620.

[5] Money for the Jupiter program had not been included in the Air Force budget after Wilson's roles and mission decision. The Department of Defense provided $35 million to sustain the Huntsville project through November. Senate Committee on Armed Services, *Satellite and Missile Program Hearings,* 1957–1958, p. 1695.

possibility of eliminating one IRBM program or combining them into a single effort. Thor and Jupiter production requirements were to be limited to their test requirements and contractor overtime was to be curtailed. The Titan priority was to be reduced. In view of the foregoing a slight delay in the IRBM program was to be expected.

These decisions were precipitated by a drastic increase in the flow of defense expenditures as many of the missile projects moved into the costly development and production phases. So torrential was the flow of expenditures that they threatened to overwhelm Wilson and muddle the fiscal picture. When the President and Congress balked at the prospect of raising the national debt limitation, Wilson was forced to attempt to bring the spending increases under control.[6]

Even as the *ad hoc* committee undertook its deliberations in August, it was evident that their options were limited and that choice would be exceedingly difficult.[7] In the first place, since rumors of Soviet missile skills already enjoyed a wide circulation in the Pentagon, a major Soviet success would render difficult the liquidation of any American project of demonstrated success or potential. Moreover, since only about ten per cent of the combined Thor-Jupiter test programs had been completed when the Committee began its consultations, relative technical advantages were hard to appraise.

Three possible courses of action were open to Holaday: (1) either the Jupiter or Thor could be eliminated; (2) components of both could be "married" into a single weapon system; or (3) dual production could be directed. Medaris and Holaday both recognized at the outset that the elimination of the Thor was not practicable in view of the fact that the Air Force was designated as the "user." Hence Medaris' efforts were entirely devoted to a demonstration of the technical competence of his Army missile team and the superiority of their product on the basis of the flight test record, of their achievement of planned

[6] Schwiebert, *History of the Air Force Ballistic Missiles,* pp. 221–22.
[7] Interviews with William Holaday, July 25, 1965 and General Medaris, August 30, 1963.

objectives, and of their solution of major conceptual and engineering design problems.[8]

The prospect of developing a single IRBM from Thor and Jupiter components was also rapidly dismissed. Any substantial interchange of components would delay the initial operational capability date of a system already recognized as transitional. Furthermore, preliminary estimates suggested that dual production would not cost appreciably more than a marriage of Thor and Jupiter components.

The operational question, therefore, was whether or not the Jupiter was to be eliminated. The Air Force contended that the missiles were greatly similar in design and components. Aside from the different approach to the reentry problem and minor differences in the theory of the guidance systems, they were basically similar liquid-fueled rockets of comparable range.[9] Air Force officials asserted that neither they nor the Army faced insurmountable technical problems in the production of a weapon. Their case against dual production was based upon the fact that hard tooling for quantity production of the Thor had already been installed at Douglas Aircraft. They insisted that they were prepared to fabricate more Thors than would be required for the foreseeable future.[10] Moreover, Air Force spokesmen estimated that the costs of dual production would be very substantial. The estimates are suggestive of the significance of vested interests for mathematical analysis. General Irvine calculated that the additional costs of manufacturing both the Thor and Jupiter would be $429 million over and above the cost of the Thor alone. Secretary of the Air Force Douglas estimated the additional costs at over $200 million. Mr. Holaday more cautiously indicated incremental cost increases of something over $100 million.[11]

[8] Interview with General Medaris, August 30, 1963.

[9] House Committee on Appropriations, *Ballistic Missile Program Hearings*, 1957, pp. 34, 99.

[10] Senate Committee on Armed Services, *Satellite and Missile Program Hearings*, 1957–1958, p. 993.

[11] *Ibid.*, p. 1503. Apparently Secretary McElroy shared Douglas' estimate of $200 million as the cost of dual production. House Committee on Armed Services, *National Defense Missiles Hearings*, 1958, p. 4708.

General Medaris was equally vigorous in defense of a decision in favor of the Jupiter or, alternatively, dual production. He emphasized that only the Jupiter had actually accomplished a fully successsful full-range flight with nose cone and guidance packages; that only the Army contractors—Chrysler, Ford Instrument Co., and North American Aircraft—merited confidence on the basis of their participation in the Redstone project; that the Jupiter alone had been designed with mobility, though it could also serve the Air Force as a tied down system; that ABMA had met every single schedule they had set for themselves; that they had solved the reentry problem in a more satisfactory and economical fashion; and that men already trained to operate the Redstone could be easily retrained to operate the larger Jupiter. Army officials maintained that the Jupiter was more rugged, less complicated to operate, less costly to site, easier to remove to other locations, and more accurate.[12]

The *ad hoc* committee held briefings and technical hearings throughout August and September. Although both Generals Schriever and Medaris held out for sole production of their own missile to the very end, the decision, when it came, was really no decision at all. Rather, Holaday asked to be relieved of having to choose between them until development tests were more conclusive. Since no clear, undeniable, obvious technical superiority had been achieved or established, no choice was forthcoming. Equally clear, however, was the fact that the failure to choose was based on more than the inconclusiveness of the technical competition. Indeed, as one of the reports of the Ballistic Missiles Committee candidly asserted: "Termination of either one of these programs will give rise to political questions of various types. (a) A local and state nature; (b) a national nature involving the major parties; and (c) an international nature involving the attitude of our allies." [13]

In short, the diplomacy of contract deployment among the forty-eight states, the anticipated harassments by Democratic

[12] House Committee on Government Operations, *Organization and Management of Missile Programs,* 1959, p. 62.
[13] Senate Committee on Armed Services, *Satellite and Missile Program Hearings,* 1957–1958, p. 1503.

legislators on the state of American preparedness, and the assumption that allies in Europe would readily accept any and all novel strategic weaponry promoted timidity, procrastination, and irresolution. Deliberate duplication was supposed to facilitate intelligent choice at some indefinite point in the future. The political pressures created by the service programs operated to foreclose precisely the choice anticipated at the outset. When the programs were initiated, the Secretary did not anticipate that they would be equally successful. As he reportedly told his colleagues, he found himself "in the position of the feller who proposed to two girls, both of whom accepted."

To be sure, Holaday's decision against termination applied only to the development phases of the Thor and Jupiter programs. Consequently, the Army Ballistic Missiles Agency was permitted to continue their research and development work on the Jupiter. They increased their procurement of test vehicles and resumed development of ground support equipment; they also withdrew all overtime restrictions.[14] These actions, in turn, prejudiced the ultimate decision for dual production despite claims of a leading Pentagon official as late as November 20, 1957, that "a decision as to which missile will be produced in quantity will be made within a few months." [15]

Secretary of Defense McElroy did hedge this prediction by admitting that the option of proceeding with both IRBM systems was being considered. The expediency of such a nondecision was enhanced by the unanticipated, technical surprise achieved by the Soviet Union in October, 1957.

THE IMPACT OF SPUTNIK AND
THE DECISION FOR DUAL PRODUCTION

Technical uncertainty, interservice and industrial rivalry, and political pressures all made a choice between the Thor and Jupiter unpalatable. The Russian launch of Sputnik I mercifully intervened, however, to spare the Secretary of Defense the

[14] Donnelly, *U.S. Guided Missile Programs*, p. 69.
[15] House Committee on Appropriations, *Ballistic Missile Program Hearings*, 1957, p. 6.

necessity for choice. Although intelligence information since early spring, 1957, pointed to an early flight testing of long-range ICBMs and an earth satellite by the Russians, the October event apparently came as a complete surprise.[16] The Administration reacted with a detached calm; yet the shock was profound.[17]

One fundamental problem for the Pentagon planner during the arms race is to specify—with respect to research and development programs—relative priorities between speed and economy. The two are not necessarily compatible. Especially when developing scientific concepts which have already been demonstrated, the speed with which a program is completed is roughly proportional to the resources expended. A decision for economy would have resulted presumably in the liquidation of the Jupiter, since, if the Thor was successful, all the missiles needed could be produced on the "hard tooling" already assembled at the Douglas Corporation. Sputnik, however, diminished somewhat the Administration's priority upon economy in the defense sector. It enhanced the significance of producing operational ballistic missiles as rapidly as possible and consequently counseled further postponement of choice between the rival missile programs. After nearly a year of vacillation, review, hesitation, discussion, and repeated assurances that one of the missiles would be chosen, the Department of Defense announced on November 27, 1957 that a decision had been reached!

[16] Deputy Secretary of Defense Quarles estimated in June, 1957, that the Soviet Union might soon obtain an intercontinental ballistic missile. *New York Times,* June 19, 1957, p. 5.

[17] The most disingenuous aspect of the Administration's response to the public outcry over Sputnik I involved the manipulation of budgetary figures related to research and development expenditures. The amount appearing in the defense budget for research and development was $1,686,000,000. Administration leaders, however, repeatedly cited the figure of $5,039,000,000. The difference was, of course, the inclusion in the latter figure of funds from the procurement and production budgets which went into research and development work. They were somewhat ambiguous since they included pay for administrative personnel, the costs of lawn mowing on research and development facilities, operation and maintenance costs of research ships conducting tests, and a variety of other items which contributed little to the actual program of research.

Both the Thor and the Jupiter were to be placed into production. In the wake of Sputnik, this was not a difficult decision. The premonitions of a missile gap, technical uncertainties, time, economy, geopolitics, domestic politics, and personalities all had an influence on the decision which was announced by Secretary of Defense McElroy to the Senate Armed Services Committee on November 27.[18]

Most interesting were the arguments adduced for the decision on economic grounds. On the one hand, it was argued that the initial outlays for production tooling were the largest part of the entire cost; hence it would be uneconomical to eliminate one of the programs at the point when the largest portion of the investment had been made, without as yet capitalizing upon it in terms of production. Others assured their critics that economies could be achieved at a later date. For the moment, it was desirable to develop a broad production base in order to be able to stimulate competition on future programs.[19] Still others conceded that money could doubtless be saved through discriminate choice between the competing projects. Since time rather than money was of the essence in November, 1957, economy might be purchased at the terrible price of national disaster. Despite the sophisticated *ex post facto* rationalizations,[20] it seems clear that the latter point was uppermost in the mind of

[18] Secretary McElroy acknowledged the relationship between Sputnik I and the decision to produce both missiles in testimony before the House Armed Services Committee. See House Committee on Armed Services, *National Defense Missiles Hearings*, 1958, p. 4012. The shock and apprehension which permeated all Defense Department activities in the weeks following Sputnik I is illustrated by the wide variety of programs and decisions undertaken by Secretary McElroy during his first weeks in office For an account of these actions, see Senate Committee on Armed Services *Satellite and Missile Program Hearings*, pp. 2080–82.

[19] U.S. Congress, House, Committee on Appropriations, *Hearings, Department of Defense Appropriations 1960*, V, 86th Cong., 1st Sess., 1959 p. 863.

[20] Such rationalizations are not necessarily to be viewed as mere acts o cynicism. The justification of hard decisions invariably entails some exaggeration of the advantages and some underrating of the liabilities of the course chosen. Bertram M. Gross, *The Managing of Organizations: The Administrative Struggle*, II (London, The Free Press, 1964), p. 766.

the man who was chiefly responsible for the decision—Secretary McElroy. He viewed the decision for dual production purely and simply as a hedge against the possibility of unforeseen delays in the development testing or fabrication of either Thor or Jupiter. He was perfectly willing to concede the somewhat greater costs involved.

Such caution may have been justifiable in the aftermath of demonstrated Soviet capabilities. The elimination of any backup project would perhaps have seemed foolhardy under the circumstances. Moreover, it might have been possible to maximize both long- and short-range interests. The success of the Jupiter test program promised to lead to early operational capability, whereas the Thor had somewhat greater growth potential for future generations of IRBMs. In the wake of the Soviet Union's dramatic demonstration of their early lead in space technology, both missiles were promising as vehicles for delivery payloads into space as well as military systems.

More immediately the decision was supported on the grounds of supply and demand. As the Soviets had already flight-tested ICBMs and since the Atlas was not expected to be tested until mid-1953, it was natural for an insular power to consider the extension of range of an IRBM by virtue of peripheral overseas bases as the equivalent of an intercontinental missile capability. As it was deemed essential not to concede the Soviets an advantage in the range of ballistic missiles, the Administration was prepared to move back into Europe, despite the fact that overseas B-47 bases had only recently been deprecated as excessively vulnerable.

Spokesmen for the Administration were not prepared to concede any basic alteration in the *balance of deterrence*. They were, however, fearful that the *balance of confidence* within the Western Alliance would be adversely tilted in the absence of some demonstration of American technological prowess. Thus it was deemed desirable to emplace missiles in Europe which could exhibit a demonstrated capability of striking targets in the Soviet heartland. It was casually assumed that the NATO allies would be all too willing to provide staging bases for these missiles since Soviet medium-range ballistic rockets were already aimed at major European metropolitan centers.

As McElroy reported to the Johnson Committee: "By making use of the production capacity now available for both the Jupiter and Thor, an operational capacity can be achieved by the end of 1958 in the United Kingdom; and, as soon as necessary arrangements can be affected, at other appropriate locations." [21]

The possibility of encountering difficulties with other allies was not entirely discounted, but it was minimized. As the Secretary of Defense told the Mahon Military Appropriations Subcommittee in the House: "We don't think we will have much difficulty in getting them deployed overseas, and we also have certain territories of our own, where we could put them, without any difficulty and we would be glad to have them." [22]

There is some question as to whether the desire to exploit all possible production capabilities was decisive. The deployment of IRBMs in Europe was considered an asset to the American strategic arsenal as an additional retaliatory system for the West, an additional trigger for SAC, and an added complication for Soviet defense plans. But Quarles informed the Johnson Committee: "I think it wasn't so much the thought that we couldn't produce the necessary quantity of either one. I believe we could have. But the danger there is that we would have been in production on one that later proved not to be a successful one, and while that was a small chance, it was, nevertheless, a real chance." [23] The fact that the persistent refusal to permit the Army to implement its Project Orbiter proposal as insurance against slippage in the Vanguard schedule now contributed to the embarrassment of the Administration doubtless strengthened the hand of those resisting the cancellation of either the Thor or the Jupiter.

Yet it seems clear that McElroy's decision was not solely based

[21] Senate Committee on Armed Services, *Satellite and Missile Program Hearings,* 1957–1958, p. 194.

[22] House Committee on Appropriations, *Ballistic Missile Program Hearings,* 1957, p. 70.

[23] Senate Committee on Armed Services, *Satellite and Missile Program Hearings,* 1957–1958, p. 2047.

on strategic, technical, or economic grounds. Political factors also influenced his thinking. Certainly it might have appeared strange to the domestic public to have eliminated a promising and glamorous project at a time of great crisis in the public mood. It seems hardly coincidental that a decision was reached only late in the evening prior to McElroy's appearance before the Senate's Permanent Defense Investigating Subcommittee headed by Majority Leader Lyndon Johnson. McElroy correctly estimated not only that the specific decision would be met with approval but that a show of decisiveness would be greatly appreciated. Senator Johnson expressed the feelings of many Congressmen when he told the Secretary of Defense: "Without passing judgment on the wisdom of the decision, I congratulate you on the fact that a decision has been made." [24]

The decision for dual production had support from other sources as well. Faced by a downward trend in the economy, dual production constituted a counter-cyclical tool of sorts. Some overtones of "pump priming" did nothing to discourage the Administration from a decision which was defensible on other grounds. For Neil McElroy, who only recently had assumed the awesome burdens of the Pentagon, it was a popular decision. No new incumbent of a trying office likes to start off in the midst of a national crisis with a decision calculated to alienate a substantial group of service partisans, industrial contractors, or supporting communities. In this case all were exerting intense pressures on those at the top. Attempting to explain the apparent indecisiveness of the Pentagon on the Thor-Jupiter dispute, one Assistant Secretary of Defense commented: "If the Defense Department suggested cancelling the Air Force's Thor program, a Congressional delegation from California would be down our necks. And elimination of the Army Jupiter program would have half the Alabama delegation plus a couple of representatives from the Detroit area fighting us." [25]

[24] Senate Committee on Armed Services, *Satellite and Missile Program Hearings,* 1957–1958, p. 225.
[25] William S. Fairfield, "PR for the Services—in Uniform and in Mufti," *The Reporter,* XVIII (May 15, 1958), 21.

The extreme difficulty of the decision is attested to by the circumstances under which it was reached. While normally such decisions would have been the province of the Special Assistant for Guided Missiles, Mr. Holaday, in conjunction with the Secretary of Defense's Ballistic Missile Committee, this forum was not officially consulted. Its individual members, Wilfred McNeil, Comptroller, Dr. Foote, Assistant Secretary for Research and Engineering, Mr. McGuire, Assistant Secretary for Supply and Logistics, Mr. Bryant, Assistant Secretary for Properties and Installations, and Dr. Reed of the Budget Bureau, may have been polled. The Joint Chiefs of Staff were not consulted specifically as to the wisdom of the decision for dual production. They were contacted later only with respect to the appropriate method of deployment. Holaday asserted that the Chairman of the Joint Chiefs had concurred with the decision and that the Air Force Chief of Staff had been the most influential dissenter.[26]

The direction of Administration thinking on the matter was suggested on November 20, 1957, when Deputy Secretary Quarles testified before the Mahon Subcommittee in the House. In spite of his assurances that a choice would probably be made, he left the definite impression that dual production was daily appearing more and more attractive. Finally, and doubtless catalyzed by McElroy's imminent appearance before the Senate Preparedness Investigating Subcommittee, a decision was reached at the White House on the evening of November 25. Prior to this meeting, which was attended by Vice President Nixon, Dr. James Killian, Mr. Quarles, Mr. Holaday, Sherman Adams, Mr. Brundage of the Bureau of the Budget, and Secretary of State Dulles,[27] McElroy had consulted with President Eisenhower to lay the main guidelines for the decision.

The decision, when it came, was unanimous. Only the extraordinary political conditions existing in the aftermath of Sputnik could have overcome otherwise persuasive reservations

[26] Senate Committee on Armed Services, *Satellite and Missile Program Hearings,* 1957–1958, p. 403–04.
[27] *Ibid.,* p. 402.

grounded both in economics and strategy; but whereas the decision to continue development suited the political and military needs of the Administration, the volume of production was to be decisively influenced by the politics of the NATO alliance.[28]

[28] If the decision appears to have been reached in haste and without systematic and thorough analysis this reflects in part the circumstances prompting it and the high level of the government at which it was resolved. James Schlesinger had ascribed the relative lack of quantitative analysis informing the highest level decisions to the multiplicity of objectives represented, the uncommensurability of many of those goals, and the fact that there one is dealing with "rare events, single events, or mere possibilities—rather than repetitive and routinized operations." "Quantitative Analysis and National Security," *World Politics,* XV (January, 1963), 312.

(6) THE DIPLOMACY OF DEPLOYMENT

"Armaments," as George Kennan once noted, "are important not just for what could be done with them in time of war, but for the psychological shadows they cast in time of peace." [1] Those shadows have never been longer than in an age of nuclear deterrence. The Russian launching of Sputnik I prompted a politically facile resolution of the Thor-Jupiter competition in favor of dual production. That decision could be made and implemented entirely within the jurisdiction of the United States Government. Deployment of the missiles, however, required the assent of foreign allies. If interservice politics influenced the structural decision for dual production, intra-alliance politics could frustrate the execution of the strategic decision to emplace IRBMs overseas. One must, therefore, inquire into the correspondence of allied and American objectives as they pertained to the deployment of these long-range ballistic rockets in Britain and on the Continent. How did converging or conflicting aims influence the payoff from the IRBM development programs? To what strategic or political purposes were the missiles to be put? What were the consequences of the proposals for European base rights upon the service missile programs, upon the parties to such agreements, and upon the Alliance? [2]

[1] George Kennan, *Russia, the Atom, and the West* (New York, Harper & Bros., 1957), p. 93.
[2] It is, of course, true that most of the difficulties encountered in seeking launching sites for Thors and Jupiters would have arisen had there been but one IRBM and no interservice rivalry.

Sputnik served to calm interservice discord at home by providing the sense of urgency required to increase spending, accelerate a variety of programs, and focus attention on external dangers. Within a matter of weeks, overtime restrictions on missile contracts were eliminated. Money withheld from basic research projects by the Defense Department Comptroller was restored to the services. The Explorer Project was resuscitated. Program schedules for Atlas and Polaris were accelerated. The authority of Special Assistant for Guided Missiles William Holaday was extended in the missile and space field. An Advanced Research Projects Agency was created. Dispersal of the Strategic Air Command's fleet of B-47 and B-52 bombers was increased. The Army was authorized to proceed with the Pershing medium-range ballistic missile and the Nike-Zeus antimissile missile system. The Air Force was authorized to proceed with the development plans for a Distant Early Warning Network. A program for reorganizing the Department of Defense was initiated. And, as previously indicated, the dual production of Thors and Jupiters was ordered.[3]

At the same time, evidence of Soviet missile developments diminished allied unity by encouraging doubts about the technological superiority, political leadership, and military power of the United States. The proposal to deploy strategic missiles in Europe crystallized a number of political conflicts within NATO, and tensions in the Alliance were exacerbated rather than alleviated by the implied interdependence of the offer. Ironically, the forces producing disarray within NATO bore a remarkable resemblance to those contributing to Army-Air Force rivalries at home. Like the Army, many Europeans tacitly expressed a loss of confidence in the senior alliance partner. They raised similar demands for control over deployment and for use of decisions regarding nuclear weapons, and maintained similar reservations with respect to the basic strategy of massive retaliation.

The intensity of European opposition to IRBM deployment

[3] *New York Times,* January 24, 1958, p. 6. See also Senate Committee on Armed Services, *Satellite and Missile Hearings,* 1957–1958, p. 2428.

on the Continent appeared to surprise Administration leaders, for the offer of America's most sophisticated missile delivery capability seemed to them a logical response to new developments. An initiative designed to achieve simultaneously several important objectives, it was hardly calculated to unleash a spate of criticism or spur active resistance from normally deferential allies. Military leaders in the Pentagon and in SHAPE were the most active proponents of the IRBM deployment. The rationale they elaborated can be briefly summarized. Needless to add, emphases varied with the advocate. First, European deployment of Thor and Jupiter missiles was consistent with NATO strategy and responsive to requirements established at SHAPE. For some time NATO military strategy had been based on the expectation that nuclear weapons would have to be employed in the defense of Western Europe. During 1957, NATO strategy had been adjusted, in what came to be known as the Radford Plan, to the premise that the West faced an insurmountable gap in manpower and, thus, permanent inferiority in conventional encounters with the Soviet hordes in Europe. Nuclear weapons were henceforth to be stockpiled on the Continent, and a double veto system was devised for their control.

While such weapons were to be of a tactical nature, tactical was defined in such a way as to permit the Supreme Allied Commander, Europe (SACEUR), to acquire a capability sufficient to destroy all Soviet weapons aimed at Europe. Thus, this doctrine would allow for weapons of a range and destructiveness almost indistinguishable from those in the arsenal of the Strategic Air Command. Such forces could actually be called tactical, as Henry Kissinger later observed, "only in the sense that they were stationed in Europe and not in the United States and that they were controlled by SACEUR rather than the commanding general of SAC." [4]

General Norstad's primary concern was the reassurance of European allies that nuclear weapons would be available to them in an emergency without at the same time encouraging a

[4] Henry Kissinger, *The Troubled Partnership* (New York, McGraw-Hill Book Co., 1965), p. 97.

proliferation of nuclear arsenals within NATO. He thus considered the stockpiled weapons as a supply system in which allies would be given delivery means and training in their deployment and use, while custody over the atomic components remained with the United States. As he later explained to the Jackson Subcommittee: "This is very similar to the system we use . . . with American forces where you have a supply system and in accord with properly authenticated orders and directions, the weapons themselves are made available to units that are trained in their use." [5]

Quite obviously the American Commander of NATO felt that Europeans had a requirement for intermediate-range rockets. He was responsible for generating at SACEUR in late 1957 a military requirement for ballistic missiles which would replace vulnerable tactical aircraft and which could be targeted against Soviet MRBMs, airbases, troop concentrations, and logistical complexes in East Germany and areas farther to the east.[6] Thus SHAPE was eager to receive IRBMs. The military requirement which they established envisaged the emplacement on the Continent of substantially more than the seven squadrons of fifteen missiles apiece which were ultimately deployed.

Nor, it may be added, were these highly vulnerable, first-generation missile systems necessarily inconsistent with the requirements of American strategy. The "massive retaliation" doctrine consisted of a decision to employ a broad mix of strategic retaliatory systems against the politico-military structure of the enemy in order to deter a wide range of contingencies. It contemplated "probable first use" of nuclear weapons, assumed "little control" over the course of hostilities, and emphasized a large number of various retaliatory systems to insure against any calculated surprise attack by the enemy.[7]

Within this context it seemed natural to deploy Thors and

---

[5] Senate Committee on Government Operations, *Organizing for National Security Hearings*, 1961, pp. 22–23.

[6] Timothy Stanley, *NATO in Transition* (New York, Praeger, 1965), pp. 162–63; Kissinger, *The Troubled Partnership*, p. 128; and Norstad's testimony in *Organizing for National Security, Hearings*, p. 34.

[7] Stanley, *NATO in Transition*, p. 93.

Jupiters overseas wherever bases could be obtained without making substantial concessions over their control. Indeed, the prospect of a significant Soviet ICBM capability seemed to revive, for an interim period at least,[8] the former justifications for the elaborate overseas base system created after World War II. The combat radius of the first strategic rockets to become available made such a base system seem absolutely essential. The wide dispersal of strategic forces, which such a base system facilitated, promised to complicate Soviet calculations for a surprise attack and compound their defense problems. This, it was hoped, would force reallocations of the Soviet defense budget away from expenditures for offensive systems. Moreover, since the degree of anticipated accuracy of early generation long-range rockets was a function of range, by permitting retaliatory attacks from close-in bases, the devastation of Russian targets seems more clearly assured.[9]

Furthermore, IRBM deployments were considered "an important psychological reassurance as to the U.S. commitment" to Europe's defense,[10] as well as an earnest indication of its intention to place the most advanced military technology at the disposal of the Alliance. It was also assumed that Thors and Jupiters might checkmate Soviet MRBMs located in Central Europe and provide an additional sanction to insure the limitation of conflicts on the Continent. Finally, the acquisition of IRBM bases appeared to be a promising experiment in NATO sharing at a time when the closer integration of the Alliance had received a new urgency and appeal.[11]

[8] President Eisenhower apparently considered the military value of the IRBM to be nearly equivalent to that of the ICBM, for, as he later wrote, "located on bases on foreign soil, [it] could strike any target in Communist areas as well as could an ICBM fired from the United States." Dwight D. Eisenhower, *Mandate for Change* (Garden City, Doubleday, 1963), p. 457.

[9] For an evaluation of these claims, see Townsend Hoopes, "Overseas Bases in American Strategy," *Foreign Affairs*, XXXVII (October, 1958), 69–82.

[10] Stanley, *NATO in Transition*, p. 191.

[11] See Malcolm Hoag, "On NATO Pooling," *World Politics*, X (April, 1958), 475–83. Hoag was not himself an enthusiast for the IRBM de-

Evidence of the vulnerability of the Thor and Jupiter systems was not considered by Administration leaders to be a decisive deficiency either, since it was widely assumed that the Soviet Union would not dare attack Europe alone and that simultaneous attack on European and American bases would prove too complicated to attempt. Should an attack not be perfectly coordinated, either the American- or the European-based component of the Alliance's strategic capability would be triggered in retaliation. In fact, in one version an attack on European missile sites was itself to provide strategic warning for SAC. "The first shot he fires," General Nathan Twining assured the House Committee on Appropriations, "SAC goes and we have him over a barrel." [12] To suggest that a strike on European targets would constitute strategic warning for U.S. retaliatory forces was perhaps consonant with the traditional sequence of American security policy—isolation, mobilization during the initial phase of hostilities in Europe, and finally intervention. It was hardly compatible with the strategic requirements of the missile age nor appropriate as an argument for interdependence. It merely dramatized the increasingly unpalatable division of labor between the Anglo-American sword and the Continental "cannon fodder." [13]

Needless to add, Defense officials were anxious to capitalize upon the considerable investment that they had made in the Thor and Jupiter development programs and to recoup American technological prestige undermined by the demonstrated Soviet prowess in missile and satellite technology. In this latter connection it was probably felt that an appropriate response had to fall within an area that would be regarded as comparable by the peoples of Europe.[14]

---

ployments in view of the reluctance of European allies to expend adequate funds for their hardening and protection.

[12] House Committee on Appropriations, *Hearings, Department of Defense Appropriations 1960*, 1959, p. 45.

[13] See Robert E. Osgood, *NATO: The Entangling Alliance* (Chicago, University of Chicago Press, 1962), p. 187 ff.

[14] For an analysis of the importance of national pride in precipitating a vigorous response to Soviet efforts in space, see Vernon Van Dyke, *Pride*

As for Secretary of State Dulles, while he approved the offer of IRBMs to Europe, he does not appear to have considered such deployments as absolutely essential either for military security or diplomatic prestige. He anticipated no immediate transformation in the military balance of power as a consequence of Sputnik. Rather he felt that the critical period was five to ten years away, and he expected that manned bombers would continue, for much of that period, to remain the preferred means of delivering thermonuclear weapons.[15] Nevertheless, Dulles did share with the President the conviction that strains on the Alliance had to be relieved by a greater emphasis upon interdependence.[16] The emplacement of Thors and Jupiters on British and European bases promised in his view to improve American deterrent power and underscore a renewed interdependence. It would also improve the understanding by American allies of the residual military capabilities of the U.S., and enhance the cohesion of the West in the face of a growing menace. Thus, there were no substantial differences between the approaches of the State Department and the Defense Department as to the substance of the offer of IRBMs. It was approved and enjoyed their consistent support.[17]

Paradoxically, it was the appearance of a revived interdependence that gave rise to European resistance. Since its inception NATO appeared more like a unilateral guarantee than a genuine multilateral alliance. Geographically, the Alliance consisted of a western peninsula on the Asian-European land mass and a North American island several thousand miles to the west. Invulnerability to direct Russian attacks had for years provided a stable basis for the credibility of American pledges to unleash massive retaliation for Soviet provocations in Western Europe. The successful test firings of ICBMs by the Soviet Union and

---

and Power: The Rationale of the Space Program (Urbana, University of Illinois Press, 1964) .

[15] See *United States Department of State Bulletin,* XXXVII (November 4, 1957) , 708.

[16] *Ibid.* (November 18, 1957), 787.

[17] Personal correspondence from the Hon. Robert Murphy, former Deputy Under Secretary of State, to the author, January 7, 1966.

their launching of Sputnik I, however, provoked anxieties that if the Russians either "acquired more intercontinental missiles than the United States or produced them before the United States could do so, the American mainland would be more vulnerable even than Russian territory." [18] The implications of such developments upon the Alliance were not altogether obvious. They were sufficiently unsettling, however, as to occasion quite disparate views as to what should be done to meet new contingencies.

THE POLITICS OF EUROPEAN DEPLOYMENT

Just as the decision to produce two IRBMs was made in haste against the backdrop of impending Congressional investigations of the satellite and space programs, a decision to seek European sites for Thors and Jupiters was made in anticipation of North Atlantic Treaty Organization Summit discussions scheduled for mid-December, 1957. Well in advance of those meetings the nature of the American offer was widely publicized in the press. Statements by leading American defense and foreign policy officials revealed a considerable optimism that base rights would be extended by a number of European states in order to counterbalance the growing Soviet ballistic missile threat from Eastern Europe.

Early assumptions as to European needs were, however, clearly based upon miscalculations. Sputnik unleashed far from uniform reactions on both sides of the Atlantic. European peoples and statesmen were, for a variety of reasons, growing increasingly self-assertive in defense of their own unique interests. Consequently, they were less disposed to quietly defer to American leadership in strategic and diplomatic matters. If Americans were inclined to consider the offer of IRBMs as a magnanimous gesture from a position of strength, Europeans were more sensitive to the renewed dependence of the U.S. for advanced bases from which to launch their newest strategic delivery systems.

[18] Raymond Aron, *The Great Debate: Theories of Nuclear Strategy* (Garden City, Doubleday & Company, Inc., 1965), p. 13.

Nor was the bargaining position of the United States particularly impressive. The sharing of new risks is never likely to be enthusiastically welcomed, especially at a time when the technological credentials of the senior partner in the Alliance are being severely challenged. Congressional control over the exchange of information relating to fissionable materials, and their zealous custody of proprietary information, significantly reduced the range of attractive concessions on the basis of which an acceptable *quid pro quo* could be arranged.

Confident of a favorable reception to the IRBM offer, shocked surprise greeted the Europeans' unexpected resistance to Secretary of State Dulles' proposal. Indeed, so strongly was such resistance expressed even before the convening of the NATO Heads of State Meeting on December 16, 1957, that the Secretary of State publicly disavowed any intention of pressuring allies to accept the IRBMs. The façade of unity was thus preserved in the face of the new Soviet menace. "There is no desire on the part of the United States," he assured the press on December 10, "to press these missiles in the hands or on the territory of any country that doesn't want them. The present thinking of SACEUR is that it would be useful to have them." [19]

Anxious to prevent the embarrassment of overt rebuff, Dulles resorted to a face-saving expedient. The military authorities in SHAPE Headquarters in Paris were asked to make a study of military requirements for intermediate-range ballistic missiles prior to any sounding out of governments as to their attitude toward emplacing strategic missiles on their territory. The onus of requesting sites was thus passed to the military leaders of the Alliance. General Norstad was fully cognizant of the political strains provoked by the American offer and he later indicated that, in NATO planning, ample consideration was given to political and psychological factors which might legitimately preclude the emplacement of Jupiter missiles in certain countries on the Continent. [20] Norstad immediately eased pressures on several important governments by announcing that there was

[19] *New York Times,* December 11, 1957, p. 4.
[20] *Ibid.,* July 21, 1957, p. 12.

"no requirement for placing these bases in any particular place in the NATO area." [21] In short, military considerations would not dictate emplacement of IRBMs in any countries where political difficulties threatened.

The United States also soft-pedaled the urgency of decision on the grounds that the long lead time involved allowed decisions on missile sites to mature slowly as the testing and production of the missiles was brought to a conclusion. That this represented submission to hard political facts rather than conclusions based on the logic of the technical process was suggested by the fact that the timing of a prior agreement with Britain for the acceptance of Thor missiles was explicitly justified by the long lead time for base construction and manpower training.[22]

At the same time, attempts were made to sweeten the pill of acceptance and to underline the prospect of renewed independence of the United States with the development of a reliable ICBM. Vague promises of assistance in the construction of Polaris submarines were also extended.

French, Dutch, and Italian officials all expressed interest in the offer, which, however, was hardly concrete in view of the very tentativeness of the American Polaris program and doubts about Congressional sympathy for such a program of technical sharing. Implicit in the successful firing of an Atlas ICBM on December 17 was the reminder that European bases were a matter of but transitory interest to the United States and were, therefore, not an indispensable asset for which major political concessions would be granted. To be sure, at the December, 1956, NATO Council meeting the Governments of Britain, France, Germany, the Netherlands, and Turkey had requested that atomic weapons be made available to European forces. Deliveries of tactical nuclear weapons and short-range missiles like the Honest John and the Corporal were now viewed as an inducement to increase the willingness of some allies to station IRBMs on their soil.[23]

[21] *Ibid.*, December 24, 1957, p. 4.   [22] *Ibid.*, December 16, 1957, p. 1.
[23] James L. Richardson, *Germany and the Atlantic Alliance* (Cambridge, Harvard University Press, 1966), p. 50.

In the end neither the carrot nor the stick was sufficient to render major allies more amenable to the acquisition of strategic missiles on the terms offered. Reservations expressed prior to the NATO summit meetings were sustained throughout those deliberations. The final communiqué contained, to be sure, an agreement in principle to deploy IRBMs in Europe. The details of that deployment were, however, to be worked out in SHAPE and discussed further in March, 1958, Conference of NATO Defense Ministers. On the agreement Secretary of State Dulles candidly commented, "I am not attracted by agreements in principle. They usually mean that the governments concerned are reserving the right to frustrate them in practice." [24] Even this agreement in principle was apparently obtained only in return for an American commitment to "review negotiations with the Russians for some kind of settlement at the highest level." [25] If this was the case the result appears the more dubious. If the Europeans accepted an agreement in principle in order to avert more specific commitments, the United States surely was not likely to muster enthusiasm for negotiations with the Russians when technological developments appeared to be eroding its strategic superiority.

BRITAIN AND THE THOR AGREEMENT

Early estimates of the demand for IRBMs were understandably optimistic; nevertheless, such optimism was excessive and ill-founded. The enthusiasm of SHAPE for weapons promising to make a significant contribution to Europe's defense was accompanied by British initiatives to obtain from the United States a first-generation, strategic missile delivery system. The numerous precedents of foreign base rights enjoyed in the past and the habit of obtaining European acquiescence in American strategic conceptions for the Alliance further diminished expectations of resistance to the offer of Thors or Jupiters.

[24] Cited in Great Britain, *Parliamentary Debates* (Commons), DLXXX (1958), col. 797.
[25] Richard Goold-Adams, *John Foster Dulles: A Reappraisal* (New York, Appleton-Century-Crofts, Inc., 1962), p. 260.

The initial stimulant of British interest in the IRBM was probably the Suez Crisis. Technical discussions regarding deployment of such missiles in the United Kingdom began as early as the late fall of 1956. By January, 1957, there was considerable public speculation about an imminent missile bases deal with the United States. In February, when Defense Minister Duncan Sandys prepared to embark on a trip to Washington, knowledgeable commentators suggested that he intended to seek a liberalization of the McMahon Act and to enlist American aid in the field of ballistic rocketry.[26]

A month later Anglo-American Summit discussions in Bermuda yielded a political agreement to supply Thor missiles to the Royal Air Force for deployment on sites in Britain under the joint control of the British and American governments. The Agreement merely formalized arrangements explored in the talks between Sandys and Secretary of Defense Wilson in early February, and under discussion at the technical level for some time.[27] Discussions between the U.S. Air Force, which had been designated executive agent for the Office of the Secretary of Defense in talks with Britain, and the Royal Air Force had begun in the fall of 1956, and were followed by more formal negotiations in February. At the time, a choice between the Thor and Jupiter as the weapon system to be transferred to the British had not been reached, although a presentation on the Thor was made to RAF officials. The key role of the Air Force in the negotiations, the compatibility of their doctrine with that of the RAF, and the close relations which had developed between the two services since World War II, nevertheless, predisposed them to accept the weapon developed by the Air Force.

That Britain was the first ally to display an active interest in the IRBM can be explained through references to a variety of political, strategic, and economic concerns. What strategy required, economics encouraged, and politics permitted! In 1957, under the impetus of a change in governments and a forceful

26 *New York Times,* January 25, 1957, p. 3.
27 *New York Times,* February 3, 1957, p. 1 for the communique issued at the conclusion of the Sandys-Wilson talks.

personality in the Defense Ministry, British defense policy acquired its own New Look. Sensitive to the humiliation of Suez, pressed by fiscal constraints, and anxious for political reasons to end conscription, the Conservative Government ardently embraced the logic of nuclear deterrence.[28]

Applying this logic, the British evinced a natural interest in the most advanced strategic delivery systems. They also became increasingly sensitive to the credibility of Amercan commitments to allied partners in NATO, the priority items on the targeting list of the Strategic Air Command, and the obsolescence of their own projected V-Bomber Force—a victim of the very advances in electronics and rocketry which had already produced the Russian ICBM. To the British the Thor weapon system appeared as an attractive prospect, albeit transitional in terms both of capability and availability.[29]

Indispensable to the realization of their preferred strategy, an independent nuclear delivery capability was also to provide a basis for an independent diplomacy and a measure of maneuverability in those instances where their interests diverged from those of the United States.[30] Aubrey Jones hinted at one of the basic concerns of government policy when he declared, "The alliance ought to have a balance of power within it. I would not like to see any lopsided alliance." [31]

Acquisition of the Thor promised not only to accelerate the development of new military capabilities but to permit a resuscitation of the "special relationship" with the United States as

[28] The new doctrine of Defense Minister Sandys was revealed in the White Paper on Defense published in March, 1957. See Laurence W. Martin, "The Market for Strategic Ideas in Britain: The 'Sandys Era,'" *American Political Science Review*, LVI (March 1962), 23–41 for an account of the genesis of that doctrine.

[29] In 1958 the British initiated their own effort to develop the Blue Streak missile as a national priority program. It was to be launched from an underground silo and would thus "be free from the principal shortcomings of Thor." Harvey A. DeWeerd, "The British Effort to Secure an Independent Deterrent," in Richard N. Rosecrance (ed.), *The Dispersion of Nuclear Weapons* (New York, Columbia University Press, 1964), p. 96.

[30] Klaus Knorr, "Nuclear 'Haves' and 'Have-Nots,'" *Foreign Affairs*, XXXVI (October, 1957), 170–71.

[31] Great Britain, *Parliamentary Debates* (Commons) DLXXXIII (1958), col. 500.

well. A liberalization of the McMahon Act regarding scientific sharing was certainly a prime objective of the British. They were inclined to consider this as a long overdue resumption of wartime collaboration in scientific affairs. The United States, on the other hand, had been persistently interested in preserving a division of labor within NATO, and keeping weapons secrets out of the hands of allies with unreliable security systems. The Conservative Government had high hopes of employing significant new discoveries in thermonuclear weaponry as leverage to extend further the liberalization of McMahon Act procedures achieved in 1954.[32]

Economic interests were certainly not negligible. The Minister of Supply candidly expressed his hopes of obtaining access to novel technology with potential for civilian applications. As he reported to his Parliamentary colleagues:

I was most impressed, when in the United States a few months ago, to observe the way in which a new industry has gathered around the ballistic missile. The ballistic missile offered to American industry a challenge. It was calling into being all kinds of new techniques, new materials, which were bound later to fertilize civil industry. We are an industrial country more than any other living on our industrial and technical skill and I ask myself, is it right that we should be excluded entirely from this knowledge?[33]

In short, a successful bid for an American-produced, first-generation IRBM promised to prolong the value of the British nuclear arsenal and to sustain their fleeting great power status and the perquisites of their still considerable prestige. It would also provide insurance that in a general war targets of special interest to them would be destroyed, and it would offer an additional basis for the reconstruction of a special relationship with the United States.

THE LOGIC OF AMERICAN ACQUIESCENCE

While President Eisenhower has not as yet fully revealed the rationale for the decision to make Thors available to the Royal

[32] See Nicholas, *Britain and the U.S.A.*, chap. 9.
[33] Great Britain, *Parliamentary Debates* (Commons), DLXXXIII (1958), cols. 499–500.

Air Force, a number of plausible arguments, in addition to the general considerations discussed above, can be deduced. In the first place, it would have been exceedingly difficult for the President to deny the logic on which the new British defense policy was grounded, since it paralleled that of his own Administration. Once the strategic premises were granted, the need for advanced delivery systems could hardly be denied. Secondly, arguments for economy clearly had force with the President, and providing assistance to the British on the production of a first-generation missile delivery system was an obvious way of capitalizing upon interdependence within NATO. Thirdly, it is probable that any reasonable request from the British would have been given the most careful consideration at a time when the Administration was anxious to reestablish close working relations with the Macmillan Government in the aftermath of the Suez debacle. Finally, a division of even strategic labors, as was implied in the Bermuda Agreement, was fully in line with the President's concept of a working alliance; that is, one in which individual efforts of the individual members were to be coordinated voluntarily, rather than a carefully calculated division of labor derived from a single comprehensive strategy for the Alliance.[34]

Congressmen, sensitive to any sharing of information or technology relating to strategic missions, were appeased by the assurance contained in the Bermuda Agreement that nuclear warheads would remain under strictly American custody. Others were pleased to learn that the Agreement would relieve some 2,300 American soldiers for duty elsewhere.[35] Above all, however, the transfer of Thors was appealing because, as in 1949, in adjusting to a technological revolution in strategic de-

[34] Nicholas, *Britain and the U.S.A.*, p. 131. See also Eisenhower, *Mandate for Change*, p. 457.

[35] Sherman Adams, *Firsthand Report*, p. 285. Actually the Agreement signed at Bermuda was of a tentative nature and contingent on the successful development of the Thor. It included also the reestablishment of Joint Intelligence and Military Planning with the British. No mention was made of these latter aspects of the settlement in the communique out of deference to French sensitivities.

livery systems, the United States found itself developing first-generation systems whose range required advanced bases for any strategic utility. And as in the late 1940s when B-29s were emplaced on British bases, the desire for immediate deployment overcame the reluctance to resume a posture of mutual dependency.

Trade-offs between territory and technology were nothing new in NATO strategy. But the ease with which agreement was consummated was to be misleading with respect to hopes for similar arrangements on the Continent. Nor was the Bermuda Agreement universally acclaimed in Britain. Indeed the public reaction in Britain imposed a considerable strain on Anglo-American relations.

PARLIAMENTARY AND PUBLIC
PROTESTATIONS IN BRITAIN

Opposition to the Thor Agreement was vigorously expressed both in Parliament and in the streets, much to the surprise of civilian and military leaders in the United States and Britain. The public outcry was based variously upon technical reservations, political apprehensions, and pacifist emotions. The Parliamentary Opposition expressed doubts as to the wisdom of procuring a relatively primitive first-generation missile system which was potentially unreliable and promised to be rapidly obsolesced when solid fuel missiles became available.[36] It was also doubted that a vulnerable, slow-reacting, and relatively inaccurate missile system was an appropriate delivery system for a coalition with defensive aims.[37] Others were troubled by what they considered an imprudent diversion of scarce resources from conventional requirements for additional air transport, tanks, and landing ships highlighted by the troubled military and

[36] Spokesmen for the Labour Party delighted in quoting from the *New Scientist* the trenchant observation: "Had the American Government not committed itself to supplying intermediate range missiles to Britain and to NATO, it is more than probably that these would by now have been cut out of the American defense programme altogether." See *Parliamentary Debates* (Commons), DLXXXIII (1958), col. 415.

[37] *Ibid.*, col. 555.

political situations in Bahrein, Yemen, and Malaya. Nor was the expression of jingo sentiment absent from the criticism from the Opposition bench. Aneurin Bevan lent his eloquence against the assumption of risks "merely to add to the sovereign power of another nation." [38] There were the predictable alarums that the Agreement would disrupt the atmosphere of peace and threaten the prospects of disarmament. Of more consequence were thoughtful queries regarding the wisdom of diluting existing control arrangements over nuclear armaments at a time when NATO strategy was ill-formulated, and the risks of accidental war were being compounded by the compression of time and space wrought by the new technology.

Parliamentary opposition was not sufficient to disrupt Government plans, and it was sustained by a 289-251 margin when the issue was brought to a vote in the House of Commons. This indicated that a few Conversatives broke ranks to vote with the Opposition, but the majority was not jeopardized.

Opposition criticisms were deftly handled by Cabinet members. They emphasized that Britain was already a major target for Soviet attack; that the alternatives of neutralism, nuclear pacifism, obsolete delivery systems, or reliance on conventional defense in the nuclear age were unpalatable; and that the Agreement would not only offer the possibility of countering any recurrence of Soviet political blackmail but enable them to tie the United States more closely to British defense. Plans for a follow on Skybolt missile promised ostensibly to restore British defense sovereignty and extend the lifetime of the planned V-Bomber force. Government spokesmen did not fail to remind their Labourite colleagues that the decision represented merely the application and extension of the logic that led the Attlee Government to initiate the atomic bomb program after the war. Nor was it forgotten that a Labour Government had allowed the basing of American bombers in Britain at the time of the Berlin Blockade.[39]

Above all, the double-veto system, operative at the Cabinet

[38] *Ibid.,* DLXXX (1958), col. 755.
[39] *Ibid.,* DXC (1958), cols. 395–97.

level, insured that the British Government would effectively have an opportunity to frustrate precipitate and rash actions which otherwise might be launched from their shores. The double-veto system, or dual-key arrangement, was devised as a means of meeting their desire for "positive control" over missile launchings from their territory. British interests in such technical controls emerged at a time when it was expected that the first two Thor squadrons would be manned by Americans while British personnel were being trained to assume those responsibilities later. Subsequently, when the British decided to man all four Thor squadrons from the outset, the advantages of positive control reverted to the United States.

Publication of the details of the Agreement served to pacify opponents in Parliament. Nuclear warheads were to be kept under the custody of the United States, though in close proximity to the missile sites in England to permit swift installation in an emergency. Missile design allegedly prevented significant risk of inadvertent or accidental detonation. The Thor squadrons were to be deployed in "small numbers on dispersed sites" —used or unused Royal Air Force fields in East Anglia, Lincolnshire, and Yorkshire.[40] Four squadrons were eventually received, with fifteen missiles in a squadron. Financial arrangements provided that the United States would provide the missiles and specialized equipment, in addition to the training costs for British personnel in the United States. Britain paid for the construction of sites and certain other unspecified items, bringing their total contribution to approximately $28 million.[41]

If the opposition in Parliament derived from strategic reservations, emotional nationalism, and technical doubts, the

[40] As the significance of securing deterrent forces from a surprise attack came to be appreciated, initial plans to locate the Thors on only four bases were revised. It appears that SAC was less interested at first in achieving a wide dispersion of the missiles than in exploiting the economies in logistic support and training obtainable by locating the squadrons centrally on a limited number of bases. Ultimately the Thors were located in complexes of three missiles on twenty separate sites throughout the United Kingdom.

[41] *Ibid.*, DLXXXIII (1958), col. 30.

general public's reaction reflected a mixture of envy, jealousy, fear, latent distrust of Americans, and an overt dislike for Secretary of State Dulles. Vocal dissenters among the public were certainly a small minority, but opinion polls indicated that on the missile bases issue, the Government enjoyed little support among the general public. Base rights for ballistic missiles was not acknowledged as analogous to the B-29 agreements during the late 1940s. Although demonstrations did not achieve the magnitude of later unilateralist-sponsored initiatives, the IRBM issue, along with other trends in British defense policy, strengthened a tide of emotional and moralistic resistance which hampered the flexibility of the British Government.

Public agitation was, needless to say, contained, parliamentary opposition subsided, and the Agreement was implemented. Yet the conditions in Britain were demonstrably unique, and optimism over emulation by Continental allies was ungrounded. The British had taken the initiative, and the element of mutual confidence which sustained Anglo-American relations could not be equaled with more remote allies. Above all, the prolonged public and parliamentary furor was a disquieting portent of resistance to be encountered elsewhere. Even in Britain the IRBM offer found the *Economist* and the *New Statesman* joined in opposition, the Labour Party embroiled in a vicious internal party quarrel precipitated by the issue of nuclear policy, and Cabinet Ministers defending the Agreement in no more than perfunctory terms. Finally, the method and timing of a bilaterally negotiated agreement were to introduce difficulties when, in December, 1957, the United States sought similar agreements from other European allies.

POLITICAL DIFFICULTIES
ENCOUNTERED IN EUROPE

In Europe the offer of missiles, designed to allay fears and bolster the cohesion of the Alliance, brought to the surface latent apprehensions, threatened the stability of several governments, and produced ripples on the never placid seas of intra-alliance relations. Ultimately only Turkey and Italy emplaced strategic missiles on their territory; meanwhile, it was a source of some embarrassment to the United States that a benevolent gesture caused such political turmoil. In Marquis Childs' felicitous phrase, it was to be "the winter of our discontent following on the autumn of our disillusion." [42]

That an agreement with the French would be difficult to achieve was evident from the outset. They consistently sought to employ an offer of base rights as a means of adjusting their own balance sheet of grievances against the United States. Those grievances included immediate policy issues related to their colonial war in Algeria and more fundamental reservations about Anglo-American conceptions of the appropriate structure for the NATO Alliance.

Although technical discussions with the French military proceeded smoothly, political conditions rendered a successful outcome unlikely. Piqued by pressure to accept IRBMs and offended by the bilateral character of the Anglo-American transfer arrangement, the Gaillard Government channeled its energy at the NATO Summit Conference into obtaining support from other allies for an agreement to comply with the American proposal only in principle. More specific acceptance would be conditional upon American willingness to contemplate nuclear sharing and the cessation of arms shipments to Tunisia.

With the accession to power of General de Gaulle in May, 1958, the political obstacles to agreement became even more pronounced. Between the General's insistence that "defense has a national character," and the United States' reservations toward proposals which would "infringe upon American control of nuclear weapons in NATO itself," there was little room for fruitful bargaining.[43] The French President immediately went far beyond previous French demands to include as a *quid pro quo* for bases, financial assistance to France's embryonic ballistic

[42] Marquis Childs, *Eisenhower: Captive Hero* (New York, Harcourt Brace & Co., 1953), p. 263.
[43] See Ciro Zoppo, "France as a Nuclear Power," in Richard N. Rosecrance (ed.), *The Dispersion of Nuclear Weapons*, pp. 113–56.

missile development program, technical assistance on problems
of nuclear warhead design, and complete assurances of a right to
share the initiative with the United States in any unleashing of
strategic rockets.[44] Gaullist obduracy was reinforced by the
differentiation in tactical concepts to be applied to Thors emplaced in Britain and projected squadrons of IRBMs in France.
With respect to the British-based Thors, there was to be joint
Anglo-American control over operations; for IRBMs based on
the Continent, decisions on use were to be lodged with the Supreme Allied Commander, General Norstad. This probably reflected not only the relationship of confidence which had long
obtained between Britain and the U.S. and the fact that the
British had taken the initiative in requesting the Thor squadrons, but General Norstad's growing conviction that integration
of the new weapon system into the command structure of
NATO could be a significant means of giving substance to
revived talk of interdependence and supranationalism with the
Alliance.

In Germany, also, the IRBM offer raised troublesome problems concerning the structure of the Western Alliance and Germany's place within it. It also temporarily threatened the stability of Chancellor Adenauer's Government by posing the unpalatable choice between the acceptance of nuclear armaments
or an admission that Germany occupied a position of less than
perfect equality with other members of the Alliance.

The opposition to strategic missile bases in Germany included the hierarchy and much of the rank and file membership
of the labor movement, a vocal group of Protestant churchmen,
a sizable and influential segment of the scientific community,
several leading military commentators, and the Social Democratic Party.[45] At home, the source of resistance ranged from a
general apprehension about renewed militarism to more specific fears that missile deployments in West Germany would

[44] *New York Times,* June 8, 1958, p. 2.
[45] *New York Times,* December 15, 1957, p. 33. In December a public
opinion poll conducted by EMNID found 74% of the respondents opposed to stationary missiles in Germany. *Die Welt* (December 14, 1957).

restrict their diplomatic flexibility on questions relating to the future of Central Europe and, specifically, reunification.[46]

German diplomacy displayed great dexterity in responding to this dilemma. Chancellor Adenauer succeeded in avoiding the necessity of having either to accept or reject the American offer.[47] He discouraged any concrete requests for bases by: (1) suggesting that any such question would be political and thus subject to determination by the Bundestag, where a strong tide of resistance was evident; (2) encouraging the expression of the military dictum that within the Alliance, Germany occupied a tactical position and was thus unsuitable for the deployment of strategic weapons; and (3) undertaking a diplomatic initiative aimed at diverting attention away from the issue and focusing the efforts of the NATO representatives in Paris away from new military deployments to new diplomatic efforts by the United States designed to lessen tensions with the Soviet Union.

On March 25, 1958, the Bundestag upheld the Government's policy of acquiescing in missile deployments on German territory *provided* that General Norstad recommended them and that his plans were approved by the Defense and Foreign Ministers of the NATO members. Since General Norstad accepted the logic of the German military argument against bases, and since he and the leading American defense and foreign policy experts were fully cognizant of the political liabilities associated with the enterprise, Chancellor Adenauer succeeded shrewdly in vowing his fidelity without fear of having to demonstrate it.

Greece was at one time considered a desirable site for Thor or Jupiter deployments. Yet as the twin problems of governmental instability and intra-alliance difficulties intruded, the project

[46] This latter argument received considerable impetus from the Reith Lectures of former American Ambassador to the Soviet Union, George F. Kennan. See his *Russia, the Atom, and the West*. Foreign opposition to the location of missiles bases on German soil was to be found especially in Britain and the Scandinavian states. For a commentary on European reactions to Kennan's Reith Lectures, see Terrence Prittie, "Have the 'Kennan Plans' Come too Late?" *New Republic* 137 (December 30, 1957), 13.

[47] *The Economist* (December 28, 1957), 1112–13.

was abandoned. The IRBM offer caught the Karamanlis Government between electoral and diplomatic imperatives. Acceptance would have aroused a storm of protests at home. Nevertheless, the Premier was fearful of invidious comparisons of the reliability of the Greeks as allies at a time when the Turks were reportedly anxious to provide bases for American missiles, and when the two countries were embroiled over the Cyprus issue.[48] The choice of eager Turkey over reluctant Greece was ultimately facilitated by the gradual downgrading of the importance of IRBMs in western strategy.

Italy, like Greece, faced early elections; hence their reaction to the IRBM offer was "agreement in principle," followed by a public attitude of embarrassed silence in the face of domestic turbulence. The Pella Government did take a positive attitude toward the offer, but negotiations to implement it were protracted and not without difficulties over political concessions and cost-sharing arrangements. When they signed an agreement with the United States on March 26, 1959, to accept one squadron of Jupiter missiles, Italy became the second NATO country to emplace IRBMs on its territory. According to the terms of the agreement, the United States was to provide the missiles, train Italians to operate them, and retain custody over the warheads at all times. The Italian Government assumed responsibility for manning the missile sites and paid the costs of base construction.

Turkey was, as usual, a grateful recipient of the most advanced military technology from the United States. Few difficulties attended the negotiation of arrangements for their acquisition of two squadrons of Jupiter missiles—bringing the full complement of deployed IRBMs in NATO to seven squadrons. In their willingness to accept the Jupiters, the Turks were as consistent with their normal posture in NATO as the Scandinavian members who requested that they be asked neither to station missiles nor stockpile fissionable materials on their soil.[49]

48 *New York Times,* April 20, 1958, p. 7.
49 *New York Times,* December 12, 1957, p. 5. The Netherlands at one point admitted a willingness to accept IRBMs if that was deemed neces-

RUSSIAN RESPONSE TO THE PLANNED DEPLOYMENT

Predictably, the Soviet Union mobilized all the resources of its diplomacy to frustrate the projected emplacement of American IRBMs in Europe. The frantic diplomatic activity which they undertook grew out of their sensitivity to the stationing of additional strategic delivery systems close to their borders, and their recognition that the general public response in Europe to the new weapons posed a unique opportunity to exacerbate the exposed fissures within NATO. Their efforts were oriented toward exploiting divisions within governments, within Europe, and between the Europeans and the United States.

In the scope and intensity the diplomatic efforts of the Soviet Union in response to the American offer of IRBMs to NATO were virtually without precedent. Specific threats were joined with vague innuendos in notes to all NATO governments and sundry neutralist statesmen. France was reminded of German *revanchist* aims and of Anglo-American dominance of the decision-making processes in NATO; Britain of the dangers of rash and provocative acts originating from their soil; Germany of the consequences that a decision to allow missile bases might have upon long-cherished hopes for reunification; Greece of possible economic sanctions; and America of responsibilities jointly shared for the peace of the world, as well as the dangers implicit in such a diffusion of authority over life and death decisions. Others were warned vividly of the certain devastation of their cities in the event of war, should they allow strategic missiles on their territory. In a general assault on overseas bases, the Russians sought postponement of decisions on the IRBM proposal by holding out vague offers of summit conferences, dis-

---

sary by NATO commanders. In response to the unfavorable reaction registered throughout most European countries to the IRBM offer, their retreat from that position came swiftly. On April 29, 1958, Defense Minister Cornelius Staf candidly expressed the limits on Dutch willingness to comply with American plans: "The Netherlands Government would grant the establishment of missile bases only if these were an imperative military necessity." *Ibid.,* April 30, 1958, p. 11. Diminished interest in Europe in the missiles also reflected the growing appreciation of the costs incurred by the British in deploying them.

armament agreements, a lessening of tension, or arms control limitations in certain "zones of peace."

Although it is impossible to calculate the precise influence the Soviet campaign had on the reticence of many European governments to respond to American overtures for missile sites, it seems clear that it did increase the public apprehension in Europe over such a development, thus contributing to the political difficulties confronted by each of the governments contemplating implementation of the American offer.[50]

STRATEGIC RESERVATIONS REGARDING
THE DECISION TO DEPLOY

European reservations regarding the desirability of deploying Thor and Jupiter missiles on the Continent reflected their fears of assuming new risks and their desires to escape the political and financial costs of accepting strategic weapons systems. In the United States there were also second thoughts about the decision to emplace IRBM sites in Europe. These were prompted by strategic analysis as well as political calculation, and they were articulated with the greatest sophistication by various "civilian strategists." [51] These theoreticians of deterrence sought to measure the utility of particular weapons systems against the essential requirements of the strategy: namely, demonstrating one's ability to do what one says he will do, threatening to do so persuasively, and preserving the capacity to communicate the decision to execute the threat to those responsible for its implementation.

Against these standards—most rigorously advanced in Albert J. Wohlstetter's famous article "The Precarious Balance of Terror" [52]—the marginal utility of IRBMs deployed in Europe

[50] For examples of the Soviet Union's extensive diplomatic effort see *New York Times,* December 12, 1957, p. 1; December 13, 1957, pp. 6, 7, 9; December 14, 1957, p. 3; December 15, 1957, p. 34; December 16, 1957, p. 1; and December 17, 1957, pp. 1, 14.

[51] For a description and appraisal of these important analysts of national security issues, see Bernard Brodie, "The Scientific Strategists," in Robert Gilpin and Christopher Wright (eds.), *Scientists and National Policy* (New York, Columbia University Press, 1964), pp. 240–56.

[52] *Foreign Affairs,* XXXVII (January, 1959), 211–34.

was adjudged to be low. An effective response to the Soviet development of long-range missiles required more than a mere matching of capabilities. It necessitated concern for the "survivability" of American deterrent forces as well as steps to mitigate the "crisis of confidence" within the NATO Alliance.

A growing awareness of the vulnerability of American strategic forces, particularly those deployed on overseas bases, began to emerge in the middle 1950s. The studies of Albert Wohlstetter and others at the RAND Corporation were especially significant in defining and publicizing within the Air Force the important distinction between first and second strike forces. Indeed, this was the main conceptual contribution of the significant RAND Report-266, *Selection and Use of Strategic Bases,* first published in April, 1954.[53] Nevertheless, although the Air Force began to adopt policies which displayed some anxiety regarding the survivability of SAC forces, the Gaither Committee later concluded in its report that "the major danger facing the country . . . was the vulnerability of the American strategic forces." [54] Thus it appears that the concern of the civilian strategists was not yet sufficiently reflected in Air Force policy.

In this connection, the vulnerability of both Thor and Jupiter missiles rendered them questionable assets. Fixed-based missile systems in Britain and on the Continent had little chance of surviving a Russian attack. Only mobile or hardened systems offered a secure probability of survival, since ballistic missile flight time is so short that warning is unreliable and accident prone. The value of the IRBMs was also compromised by the fact that rapid launching of first-generation, liquid-fueled mis-

[53] This report was jointly authored by Wohlstetter, F. S. Hoffman, R. J. Lutz, and H. S. Rowen. The substance of the study had been circulated in slightly different form earlier, and its major conclusion, that the formerly programmed system of advanced overseas operating bases would be extremely vulnerable to enemy attack by 1956, had been accepted as the basis for future Air Force basing policy in late 1953. For a detailed study of the nature and impact of this report, see Bruce L. R. Smith, *The Rand Corporation* (Cambridge, Harvard University Press, 1966), chap. 6.

[54] Morton Halperin, "The Gaither Committee and the Policy Process," *World Politics,* XIII (April, 1961), 365–66.

siles was uncertain; active defense futile, particularly in the absence of serious efforts to harden the sites; and passive defense remote in view of the range, accuracy, and warheads of Soviet medium-range ballistic missiles presumably directed at targets in western Europe.[55]

Defenders of the Administration dismissed such arguments on the grounds that the Soviet Union would not be likely to commit the rank folly of attacking Europe without simultaneously attacking the United States. Plausible as the contention may have sounded, Wohlstetter was not prepared to concede that the problems of coordinated attack, while complicated, had been rendered insoluble. "Times of firing," he noted, "can be arranged so that impact on many dispersed points is almost simultaneous." [56]

Mobility was eschewed by the primary users of the IRBM— the U.S. Air Force and the British Royal Air Force. Concealment was virtually impossible. Hardening was rejected since speed of deployment was contingent upon emplacement in a soft configuration, and the cost of hardened sites for relatively primitive liquid-fueled systems was deemed extravagant. Needless to say, this reluctance to spend money for the protection of missiles to be deployed in Europe sharply reduced their value as retaliatory weapons. That this was recognized by members of the Gaither Committee was implied by comments in the report regarding the marginal utility of "acquiring missiles which were difficult to fire and which were exposed to enemy bombing." [57]

Many civilian strategists, including Townsend Hoopes, George Rathjens, Albert Wohlstetter, Bernard Brodie, and others, did not discount the importance of matching technolog-

[55] George W. Rathjens, Jr., "Notes on the Military Problems of Europe," *World Politics*, X (January, 1958), 191. These missiles were apparently also vulnerable to snipers equipped with rifles and telescopic sights. This was perhaps of some significance since little effort was made to conceal the location of the bases.

[56] Wohlstetter, "The Precarious Balance of Terror," *Foreign Affairs*, XXXVII (January, 1959), 225.

[57] Halperin, "The Gaither Committee and the Policy Process," *World Politics*, XIII (April, 1961), 366.

cal accomplishments for purposes of sustaining American prestige. But they were principally concerned with dissipating the confusion that was apparent at the highest levels of Defense planning between matching capabilities and preserving adequate deterrence. Of limited value as retaliatory weapons, the IRBMs, in their view, did not rate as very impressive systems even as a complement to NATO's counterforce capabilities. Political constraints implicit in the double-veto system devised to govern their use made it extremely unlikely that the weapons would be used for premeditated or preemptive strikes. Yet if the Europeans could veto use for first-strike purposes, a similar veto remained with the United States when their use was contemplated in retaliation for oblique, indirect, or ambiguous challenges to the security of individual states of Western Europe.

Those who were inclined to favor a conventional buildup on the Continent as the most plausible response to the recent evidence of additional Soviet strategic capabilities also regretted the decision to emplace vulnerable IRBMs in Britain and on the Continent. Anxious to develop more flexible means for responding to local crises, they expected that an emphasis upon additional strategic forces in Europe would further reduce the already flagging zeal of NATO allies to increase their conventional contributions to the Alliance. Nor could first-generation IRBMs be accommodated to the requirements of a limited war situation. More unlikely weapons for use in limited conflicts could hardly be imagined. As Wohlstetter commented, "The inaccuracy of an IRBM requires high-yield warheads, and such a combination of inaccuracy and high-yield, while quite appropriate and adequate against unprotected targets in a general war, would scarcely come within even the most lax, in fact reckless, definition of limited war." [58]

Neither was the case for the Thor and Jupiter deployment considered especially sound when viewed from the standpoint of European local defense needs. Henry Kissinger was perhaps the most prestigious strategist advocating the use of missile

[58] "The Precarious Balance of Terror," *Foreign Affairs*, XXXVII (January, 1959), 227–28.

forces to enhance European capabilities for local defense and to increase the cohesion of the Alliance.[59] His primary concern was with the political impact of the new weapons. As a means of bolstering the credibility of American pledges to the Europeans, he was sympathetic to the quest for IRBM bases, although he considered this increment to the American strategic forces an "added advantage rather than a military necessity." [60] Recognizing the implications of Soviet intercontinental delivery vehicles for the cohesion of the Atlantic Alliance, he was convinced that medium-range missiles might have considerable utility in enabling Europeans to resist local threats and in reassuring them that the most modern weaponry would be placed at their disposal. They would also encourage the Europeans to assume greater responsibility for their defense even as their desires to influence allied policy making were accommodated.

In his view a European missile force was a feasible project, since it was assumed that even a numerically inferior force could serve to deter attack if it could guarantee significant reprisals upon an aggressor. He also acknowledged, however, that a defensive force required qualitatively more advanced missile technology in order to insure its survival against surprise attack. Concerned about the maintenance of the Alliance, he was anxious also that a European missile force should be deployed directly under NATO control. Unreliable, highly vulnerable, and indiscriminately destructive first-generation Thors and Jupiters certainly did not possess the attributes Kissinger deemed essential.

Since many of these reservations toward the IRBMs were directly related to a concern for the stability of deterrence and the effective management of the military environment, it is surely of interest to note that they were expressed mainly by civilian strategists outside the Government rather than arms control specialists within the Defense and State Departments. Explana-

[59] See his article, "Missiles and the Western Alliance," *Foreign Affairs,* XXXVI (April, 1958) , 383–400.
[60] *Ibid.,* p. 388.

tions for this must be somewhat speculative. It appears, in the first place, that arms control was still considered to some extent an alternative to armaments policies rather than a means of tacitly coordinating the military policies of potential adversaries. Certainly the priority of even limited measures of arms control was diminished by the apparent erosion of Alliance cohesion and the Soviet challenge to American strategic superiority. Secretary of State Dulles was inclined to discount the likelihood of significant progress in the arms control field until a new political climate had been created. Moreover, the fortunes of Harold Stassen, the President's Special Assistant for Disarmament, were low within the Administration as a consequence of politically damaging indiscretions which he had committed during the London Disarmament Conference in the spring of 1957.[61] Dulles, with his profound skepticism toward arms control and disarmament schemes, was extremely jealous of the prerogatives of Stassen and consistently sought to diminish his standing with the President. Nor was Stassen in a position to mobilize institutional support for his preferred policies since he had developed only the most tenuous relations with the Departments of State and Defense and the Atomic Energy Commission. In this particular case, while sentiment in Stassen's group regarding the IRBM deployments ran from lukewarm to cool, they may have been somewhat disarmed by virtue of the fact that such deployments were justified in part as a response to heightened fears of surprise attack—at the time one of the principal concerns of arms control specialists. In any event, a coordinated approach to the problems of alliance policy, strategic policy, and arms control policy was rendered difficult inasmuch as the State Department had only a small number of persons directly preoccupied with arms control and military subjects. Bernard Bechhofer, a careful student of American arms control efforts in the postwar period has concluded that

[61] See Saville R. Davis, "Recent Policy Making in the United States Government," *Daedalus* (Fall, 1960), 951–66, for an analysis of the intragovernmental politics of arms control initiatives during this period.

by 1957 "no broad over-all American policy that comprehended within itself both the unity of the West and a negotiable position towards armaments regulations" had emerged.[62]

To sum up, a deployment of Thor and Jupiter IRBMs in Europe seemed to promise a possible matching of sorts of a new Soviet military capability, a demonstration of American missile technology at a psychologically important moment, and a means of involving the Allies in such a way as to give some substance to revived talk of interdependence within NATO. The contributions IRBMs could make, however, to European defense, American deterrence, and the cohesion of the Alliance were substantially overrated. Consequently it appears that the request for overseas bases for the Thor and Jupiter missiles was prompted at least as significantly by the political advantages of immediately capitalizing on available weaponry as by a sober and systematic evaluation of the strategic requirements of the situation. Even the political advantages subsequently proved illusory, since the request for bases underscored the fact that one side had intercontinental missiles while ballistic rockets of only intermediate-range were available to the other, and it implied that the United States was now forced to solicit the assistance of the very allies whose protector it had been since World War II in order to restore a threatened balance of deterrence.[63]

SECOND THOUGHTS ON DUAL PRODUCTION

The chilly European reaction to American requests for IRBM base rights called again into question the major premise of the November, 1957, decision to produce both Thors and Jupiters. It now appeared that two services and two industrial complexes had committed their prestige and their production capabilities respectively to a project for which there was little demand. Moreover, enthusiasm for the first-generation IRBMs was bound to wane further as time passed, since the intial cost estimates of the system had been greatly underestimated and

[62] Bechhofer, *Postwar Negotiations for Arms Control* (Washington, The Brookings Institution, 1961), p. 431.
[63] Aron, *The Great Debate*, pp. 13–14.

more sophisticated, invulnerable, and more reliable second-generation IRBMs would soon appear on the technical horizon. The Budget Bureau Director, among others, now raised pointed questions about the importance of Thor and Jupiter missiles in view of the difficulties encountered in obtaining base rights.[64]

Although production funds had been temporarily withheld from the Army, they had negotiated a $30 million contract to Chrysler Corporation for the installation of production tooling in their Warren, Michigan plant in early January, 1958. Production levels now had to be determined, and Secretary Douglas was asked to make appropriate recommendations to the Secretary of Defense. Renewed consideration was, consequently, given to the cancellation of the Jupiter project altogether.[65] Such a projected cancellation would have become effective upon the completion of two Jupiter squadrons.[66]

In reviewing the dual production decision in the light of the marginal interest of European allies, the Air Force was convinced that excessive costs of dual logistic systems, supply, spare part requirements, and manpower training could be eliminated only by liquidating one of the competing weapons systems.[67] Moreover, time was swiftly eliminating the dangers of technical failure in the Thor program, as evidenced by their highly successful December test.[68] Should only one system be produced,

[64] Senate Committee on Armed Services, *Hearings, Major Defense Matters,* 86th Cong., 1st Sess., 1959, p. 245.

[65] *New York Times,* February 13, 1958, p. 13.

[66] At this time there were no agreements with the Europeans beyond the accord with the British, who were already committed to accepting Air Force-developed Thors. The Budget Bureau apparently questioned the importance of Thors and Jupiters in view of the difficulty of obtaining base rights in Europe and the prospect of more sophisticated second-generation delivery systems. Senate Committee on Armed Services, *Hearings, Major Defense Matters,* 86th Cong., 1st Sess., 1959, p. 245.

[67] See Douglas' testimony before the House Armed Services Committee, *National Defense Missiles Hearings,* 1958, p. 4710.

[68] On a test carried out on December 7, 1957, the guidance system malfunctioned. On the 10th, in a follow-up test, the all-inertial guidance system operated successfully. See House Committee on Science and Astronautics, *A Chronology of Missile and Astronautic Events,* 1961, pp. 36–37, 161.

the Thor continued to enjoy the favored position. The Air Force was to be the user, and Douglas had obtained a considerable headstart in tooling for quantity production. The Air Force also enjoyed a lead in the development of ground-launch equipment and manpower training.

Representative Carl Vinson, venerable Chairman of the House Armed Services Committee, urged in a letter to Secretary McElroy in February that if the requirement was for no more than two squadrons of Jupiter missiles, production should be handled at the Redstone Arsenal in Huntsville.[69] Previous testimony to the Committee confirmed the fact that there was sufficient capacity at the Arsenal to produce one squadron by early 1959. If additional demand developed, Vinson indicated his support for a production contract to Chrysler Corporation. He also urged the Air Force to eliminate uncertainties on their training requirements and to cease their efforts to undercut Defense Department decisions related to the Army missile program.[70] Vinson's proposal alarmed scientists as well as military officials at Huntsville, for they were committed at all costs to preventing the Arsenal from becoming absorbed in the production of a transitional weapon at the expense of development work on more promising projects. Their resistance to production contracts, however, proved more successful than their capacity to attract resources and authorizations for revolutionary new development work.

PHASE OUT ON THOR AND JUPITER PROCUREMENT

Ultimately seven squadrons of Thor and Jupiter missiles were procured for overseas deployment. Douglas Aircraft Corporation had production capacity far in excess of actual requirements. Limited procurement was based, however, on more than merely the reluctance of potential European recipients to assume new strategic risks. Opportunities for the emplacement of IRBMs within striking range of major Soviet targets, while per-

[69] House Committee on Armed Services, *National Defense Missiles Hearings*, 1958, p. 4797.
[70] *Ibid.*, p. 4798.

haps not legion, were, nevertheless available. Alaska, Okinawa, Guam, Formosa, and the Philippine Islands were all mentioned at one time or another as possibilities for rocket launching sites. The pros and cons of basing IRBMs in the Azores, North Africa, and Thule were also considered, although Donald Quarles, Deputy Secretary of Defense, conceded that such an extension of range requirements would reduce their effectiveness "very substantially." [71] Such deployments were eschewed, and both weapons were phased out of production.

In the end, all the various elements of a program decision— external threat, technical state of the art, cost, and time— combined to render additional deployment both unnecessary and uneconomical. Fresh intelligence reports on the progress of Soviet missile programs suggested that earlier estimates had been exaggerated. The most up-to-date information implied that their long-range missile testing during 1957 and 1958 had been infrequent and sporadic. Although some critics contended that this was because problems had been solved and production ordered, more optimistic appraisals by Defense Department officials concluded that infrequent tests were an indication of unanticipated technical difficulties.[72] At about the same time breakthroughs in the guidance systems of American ICBMs and an equivalent reduction in their estimated Circular Error Probability led to new calculations of the numbers of ICBMs the Soviets would require for any reasonable chance of successfully destroying the American retaliatory force.[73] When Soviet missile tests became even more sporadic in the spring of 1958, estimates of their projected initial operational capability date slipped from six months to a year, and the urgency of the need

[71] *Ibid.*, p. 4091.

[72] That production would be ordered before reliability had been ascertained was considered unlikely. Furthermore, the deceptive precedent of token production of the Bison long-range bomber produced an understandable desire on the part of the Administration not to be induced into a premature production of first-generation missiles to counter a purely "Potemkin Village"-type threat.

[73] Charles J. V. Murphy, "The Embattled Mr. McElroy," *Fortune,* LIX (April, 1959), 244–46.

for an interim IRBM capability correspondingly diminished.[74]

State of the art developments served also to restrain demands for substantial procurement of land-based, liquid-fueled IRBMs. Indeed, one of the forces compelling McElroy toward the dual production decision was the recognition that follow-on weapons were on the horizon, and unless Thors and Jupiters were immediately procured, delays and stretchouts would obsolesce both programs before any utility had been obtained from them.[75] Hopes were high with respect to both the Polaris IRBM and Atlas and Titan ICBM systems. Fiscal prudence induced a willingness to rely on the early availability of these systems.

In late January, 1958, the National Security Council accorded the Polaris program a top national priority, the Navy obtained additional appropriations for the Fleet Ballistic Missile System, and the earlier availability of operational Polaris missiles was insured by easing considerably the technical parameters of the weapon system.[76] In light of recent experiences in negotiating base rights for land-based IRBMs on the Continent, the acceleration of the Polaris program was the more felicitous, since it promised to "remain unobtrusive and politically inoffensive in the public forums of the world." [77] The Navy described the Polaris as the perfect retaliatory weapon. Concealed, mobile, dispersed, it could survive an atomic attack without

[74] *Ibid.,* pp. 246, 248.

[75] Interview with Wilfred McNeil, August 26, 1963.

[76] See House Committee on Armed Services, *National Defense Missiles Hearings,* 1958, p. 4654. The range requirement was reduced from 1,500 miles to 1,200 miles for the first-generation Polaris. A test navigation system and fire control system originally designed for the Jupiter-S program was redesigned for the earliest missile-bearing submarines. A less powerful propellant, also developed for the Jupiter-S, was adapted for use in the first-generation missiles, since in the accelerated program "materials had to be used which could not stand the higher temperatures of more powerful propellants." Baar and Howard, *Polaris,* p. 95.

[77] See Admiral Arleigh Burke's statement: "Regarding the Military Posture of the United States Navy with Respect to Missiles, House Committee on Armed Services," *National Defense Missiles Hearings,* 1958, pp. 4609–11.

subjecting decision makers to intolerable pressures for precipitate choices on the basis of ambiguous evidence of an imminent attack.[78]

Progress on the Atlas Program was also heartening as on December 17, 1957, a successful flight was negotiated over a 600-mile range. This was followed by a successful limited flight on January 10, 1958. Although two February test flights were to abort, optimism ran high at the project level, and progress was encouraging.[79]

The liabilities of the Thor and Jupiter became more evident to the Air Force early in 1958 when, in the process of developing support for their solid-fuel Minuteman concept, the Air Staff elaborated more refined cost-effectiveness tests for comparing alternative methods of performing equivalent missions. Those analytic techniques, designed to demonstrate the superiority of the Minuteman to the Atlas and Titan, simultaneously demonstrated the relative inefficiency and excessive cost of the first-generation IRBM, and to this extent contributed to the decision to limit procurement.

Interest in the Thor and Jupiter also waned as the potential of a mobile, land-based European MRBM acquired recognition. By October, 1959, the United States had announced its intention of not establishing any further bases for liquid-fueled missiles in Europe. In part this was based on the conceded vulnerability of such weapons by leading American defense officials, in part on the possibility "that the Western European nations

[78] Meanwhile, Army strategists shifted their attention from the Jupiter to mobile, land-based missiles possessing similar advantages. While General Taylor contended that a mobile version of the Jupiter could provide, in conjunction with the Polaris system, insurance against any "deterrence gap," this advocacy was becoming increasingly perfunctory, and the priority of Army concerns shifted to limited conventional war and its matériel and tactical requirements. Since economics ruled out the Jupiter as a delivery vehicle for nonatomic warheads, the shift in Army priorities led to a downgrading of the significance of an essentially strategic weapon. See Taylor, *The Uncertain Trumpet*, pp. 140–42.

[79] House Committee on Science and Astronautics, *Chronology of Missile and Astronautic Events*, 1961, pp. 163–65.

[might] get together . . . in the manufacture of a land-based, solid-propellant IRBM." [80] The proposal for such a missile system was conceived by General Norstad in a far-sighted acknowledgment of the problems which the Alliance faced in the missile age.

An early enthusiast of the IRBM, Norstad went on to develop a carefully staged proposal designed both to provide for NATO's medium-range defense needs and to encourage the political integration of the Alliance. In the first stage, the objective was to be a rapid buildup in mobile surface-based missiles suitable for deployment on barges and railroads. He was hopeful of designing such a missile around promising Polaris concepts. The system would be developed and produced in the United States, though some components could be assembled in Europe. As a second-generation, follow-on system, he anticipated a new improved version acquired on the basis of American technical know-how and developed components but actually fabricated on the Continent. At the same time, he was eager to begin immediately a research and development program for a European missile for NATO.

In late 1957, paper studies on these problems were carried out. Strategic studies were run for numbers, types, and operational requirements. Technical feasibility studies were also run, though not in great detail. Manufacturers were brought in to suggest possibilities of European participation based on their technical and industrial capabilities, and scientists were consulted for their evaluations of the proposal.[81]

While SHAPE planners conceded the difficulties of devising an acceptable political mechanism to control a NATO medium-range ballistic missile force, Norstad was confident that this did not constitute an insurmountable barrier. He was also optimistic about the feasibility of a technical design which would reduce political difficulties by providing for fail-safe abort proce-

[80] House Committee on Appropriations, *Hearings, Department of Defense Appropriations 1960,* 1959, p. 143.

[81] Interview with General Norstad, former Supreme Allied Command Europe, August 26, 1963.

dures and would include safeguards against accidental firing.[82]

At NATO Headquarters, Thor and Jupiter systems had originally been conceded a useful lifetime of from three to five years. Due to delays in production, unanticipated costs, and the unexpected progress in the Polaris program, they were considered obsolete earlier than initially estimated. The fate of General Norstad's plans for a more sophisticated NATO MRBM system is not our concern. Suffice it to say that growing disenchantment with liquid-fueled IRBMs was first related to the high expectations of a solid-fuel follow-on missile.[83] Later, such doubts were reinforced by a fundamental adjustment in American strategic thought and its new emphasis upon stabilized deterrence.

With respect to deployments of IRBMs in non-European areas, the Air Force made studies of the matter and reached the conclusion that logistic costs militated against them. But above all, there were persuasive reasons for emplacing strategic weapons either at sea or at home. By locating retaliatory forces as far as possible from Soviet missiles, their chances of achieving a successful surprise attack would be rendered more unlikely. Basing them in the heartland of continental United States would ease the political control problem. Such a decision would be politically appealing as well, since it seems plausible to suppose that contractors and Congressmen anxious to capitalize on construction contracts for expensive hardened silos would heartily endorse such a step.[84]

There was an understandable element of confusion, panic, and haste in the initial decision to deploy IRBMs overseas. Concern over Sputnik aroused fears as to the sufficiency of our deterrent forces. Concern over apparent deficiencies in American military technology counseled rapid deployment of any available hardware. Concern over an extension of range in So-

[82] *Ibid.*
[83] Charles J. V. Murphy, "NATO at a Nuclear Crossroad," *Fortune,* LXVI (December, 1962) , 223.
[84] Though one can but speculate on such matters, it seems likely that this consideration was of more than marginal significance.

viet missile delivery systems dictated a marriage of first-generation IRBMs with the advanced European bases to give the West a comparable capability. Yet gloomy predictions of a dangerous missile gap failed to provoke the Eisenhower Administration into a massive production program for first-generation missiles. As time confirmed the prudence of that decision, other issues emerged. A heightened concern with arms control, a growing awareness of the implications of the ballistic missile for command control arrangements, and a chastened sense of the costs of the new strategic systems all reinforced the disposition to cancel plans for any further deployments of Thors or Jupiters.[85]

The Thor-Jupiter controversy never ultimately came to a head; it simply petered out. Anticipated decisions for cancellation of the Jupiter and mass production for Thor never materialized. The number of Jupiter squadrons was indeed reduced to three in the spring of 1958. Yet this revision in the IRBM program which was officially programmed in April by the National Security Council, while considered by some commentators as a welcome though incomplete victory for the Air Force, fell considerably short of their desire for full Jupiter production cancellation. Eventually, only four Thor squadrons and three Jupiter squadrons were in fact produced. Thus, to the end, a decision between the two missiles was successfully evaded at an expense which Secretary McElroy set at $100,000,000. "That," he said, "is the price being paid for the compression of time." [86] It was also, one might add, the price paid for harmonizing the conflicting purposes of Air Force and Army in the burgeoning field of missile technology.

[85] Negotiations for the emplacement of Jupiter missiles in Turkey and Italy had not yet been completed by late 1958. Yet by this time it was perfectly clear that additional basing locations would not be sought.

[86] *Ibid.,* May 9, 1958, p. 7.

(7) THE POLITICS OF REORGANIZATION

Within NATO the offer of Thor and Jupiter IRBMs served to crystallize and reinforce that widespread concern with the credibility of American deterrent capabilities which has since marked discussions of the long-range relationship between the United States and its European allies. At home the humiliation of an apparent loss of technological superiority to the Soviet Union in missile development and the appearance of what many considered "wastefully duplicative" efforts in the development and production of missiles of dubious military utility both contributed to a climate of opinion in Washington which undergirded a major effort at Defense Department reorganization.

One element of the prevailing post-World War II mythology pertained to America's presumed intrinsic technological and industrial superiority over the Soviet Union. Systematized crudely in the immediate postwar years into a comfortable dichotomy between totalitarian and democratic science and industry, such complacent illusions were initially sustained by ascribing Russian successes to either a ubiquitous espionage network or to the efforts of captured German scientists and engineers. Such myths were of little comfort in the aftermath of Sputnik. The United States had obtained the services of the most eminent German rocket engineers, and they had as yet developed little to imitate. A tightening of security regulations would have been a transparently irrelevant response to this challenge posed by the revolutionary advances of Soviet science and technology.

Another element in the postwar climate of opinion related to the appropriate means for insuring a vigorous pace of qualitative innovation in military weaponry. Maintaining a generally respectful attitude toward the pitfalls of planning and prediction on the uncertain terrain of technical choices, military and civilian defense leaders were inclined to consider intuitive judgment as appropriate as a basis for program decisions as attempts at precise analysis. Amid the cacophony of competing claims advanced by the services and industrial suppliers, the simplest and safest resolution of conflicts appeared to involve a prudent hedging of one's bets as far as research and development were concerned. As the services came to recognize that technological innovation was the prerequisite of their survival and as industries vigorously sought to enter the lucrative market of weapons development, no dearth of technical proposals was likely.

The technological climate of opinion was thus that of the market situation of competitive oligopoly in which "firms that fail to innovate get hurt, and hurt severely." [1] Like the oligopolistic situation, the services were sufficiently concentrated to support research, sufficiently competitive to promote innovation. Just as the economic inducement for innovation in the market is the prospect of a temporary monopoly in the sale of a new product, the promise of expanded roles and missions as well as budgets spurred the services on in their quest for new delivery capabilities.

The prevailing attitudes toward service rivalry, however, were not favorably disposed toward the type of competition that emerged. A different, and somewhat contradictory, set of prejudices operated on this plane. Congressional concern and the President's ire were directed against "wasteful duplication," the indecisiveness of policy makers confronted by technical alternatives, and the evidences of secrecy and poaching permeating the services' efforts at weapons development.

[1] Henry Villard, "Competition, Oligopoly, and Research," *The Journal of Political Economy*, LXVI (December, 1958), 493.

Such perspectives were not without a touch of irony. They were not only antithetical to the cultural norms of a market economy where decentralization over research and development decision making, inter-firm rivalry, and secrecy sanctioned by patent and trade secret legislation were simply acknowledged as the necessary costs of a system producing an impressive rate of technological growth; but attempts to eliminate duplication, increase centralization, and provide planning from the center would have likely increased rather than diminished service rivalries.

Suffice it to say, the Russian success in sending Sputnik I aloft and the prospect of an impending missile gap convinced Administration leaders, as well as many prominent Congressmen, that while the present organizational environment prompted vigorous competition among the services for new weapons, this in itself did not guarantee that American military technology would keep abreast of Soviet achievements. In addition there was a growing consensus that the by-products of such competition were both costly and potentially damaging.

The crisis prompted a renewed concern over delays in the decision-making cycle as they related to the process of weapons innovation. Dr. James R. Killian had publicly defined the problem more than a year before to the Symington Subcommittee:

So far we have not been able, in the definition of the roles and missions of the services to keep pace with evolving weapons systems technology, and as a consequence, we lengthen out lead-time, we make more difficult our decision-making processes, we needlessly increase costs, and we find it difficult to avoid friction and duplication of effort.[2]

These ills were associated with a diffuse structure of defense administration. Now the growing complexity of weapons, their increasingly rapid rate of obsolescence, the seeming exponential increase in weapons costs, the multiplication of systems, and the consequent realignment of public expenditures all encouraged centralization of the vast military research and development

2 Senate Committee on Armed Services, *Airpower Hearings*, 1956, p. 1186.

effort. Such centralization appeared especially prudent in view of imminent jurisdictional clashes over novel space systems. Ironically, a centralization of managerial control accompanied, and was facilitated by, a slight proliferation of research and development agencies within the government.

Confronted by the conflicting demands to accelerate technological development rates while sublimating rivalries among the services over jurisdictional issues, Secretary of Defense McElroy responded by (1) immediately authorizing several important new projects; (2) refashioning the Department's handling of advanced research and development work so as to facilitate such jurisdictional assignments with a minimum of friction in the future; and (3) reviewing the disposition of the most creative scientific-technical teams and their contractual relations with the services and with industry. The thrust of policy was toward a deflection of Army interest away from the strategic missile field, a strengthening of the Secretary of Defense's hand for project assignments, and a general weakening of resistance to his proprietary decisions.

PROJECT ASSIGNMENTS IN MISSILES AND SPACE

The Jupiter system was an intermediate missile both in terms of range and availability. By late 1957, therefore, Army officials were concerned about future projects. Preoccupation with this problem increased as the prospects of significant production diminished. In the search for new projects—a search conducted by Army leaders and civilian officials in the Office of the Secretary of Defense—the Pershing and Nike-Zeus programs appeared increasingly attractive.

The Jupiter project had been doubly damaging to the Army. The product enjoyed but limited sales, and operational control passed to their major competitor. Opportunities for further developments in the ballistic missile field, however, remained. The ranges from 200 to 1,500 miles were unexploited; experimentation on long range rockets would now be a major asset in more modest ventures.

Within the Army, General Staff interest revived in proposals for a missile which would extend the range of their only available field missile, the Redstone. The Pershing program—directed toward the development of a solid-fueled, mobile, medium-range ballistic missile—was especially attractive. The onerous range restrictions of the Wilson Memorandum could be subtly circumvented by submitting to new technical restrictions related to propellant and weight. By subcontracting most technical and production work to Martin-Orlando Corporation, the Army may have nurtured hopes of diminishing the airframe industry's dependence upon the Air Force and neutralizing their political influence on future proprietary disputes. More importantly, by retaining "in-house" at Huntsville only the overall technical direction and development responsibility for the guidance package, the Army Ballistic Missile Agency could free their technical resources for space projects while their tactical missile requirements were being satisfied.[3] Although failing to appease Army hopes in the strategic missile field, the Pershing promised to provide a tactical support capability directly under the control of the ground commander. It also constituted an improvement upon the Tactical Air Command's support by providing an all-weather capability.[4] Nor was the Army precluded from making subsequent efforts to again extend the range of their missiles.[5]

Although the Army was pleased to acquiesce in the decision to authorize the Pershing missile program, they cannot be exclusively credited with the genesis of that system. The initiative was rather provided by Defense officials anxious to divert the

[3] Medaris, *Countdown for Decision*, p. 232.

[4] Describing the Pershing missile's capabilities, the Secretary of the Army noted that it could attack all "deep targets which are of interest to the ground force commander and which influence his scheme of maneuver or plan of defense." U.S., Congress, House, Committee on Appropriations, *Hearings, Department of Defense Appropriations 1962*, 87th Cong., 1st Sess., 1961, p. 4.

[5] Army Director of Research and Development, Richard Morse, later sought approval for research and development funds for a longer range Pershing. He also entertained hopes for a land-based Polaris missile system to counter Soviet medium-range capabilities in Central Europe. *Ibid.*, p. 214.

Army rocket development effort away from areas of direct conflict with the Air Force. As mentioned previously, Generals Medaris and Gavin and Dr. Werner von Braun were especially interested in the development of booster rockets capable of putting payloads into space. In the mid-1950s solid propellant rockets did not promise sufficient thrust to fire large payloads into orbit. As General Medaris stated: "It was a virtual certainty that liquid propellant engines would dominate that field until nuclear propulsion could become a reality at some point in the distant future." [6] Moreover, the Army had already developed an expensive facility for testing liquid engines, and their technical personnel had come of age with the big liquid engines. Indeed, Medaris contracted for the services of Martin-Orlando on the Pershing only after he had obtained some prior assurances from Secretary McElroy that additional space work would be forthcoming.

In the Secretary's Office, however, there was a feeling that the Army had invaded a field of legitimate Air Force responsibility at the expense of their own primary missions and requirements.[7] Acknowledging, on the other hand, the utility for Army purposes of a mobile, tactical missile, Director of Guided Missiles William Holaday concluded that the maximum possible weight for a field combat weapon would be 10,000 pounds. He was further convinced that only a solid-fuel rocket would be safe and maneuverable on the battlefield. To the extent that the range potential of a 10,000 pound solid-fuel missile might extend beyond the arbitrary 200-mile limit imposed in November, 1956, Army morale could be bolstered even as a tactical requirement was met. Yet it would permit no major challenge to the Air Force in the strategic missile or space field. President Eisenhower was drawn in on the discussions in the fall of 1957 and heartily approved these technical limitations which promised to improve Army capabilities without generating new jurisdictional disputes.

On January 7, 1958, Secretary McElroy authorized the Army

[6] Medaris, *Countdown for Decision*, p. 232.
[7] Interview with Wilfred McNeil, August 26, 1963.

to develop a solid-fuel missile named Pershing to "satisfy the Army's urgent requirement for a completely ground, mobile, combat-zone, air-transportable, surface-to-surface ballistic missile system to provide the field Army with nuclear firepower at long ranges." [8] Apparently concerned that his action in authorizing work on a new, extended-range missile might be interpreted in some quarters as a complete reversal of the Wilson Memorandum on roles and missions, Secretary McElroy subsequently notified Secretary Brucker and Secretary Douglas that it was not to be so understood: "In order to avoid any misunderstanding regarding the responsibility for the future research and development in the field of land-based IRBMs and ICBMs, it should be understood that this function is the responsibility of the Department of the Air Force." [9]

Army hopes were also buoyed by the announcement on January 16, 1958, that they had been assigned responsibility for developing the Nike-Zeus ballistic missile defense system. Studies of the system had been initiated as early as 1955 under a contract to Bell Telephone Laboratories. A total of $30 million had been spent on exploration of the possibilities of such a system through 1958. Although overall authority for the system was assigned to the newly created Advanced Research Projects Agency, the Army received technical responsibility and was to fund the project from its own budget.[10] Thus, the elimination of the Jupiter program was softened as the Army obtained new project responsibilities and budgetary support.

This is not to say that perfect clarity of mission assignments

[8] U.S. Congress, Senate, Committee on Appropriations, *Hearings, Department of Defense Appropriations for 1959*, 86th Cong., 1st Sess., 1958, p. 49. The JCS had approved the Pershing, and indeed the Secretary merely attached the JCS paper to his directive authorizing the Army to proceed with the project. Both the Secretary and members of the JCS were anxious to remove the rigidity of the Wilson Memorandum restrictions. House Committee on Armed Services, *National Defense Missile Hearings*, 1958, p. 4041.

[9] *Army-Navy-Air Force Journal*, March 15, 1958, p. 3.

[10] House Committee on Government Operations, *Organization and Management of Missile Programs*, 1959, p. 125.

was achieved. Indeed the ambiguity of functional divisions of labor was compounded by project assignments in air defense. Though the Army was authorized to proceed with the Nike-Zeus, the Air Force acquired a mission for a ballistic missile early warning system. Air Force representatives made no secret of their ambitions of eventually obtaining responsibilities for the entire ballistic missile defense mission. Meanwhile, progress by the Navy in the area of long-range radar presaged their own interest in the defense mission. Army developers of the Nike system were naturally eager to establish their claims as the logical users of the products of their labors.[11] The satisfaction of Army desires for a continuing role in the ballistic missile field was not, then, sufficient to obviate contentiousness among the services; rather, it opened an entirely new vista of competition. This prospect of renewed interservice strife lent urgency to Secretary McElroy's plans for Defense Department reorganization.

CREATION OF THE
ADVANCED RESEARCH PROJECTS AGENCY

One of the earliest avowed intentions of the Defense Secretary after Sputnik was the creation of an agency within the Pentagon to handle advanced research projects. "The vast weapons systems of the future," McElroy told the House Appropriations Committee, "in our judgment need to be the responsibility of a separate part of the Defense Department." [12] Such an arrangement was to assure that will o'-the-wisp projects could be followed through outside the service framework at least to a determination of technical feasibility and financial costs. On January 7, 1958, the President requested from Congress $10 million in the 1958 Supplemental Appropriation Bill to finance the creation of the Advanced Research Projects Agency "including acquisition and construction of such research, development and test facilities, and equipment, as may be authorized by the Sec-

[11] Senate Committee on Armed Services, *Satellite and Missile Program Hearings,* 1957–1958, p. 201.
[12] House Committee on Appropriations, *Ballistic Missile Program Hearings,* 1957, p. 7.

retary of Defense." [13] The Agency was actually established by a departmental directive on February 7, 1958; it was later accorded statutory recognition by Congress.[14]

The Advanced Research Projects Agency was born out of the bitter experience of indecision in the Thor-Jupiter controversy, the deep humiliation of the early Vanguard failures, and the expectation of jurisdictional disputes in space weapons technology. The missile controversy illuminated some of the costly and unpleasant by-products of a laissez faire research and development environment. "Once these programs get under way," Secretary McElroy conceded to the Senate Armed Services Committee, "the problem of diverting that very vigorous attention that is being given by an individual service is not a simple one." [15]

The Secretary of Defense foresaw a solution for such situations in the creation of an agency to be responsible for novel proposals during the early planning stages. While feasibility and cost were evaluated in an objective and detached manner, the services would be precluded from acquiring proprietary interests in "their projects." Roy Johnson, Director of the Advanced Research Projects Agency, reported to the House Government Operations Committee: "The Defense Secretary is very concerned about programs where all three services have a common interest, to prevent duplication. He wants one space program, not three. He wants one basic research [sic] in how to defend ourselves on the next system down the road from ballistic missiles." [16] By placing such an agency in the Office of the

[13] House Document No. 298, 85th Cong., 2nd Sess., 1958; cited in House Committee on Government Operations, *Organization and Management of Missile Programs*, 1959, p. 133.

[14] House Committee on Government Operations, *Missile Program Hearings*, 1959, p. 513.

[15] Senate Committee on Armed Services, *1958 DOD Reorganization Act Hearings*, 1959, p. 15. As Albert Hirschmann has observed: "The sharpened motivation to do something about a problem finds a welcome outlet through the establishment of an agency to which the problem-solving task is delegated." *Journeys Toward Progress* (New York, The Twentieth Century Fund, 1963), p. 238.

[16] House Committee on Government Operations, *Missile Program Hearings*, 1959, p. 532.

Secretary, its central location, familiarity with advanced technology, and information as to what other research and development organizations were pursuing, would, it was anticipated, facilitate the elimination of wasteful duplication.

The humiliation of Sputnik highlighted another aspect of the new Agency's appeal. Recognizing the difficulty in assuring budgetary support for research which did not promise early results for the services, McElroy was sensitive to the utility of an agency with a broad conception of technological requirements:

If we depend on one service or another to look at some of this very advanced technology and decide that its responsibility is to pick up this at a very early stage and develop and chase it down to whatever ultimate system may come out of this . . . some of these important projects drop in the spaces between the services and [are not picked up] at all until it is late in the game.[17]

The Advanced Research Projects Agency was to provide the Secretary of Defense with a staff responsible for administering advanced "state of the art" research and an organization that could "deal in the more speculative, longer-range, further-looking situations, and undertake advanced research and development in those areas." [18]

The new Agency was additionally to be endowed with a number of specific tasks. In conjunction with plans being discussed to loosen further the relations between the services and the unified and specified commands, it was conceived of as a research and development organ which could attend to the needs of those commands independent of the services.[19] Parochial service divisions would at long last be transcended in military research and development.

The Agency might also transform the role of the Secretary of Defense's Office in the field of research and development. Relying upon the services for proposals, the Secretary was pro-

[17] Testimony of Secretary McElroy, House Committee on Armed Services, *National Defense Missiles Hearings*, 1958, p. 4062.

[18] Testimony of Deputy Secretary of Defense, Donald Quarles, House Committee on Government Operations, *Missile Program Hearings*, 1959, p. 483.

[19] Hammond, *Organizing for Defense*, p. 371.

pelled into the role of arbitrator and auditor. Such a function of review, revision, and resistance induced perspectives more characteristic of the prudent judge than the dynamic innovator. Provided with his own technically competent staff, the Secretary and his staff might be transformed into initiators, surveying the entire field of military technology in search of gaps, suggesting new fields of inquiry, and promoting competition and parallel approaches compatible with overall defense needs.

An interim agency was also needed to initiate and develop space projects while the impact of space technology upon service interests was analyzed. As service rivalry in space became more imminent and jurisdictional assignments more controversial, the Advanced Research Projects Agency offered a means of contracting for projects on the basis of acknowledged capability rather than avowed mission.[20] Prior to the passage of the 1958 National Aeronautics and Space Act, the Agency was also responsible for the development of a variety of space projects subsequently diverted to the National Aeronautics and Space Administration (NASA). Among the projects it approved were the 1.5 million-pound single engine space booster and studies of a man-in-space project.[21]

A prime objective of the new agency was the elimination of *wasteful* duplication. Roy Johnson, appointed the first Director of the Advanced Research Projects Agency, anticipated the channeling of duplicative efforts into more economical directions. When, for example, the President's Scientific Advisory Committee gave him the responsibility for achieving a breakthrough in solid-propellant chemistry, Johnson solicited bids from forty chemical companies. He then parcelled out their proposals to the service research and development agencies for cross-checking and evaluation before ultimately reducing the number of feasible approaches to four.[22] Johnson was also hopeful of channeling service competitiveness in more produc-

[20] Senate Committee on Aeronautical and Space Sciences, *Government Organization for Space Activities Hearings,* 1959, p. 238.

[21] *Ibid.,* p. 109.

[22] House Committee on Government Operations, *Missile Program Hearings,* 1959, pp. 498–99.

tive directions. He even considered the creation of the Advanced Research Projects Agency an indirect means of advancing unification. As he explained to the Senate Committee on Aeronautical and Space Sciences: "It is almost impossible to tell the Air Force that, 'You have got to have the Army and Navy working for you.' But it is possible to tell ARPA to get the Army, Navy and Air Force 'working for you.' This is a matter of psychology which is very important." [23]

Johnson was also confident that economies would be attainable through the expedient of contracting with the most capable and efficient technical teams, irrespective of their service or industrial affiliation.[24] Therefore, he resolved to limit the new Agency to the role of coordinator, expeditor, and overseer rather than empire builder, carrying out in-house development work on facilities which duplicated those available elsewhere.

Granted a broad and general charter with powers derived essentially from the mandate of the Secretary of Defense in the field of advanced weapons development, the Director was responsible for the direction or performance of such projects in the field of research and development that the Secretary of Defense might designate. Above the services, Johnson had his own budget and independent contractual authority. Endowed with the perspectives of a small task force of research administrators, they were able, when dealing with universities and private industry, to request a contract agency of a military service to execute and administer a contract citing ARPA funds. Alternatively, they could execute the contract and assign it to a military agency for its administration.[25] In effect, the Advanced Research Projects Agency replaced the Secretary's Ballistic Missiles Committee as the agency in the Pentagon responsible for looking after long-range needs in the missile and space field.

[23] Senate Committee on Aeronautical and Space Science, *Government Organization for Space Activities Hearings,* 1959, p. 143.

[24] He also anticipated that service rivalries might be eased considerably by circumventing the command structures in favor of direct communication and intimate ties with the contractual agencies of the Army, Navy, and Air Force.

[25] House Committee on Government Operations, *Organization and Management of Missile Programs,* 1959, p. 137.

That Committee and its incumbent Director, William Holaday, were thus reduced to facilitating the transition from development of missile projects to their production phase, or from procurement to deployment.[26]

The Advanced Research Projects Agency was not universally welcomed in the Pentagon. The Army proved quite content after Director Johnson made it clear that he did not intend to duplicate facilities, bid for the services of the Huntsville team, or become an operational rival. When the new Agency became the vehicle through which promising projects were acquired, the Army's delight could not be concealed.

Opposition came primarily from the Air Force, Navy, and industry. General Schriever, Commander of the Western Development Division, was not only unenthusiastic, he called for the early dissolution of the Agency. The reasons for his opposition may be surmised from Air Force experience in weapons development. Roles and missions decisions, on which they considered their chances good, were to be deferred. The divorce of developer from user was especially deplored. Indeed such a separation amounted to rank heresy from the standpoint of Air Force development philosophy. The doctrine of concurrency required simultaneous planning of a comprehensive program for development, manpower training, ground handling environment, and deployment concept. They therefore anticipated a dangerous "slippage" from the postponement of decisions on service mission responsibilities on advanced projects.[27] On the one hand, Air Force officials feared that the Agency would increase duplication by setting forth on a career of empire building. Alternatively, they assumed that should ARPA concentrate its energies on coordination, an additional layer of enervating bureaucratic review would develop. Irrespective of its course, it would be a competitor for scarce money, manpower, and influence in weapons decisions.

Director Johnson exercised prudential wisdom in rejecting

[26] House Committee on Government Operations, *Missile Program Hearings*, 1959, p. 501.
[27] Senate Committee on Aeronautical and Space Science, *Government Organization for Space Activities Hearings*, 1959, pp. 431, 405.

proposals that he take over the Redstone Arsenal facilities and other government in-house capabilities for space development programs. Nevertheless, the Agency was ultimately absorbed in the Office of Director of Defense Research and Engineering, created in the more comprehensive plans for reorganization which came to fruition in 1958.

DEFENSE DEPARTMENT REORGANIZATION 1957–1958

Even as the creation of the Advanced Research Projects Agency was being discussed and implemented, more fundamental reforms in research and development administration began to evolve. Some of the changes were stimulated by public restiveness over the apparent gap in space capabilities. Some were in response to the public appearance of harmful service rivalry. Some were the product of serious reflection as to the appropriate relationship between the military services and the administration of research. Desires for a simple solution to the manifestly complex problems of organization were articulated in the form of demands for a "missiles czar." In hopes of appeasing such ill-considered popular clamor, William Holaday's title as Special Assistant for Guided Missiles was altered to Director of Guided Missiles in November, 1957.[28]

On paper, Director Holaday's new responsibilities appeared impressive. He was to "direct all activities in the Department of Defense relating to research, development, engineering, production and procurement of guided missiles."[29] In the performance of these duties he was to enjoy the confidence of the Secretary of Defense and the assistance of such staff and supporting personnel as was deemed necessary.

Yet rather than clarifying with precision the location of administrative responsibility for the missile programs, Holaday's "promotion" merely beclouded further the dubious clarity of the organizational chart and left virtually everyone, including

[28] Department of Defense Directive 5105.10, dated November 15, 1957. See House Committee on Government Operations, *Missile Program Hearings,* 1959, p. 763.

[29] House Committee on Government Operations, *Organization and Management of Missile Programs,* 1959, p. 17.

Holaday, uncertain as to what his prerogatives under the new mandate were. Director Holaday claimed the authority to decide which missiles to place in production; to recommend suitable levels of expenditure on research, development, production, and deployment; to order the cancellation of programs; and to reprogram funds within the missile budget. The assertion of such perquisites of his Office, however, was made reluctantly and without great self-assurance. He was certain neither of the relationship of his Office to that of Dr. James R. Killian, the Director of the Office of Science and Technology, nor to that of Dr. Paul B. Foote, Assistant Secretary of Defense for Research and Engineering.[30] Indeed, he had great difficulty in explaining the departmental delineation of responsibilities for space and missile work.[31] Secretary McElroy, moreover, considered him a coordinator rather than an executive, and Holaday later described his functions as those of a negotiator rather than a czar.[32]

As an expediter, bureaucratic politician, and dynamic administrator Mr. Holaday's skills were as limited as was his taste for politics. He had no personal power over funding levels, the weapons projects remained with the services, and Secretary McElroy believed that genuine reorganization of the missile programs would be disruptive. Rather than becoming a missiles czar Holaday continued as Chairman of the Ballistic Missiles Committee, facilitated the transition to production of the ICMB and IRBM programs, and served as right-hand man for the Secretary on missile matters. Even as the Secretary's personal troubleshooter, his influence was dubious because of his limited staff, the imprecise outline of his responsibilities, and the skepticism with which he was viewed at the operating level, where his Office appeared to be merely an additional layer of bureaucratic inertia through which decisions had to be forced.

[30] Senate Committee on Armed Services, *Satellite and Missile Program Hearings*, 1958, pp. 426–33.
[31] *Ibid.*, p. 432.
[32] Interview with William Holaday, former Director of Guided Missiles, July 1, 1965.

THE DEPARTMENT OF DEFENSE
REORGANIZATION ACT OF 1958

The upgrading of Special Assistant Holaday appeased Congressmen and the public; the creation of the Advanced Research Projects Agency permitted a contemplation of more extensive changes in departmental organization for the technological revolutions of the future. Major reforms were not long in emerging. In the Reorganization Act of 1958 the President and Secretary of Defense adopted a subtle and indirect approach to the problem of encouraging technological development without incurring jurisdictional controversies.

The President was an avowed opponent of wasteful spending; he was determined to eliminate the public impression that service rivalry was pervasive and harmful; and, convinced that wars of the future would not permit the relative autonomy of operations enjoyed in the past by those responsible for conducting air, land, and sea warfare, he was eager to create a command structure which allowed for the centralized conduct of diverse operations. Increasingly disposed to centralize authority in the Defense Department, he considered the budget the key to any significant centralization. He was prepared to remove the Service Secretaries and Chiefs of Staff from the chain of command, to give to the Secretary of Defense authority to use money for specific purposes *within* the service budgets, and place responsibility for all research and development work directly under him.[33] In short, in the face of the growing superfluousness of the traditional Services, command, planning, and weapons development responsibilities were centralized in the Office of the Secretary of Defense.[34]

The centralization of direction over research and development, inspired by the desire to "eliminate duplication," was not without irony. To be sure, the technological revolution, the proliferation of new weapons, the growing sensitivity to problems of command and control, the revitalization of tactical

[33] Adams, *Firsthand Report,* pp. 404–05.
[34] Ries, *The Management of Defense,* p. 172.

doctrine, and the mushrooming of strategic options encouraged the concentration of responsibility in the Department in order that firm decisions might be reached. Yet the growing uncertainties and complexities of strategic and technical choices also cast doubt on the capacity of a centralized leadership to prescribe comprehensive solutions to defense problems.

Aware of the difficulties of canceling costly programs, even if they promised only marginal benefits, McElroy diagnosed the main problem as one of avoiding the initiation of research programs "that are duplicative, overlapping or of marginal usefulness. The thing that is important in order to avoid getting into duplication and waste," he went on to suggest, "is to think it through right at the very beginning." [35]

In this connection, the most significant reform included in the reorganization plan was the creation within the Office of the Secretary of Defense of a Director of Defense Research and Engineering.[36] Dr. Herbert York, first incumbent of that Office, was directed to expedite decisions on research and development matters while reducing the extent of duplication in service programming. An appointee of the Secretary of Defense, he was to enjoy precedence over all other Assistant Secretaries in the Department. In addition to providing immediate technical staff assistance to the Secretary, his statutory duties included supervision of all research and engineering activities in the Department, direction and control of those projects in research and engineering which the Secretary deemed appropriate for centralized handling, delegation of authority to issue instructions to the military departments "to approve, modify, or disapprove programs and projects of these departments and other Defense agencies in the interest of eliminating 'unpromising or unnecessarily duplicative programs,' and the right to initiate or

[35] House Committee on Appropriations, *Department of Defense Appropriations for 1960, Hearings*, 86th Cong., 1st Sess., 1959, pp. 194–95.

[36] The inspiration for this Office apparently came from President Eisenhower's recently appointed Special Assistant for Science and Technology, Dr. James R. Killian, See Robert Gilpin, "Introduction: Natural Scientists in Policy Making," in Gilpin and Wright (eds.), *Scientists and National Policy Making* (New York, Columbia University Press, 1964), p. 10.

support promising programs and projects for research and development." [37]

Authority for making both program and proprietary decisions relating to advanced weaponry now lay indisputably with the Secretary of Defense.[38] As it enhanced the authority and competence of the Secretary, the reorganization act subtly accelerated the obsolescence of the services as operating military arms. Six unified and two specified commands were brought under the direct control of the Joint Chiefs of Staff, and the line of command was altered so as to eliminate the Service Secretaries as intermediaries. Consequently, the services were transformed into supply agencies providing weapons, manpower, and logistic support to the joint commands.[39] In this respect, two able commentators on defense policy applauded the Act for producing a "mixed system which contains both unified commands and the traditional Services," asserting that it should be able "to capture the advantages both of output oriented organizations seeking to accomplish definable missions and of competing separate services looking for ways of expanding their usefulness." [40] Superseded by the Secretary in the development of advanced weaponry, the services were now preempted in planning by the Joint Staff and in strategy implementation by the unified and specified commands.

By unifying the services at the combat level, the users of military hardware would no longer be exclusively identifiable with a single service. Simultaneously, by demoting the services into supply agencies of the joint commands, it was hoped that the

[37] House Committee on Government Operations, *Organization and Management of Missile Programs*, 1959, p. 19.

[38] This seemed to meet with the approval of most Congressmen who appeared to share the sentiment of Melvin Price of Illinois, who commented: "We are all interested in strengthening . . . the authority of one man who can say yes or no quickly to a project involving research and engineering and development." House Committee on Armed Services, *DOD Reorganization Hearings*, 1958, pp. 6173–74.

[39] Hammond, *Organizing for Defense*, p. 371.

[40] Alain Enthoven and Henry Rowen, "Defense Planning and Organization," in *Public Finances: Needs, Sources, and Utilization* (Princeton, Princeton University Press, 1961) , p. 416.

sort of relationship which Army Ordnance had traditionally enjoyed as supplier to several combat arms might be reestablished.
Close ties between *supply* and *use* of new weapons, i.e., between
development and *deployment,* were thence undermined from
two directions. Decisions between competing concepts would be
facilitated in the Office of the Secretary through the advice of
the Director of Defense Research and Engineering, who would
have not only the legal capacity but the technical competence to
decide. In addition, the mounting costs of novel developments
imposed a constant incentive to decide, and the lodging of
initial development responsibility with the Advanced Research
Projects Agency diminished the prospect of irresistible pressures
against consequential choices.

The 1958 Reorganization Act reflected the quest for *program*
as well as the desire for efficient managerial *control*. The confusion and disarray of a displaced business management team
was to give way to the coherence of strategy, command, and
logistic and technical support expedited by the creation of the
Advanced Research Projects Agency, the new office for the
Director of Defense Research and Engineering, and the more
intimate links fashioned between the Joint Staff and the Joint
Commands.

That this organizational innovation was carried out successfully was attributable to the following facts: (1) In the research
and development area military leadership was not a serious
force for resistance; (2) the Secretary of Defense was newly appointed and unattached to previously existing arrangements;
and (3) the new leadership in the Office of the Secretary of Defense did not aspire to personal control of research and development from the center, but rather was prepared to rely upon
leadership derived from the administration of the function
itself, e.g., the Advanced Research Projects Agency, the Director
of Defense Research and Engineering, and the remaining service research and development agencies.[41]

[41] With the creation of the Office of Director of Defense Research and
Engineering, the position which William Holaday had formerly occupied
became rather redundant. Hence, his office was abolished, and he was

TRANSFER OF THE ARMY MISSILE ENGINEERS
TO THE NATIONAL AERONAUTICS
AND SPACE ADMINISTRATION?

Even as research and development activities in the Defense
Department were being centralized, some projects related to
missile technology were being transferred to the newly created
National Aeronautics and Space Administration. The primary
incentive for the creation of the new civilian agency was the desire to avert an extension of the arms race into the stratosphere.
This agency was to be entrusted with responsibility for space
exploration, excepting "activities peculiar to, or primarily associated with the development of weapons systems, military operations, or the defense of the United States." [42]

From the standpoint of the Army, NASA was immediately recognized as a threat, inasmuch as their ambitions in space rivaled
those of the von Braun team. Even more significantly, leaders of
the Space Agency quickly put together a comprehensive and
ambitious program which, it appeared, would be generously
funded. NASA's first director, Dr. T. Keith Glennan, believed
strongly that the essential elements of a successful space effort
were program, funds, and an organization of capable scientists,
engineers, and technicians plus supporting personnel and facilities. It became evident very early that they would not be satisfied
to operate as a directing agency in the image of the Advanced
Research Projects Agency, but rather had ambitions of becoming a major operational agency—letting contracts, disbursing

---

again made a Special Assistant to the Secretary, with limited jurisdiction
over the transition of the missile programs from developmental to production phases. Most of his staff was transferred to Dr. York's office. With
the establishment of the National Aeronautics and Space Administration,
Holaday also became Chairman of the Civilian-Military Liaison Committee which coordinated civilian and military interests in the embryonic
space program. Chairmanship of the Department of Defense Ballistic Missiles Committee passed from Holaday to Thomas Gates, the newly appointed Deputy Secretary of Defense.

[42] U.S. Congress, Senate, NASA Authorization Subcommittee of the
Committee on Aeronautical and Space Sciences, Hearings, Transfer of
von Braun Team to NASA, 86th Cong., 2nd Sess., 1960, p. 14.

funds, supervising space probes, and acquiring major missions in the space field. While Glennan had inherited 8,000 scientists, engineers, and support personnel from the National Advisory Committee on Aeronautics, he faced serious shortages of technical competence in the fields of electronics, guidance, and launch vehicles—in short, in the very fields in which the von Braun team had demonstrated outstanding abilities. The Huntsville team was desired as "a highly imaginative and competent engineering and design group, capable of serving as an integral part of the NASA organization in the planning and executing of both short-hand long-range programs in the development of launch vehicle systems." They were also desired to "monitor contracts with other governmental agencies and with industry, and to provide necessary ground testing and assembly capability, and finally, to supervise space vehicle launching operations for NASA." [43]

Apprehensions mounted at Huntsville. Through the Jupiter program, the Army had acquired a platform from which to enter the competition for space projects and missions. They were endowed with a superb technical team, restless energy, and ambition to explore the outer reaches of the earth's atmosphere. Their managerial team had exceptional devotion to the Army and exceptional grit in the "in-fighting" of Pentagon politics; they were anxious to bid for the Nike-Zeus ballistic missile defense system and the large booster project, subsequently designated Saturn.

Predictably, General Medaris expressed vigorous resistance to proposals for von Braun's transfer when they first were circulated in mid-1958. He was satisfied that the Advanced Research Projects Agency could manage developments in outer space through their contractual authority and intimate connections with the technical talent in the country.[44] He was most concerned over the additional competition for men, money, and scarce materials which would follow the creation of a new agency. Above all, he loathed the thought of the additional required reviews and coordinating mechanisms, interagency coor-

[43] *Ibid.,* pp. 14, 16.   [44] Medaris, *Countdown for Decision,* p. 243.

dination meetings, additional complications in the exchange and sharing of technical information, and increased problems of decision making posed by the creation of another agency. His concern was heightened when, in conversations with Glennan, it began to appear that felicitous contractual relations with NASA would be difficult because of Glennan's fears of involvement in interservice and industrial rivalries if a significant portion of their space work were assigned to the Huntsville team.[45]

Two additional concerns reinforced the natural reluctance of a successful technical administrator to see his engineering staff transferred. In the first place, Medaris feared that rather than a complete transfer, the team faced ultimate dissolution. Initially, Glennan requested only about half of the members of the Redstone Arsenal in-house team. Since Medaris was convinced that the Army's success was contingent on the combined contributions of a team rather than the brilliance of individual members, he was determined to keep them together. Furthermore, in the fall of 1958 the plans for Saturn were not finalized; there was no firm booster program, and the funding available to support a vigorous space effort was an unknown variable. Under the circumstances, it appeared prudent to leave the Army Ballistic Missiles Agency in the Defense Department, for it appeared that they would continue to bear major responsibilities for financing space projects. Finally, the energies, time, and funds of the Army Ballistic Missiles Agency were still devoted to military missiles to the extent of about 95 per cent, with 5 per cent in space projects. This ratio did not change significantly until they were well into the Saturn booster program, whereupon the percentage allocated to space work increased to about 35 per cent.[46]

By the fall of 1958 the transfer of the Redstone team to NASA appeared to be imminent. Such a move had the support of the Air Force, of Deputy Secretary of Defense Quarles, and even of Director of Defense Research and Engineering, Herbert

[45] Ibid.
[46] Senate Committee on Aeronautical and Space Sciences, Hearings Transfer of von Braun Team to NASA, 1960, p. 36.

York. NASA had already acquired about three hundred people who had worked on the Vanguard and other Navy space projects, and had bid not only for ABMA but Jet Propulsion Laboratories as well.[47] They received unexpected support from the latter quarter. Scientists from Jet Propulsion Laboratories, repelled by occasionally oppressive procedural rigidities at the hands of their military administrators and lured by the prospect of attractive space probes, were eager to associate with the new civilian space agency.

Fearing that the transfer would be accomplished swiftly and without warning, allowing for no redress of Army grievances, Medaris risked a calculated leak to the press through his long-time friend, Mark Watson, of The *Baltimore Sun*.[48] Capitalizing on the public's concern with military missile projects and emphasizing the possibility of the dissolution of a "national resource," should the von Braun team be split up, they prevented a *fait accompli*. Negotiations with the NASA organization replaced the plan for immediate transfer. On December 3, 1958, Jet Propulsion Laboratories was transferred to NASA; the Army Ballistic Missiles Agency was to be "completely responsive to the requirements of NASA" according to the terms of an agreement signed by Dr. Glennan and Secretary Brucker.[49] Brucker and McElroy explained that had the transfer taken place, the nation's defenses would have suffered. They required the retention of the Development Operations Division of the Ballistic Missiles Agency in the Army, at least temporarily.

Subsequently, the fate of the von Braun team was tied inextricably to the funding fortunes of the Saturn project, the outcome of deliberations relating to future space roles and missions and the growth of NASA. Throughout 1959, an intense fight was in progress over the future direction of the space program. NASA and the Air Force were the chief adversaries. The problems of organizing interagency collaboration in connection with the Mercury program brought to the surface pressing questions

[47] *Ibid.*, p. 16.   [48] Medaris, *Countdown for Decision*, p. 246.
[49] Senate Committee on Aeronautical and Space Sciences, Hearings, *Transfer of the von Braun Team to NASA*, 1960, p. 16.

on the organization of such collaborative ventures in the future. While the Army and Navy favored Joint Commands including representation from all services, the Air Force sought to secure exclusive command and control of the space mission. When the Joint Chiefs of Staff produced a split paper on the subject, the Secretary of Defense was forced to decide for himself, assisted by the advice of Director of Defense Research and Engineering, Dr. York. Further staff consideration prompted the conclusion that the magnitude of anticipated space efforts did not justify the creation of another joint command. The development, production, launch, and allied operational activities related to space vehicles were consequently assigned to the Air Force.[50] While the Army and Navy each acquired responsibility for the payload of a satellite project,[51] launch vehicles and related equipment and services would have to be purchased from the Air Force.

Foreclosed from substantial missions in outer space, the Army Ballistic Missiles Agency saw its other projects languish throughout 1959. The Saturn project was inadequately supported. A total of $140 million was allocated to it in the Department of Defense budget for the 1959 fiscal year. According to Medaris, this was cut to $70 million by the Budget Bureau. Subsequently, a request for an additional $90 million was presented, but it was granted only after the transfer of the Saturn Project to NASA. The program had not changed, but the priority it received increased as the internal competition for funds within the agency sponsoring it declined.

Redstone and Jupiter were rapidly being phased out, and the Nike and Pershing programs had been contracted out to industry. In mid-October the Saturn was confirmed as a national requirement, but moved under the jurisdiction of NASA; Nike-Zeus was continued as a developmental project, but its budget was trimmed. There appeared to be no prospect of production

---

50 Medaris, *Countdown for Decision*, p. 254. See also the testimony of General Arthur Trudeau, Senate Committee on Astronautical and Space Sciences, *Government Organization for Space Activities Hearings*, 1959, pp. 240–41.

51 The Army received responsibility for the Transit—a communications satellite; the Navy acquired Notus—a navigational satellite system.

for the foreseeable future. Secretary McElroy at this point requested information from Glennan as to his continuing interest in obtaining the services of the von Braun team.[52]

Army resistance to the transfer dissolved in the face of fiscal austerity. Dr. York favored the transfer as a means of simplifying the administrative arrangements appertaining to the big booster program, for which the Army Ballistic Missiles Agency, the Advanced Research Projects Agency, and the National Aeronautics and Space Administration shared responsibility. A start toward placing all the projects under a single agency had been made with the incorporation of the Advanced Research Projects Agency into York's office in late 1959.[53] The Defense Department was satisfied that there was no immediate military requirement for a big space booster, although they did not discount the prospect of a long-range requirement, and that while there was an urgent requirement for such boosters in the field of space exploration, NASA was perfectly capable of handling the developmental job.

In the end, even General Medaris and the Army Staff accommodated themselves to the transfer. It began to appear that the alternative to transfer was the concellation of the Saturn in the face of Dr. York's apparent lack of enthusiasm for the Saturn plans and the prospect of project competition from the Air Force.[54] Feeling that the Army technical team constituted a national asset, Medaris ultimately supported the Secretary's proposal out of concern for the continuity, support, money, and environment needed to sustain von Braun's team. In any event, transfer to NASA appeared preferable to their transfer to the Air Force, where that service's philosophy threatened the dissolution of the team and their dispersal into private industry or alternatively their restriction to systems design and technical direction work without opportunities for production engineering.[55] While Medaris supported the transfer as finally effected, he did so without enthusiasm. His objections were related to his

[52] Senate Committee on Aeronautical and Space Sciences, Hearings, *Transfer of the von Braun Team to NASA*, 1960, p. 17.
[53] *Ibid.*, p. 29.   [54] *Ibid.*, p. 37.
[55] Medaris, *Countdown for Decision*, p. 267.

fears that the distinction between military and civilian space programs was untenable and his anxieties that, as in the Unification Act of 1947, what passed for centralization was merely the verbal façade for the proliferation of agencies contending for missions and budgets.

In the ensuing negotiations between the Army and NASA over the terms of the transfer, General Schomburg, Medaris' successor as Commanding General of the Army Ordnance Missile Command, doggedly saw to it that current programs, i.e., the Redstone and Pershing, were not simply abandoned by the Huntsville personnel involved in the transfer. Otherwise, their joint concern was to sustain the momentum and avert the fragmentation of the Army team. While the Army Ballistic Missile Agency lost some facilities, it was the prospect of rebuilding an in-house technical capability that would be competitive with private industry and the other services which left Army officials with a pessimistic outlook on the future. The Army had been stripped of its primary resource in the scramble for opportunities, prestige, roles, missions, and dollars in the defense program of the 1960s. While the transfer would presumably mitigate Air Force vs. Army rivalry, it could be predicted that NASA would compete with the Air Force for space missions with a vigor reinforced by civilian-military overtones. Nor was the conflict between development philosophies entirely liquidated, since the in-house capability was left intact and merely transferred to another agency of the Federal Government.

THE AIR FORCE, THE "ARSENAL PHILOSOPHY,"
AND SPACE TECHNOLOGY LABORATORIES

As indicated above, the relationship between the Air Force and Ramo-Wooldridge, Inc., had been worked out somewhat hastily at the inception of the Atlas program. It became increasingly unsatisfactory to Air Force contractors during the ensuing years, as they recognized the competitive advantages accruing to a company which continued to nurture ambitions of obtaining production contracts despite the hardware ban imposed upon them by the Air Force. Associate contractors became more and more critical in early 1958, but the Air Force, fearful of the disruption of the ballistic missile program that might attend any major overhaul in their management arrangements, resisted suggestions regarding the status of STL. Moreover, bidding as they were to become executive agent for major assignments in the space field, they could hardly contemplate with equanimity the loss of their technical team to industry. Salary differentials made it unlikely that STL personnel could be induced to become civil servants in the Air Force Department.

In order to postpone a showdown and divert attention, they encouraged Space Technology Laboratories to become a separate corporation, thereby divorcing themselves from their industrial affiliates.[56] The remainder of the firm merged with Thompson Products to become Thompson-Ramo-Wooldridge, Inc. It was hoped that this would demonstrate that Space Technology Laboratories was a completely independent operating company with its own board of directors, strictly enjoined by its parent corporation to conduct its business so as "to insure that TRW receives absolutely no special advantages in competition for any Air Force project as a consequence of its financial investment in STL."[57] Only financial and accounting reports were to flow between the two corporate entities. The basis of the *quid pro quo* was evident. The Air Force hoped to recreate the appearance of objectivity; the Space Technology Laboratories hoped to be able to remove the hardware ban from its parent company. Neither was successful.

Subsequently, divestiture began to appeal to some company executives. It did not appeal to Secretary Douglas, for it would have merely replaced one group of private owners with another. While it would have handled the problems of Ramo-Wooldridge, it offered little in the way of a solution to the Air Force.[58] Ultimately, as a result of the suggestions of the House

[56] Space Technology Laboratories was incorporated as an independent company on November 1, 1958.
[57] House Committee on Government Operations, *Air Force Ballistic Missile Management*, 1961, p. 7.
[58] *Ibid.,* p. 8.

Committee of Government Operations, the conclusions of the Millikan Committee,[59] and the continued concern of industrial contractors, a nonprofit corporation, Aerospace Corporation, was created to handle in-house technical direction work on future Air Force weapons systems.

From the vantage point of our interests, the growing similarity between the Army arsenal system and the Air Force's relations with Space Technology Laboratories is striking. Though they ridiculed such comparisons, the language with which Air Force partisans defended the relationship bears marked similarity to the earlier statements of General Medaris on the advantages of the Huntsville arrangement. Air Force officers praised Space Technology Laboratories' objectivity, their high technical competence, their permanence and stability, and their vision in anticipating the problems and prospects for weapons of the future. They also provided a link with the scientific and technical resources of the country.[60]

Owing to the pressures of time, their peculiar competence, and their knowledge of Air Force thinking, Space Technology Laboratories was asked to build and install instrumentation packages in the nose cones of Project Able-O, a reentry test effort; to fabricate electrical and electronic systems; to assemble and check out three Able second stages; and to build test support equipment.[61] They also did design and fabrication work on Able-Star second-stage rockets for the earth satellite program and designed, built, and operated a mobile, downrange tracking station advertised as the biggest of its kind in the world.

Thus, Space Technology Laboratories was not only anxious to demonstrate virtually the same capabilities that the Huntsville team had so proudly claimed for years, but they appeared subtly to be becoming an arsenal of sorts themselves. They were, doubtless, uniquely equipped for such advanced produc-

<hr>

[59] A committee created by the Secretary of the Air Force to look into the contractual relations between the Air Force, Space Technology Laboratories, and industry.
[60] *Ibid.,* p. 17.   [61] *Ibid.,* p. 12.

tion work because of their ability to move rapidly, simplify complex designs, and demonstrate new techniques.

The ultimate outcome was fortunate from both the stand-point of industry and the Air Force. The former eliminated a potentially disturbing situation involving the competitive ad-vantages enjoyed by an industrial rival. The Air Force, for its part, postponed any disruption in its technical team until the roles and missions in the space field were well established. It also retained the services of Space Technology Laboratories for their ballistic missile programs. Aerospace Corporation was created in order to assist the Air Force in a staff capacity on its space assignments.[62] They were commissioned by the Air Force to "aid in applying the full resources of modern science and technology to the problem of achieving those continuing ad-vances in ballistic missile and military space systems which are basic to national security." [63]

Subsequent events confirmed the trend toward fragmentation of service, industrial, and technical team loyalties. Having lost out on advanced space systems work to Aerospace, Space Tech-nology Laboratories was in the position of having to broaden its base of operations. In the process it ceased to be merely the in-dustrial or technical arm of a single service. Indeed, some rather bizarre managerial relations resulted from their diversification. On the Advent Communications Satellite Project, for example, Space Technology Laboratories and Aerospace Corporation were linked to different services. The former, as technical ad-viser of the U. S. Army Advent Agency at Fort Monmouth, New Jersey, was higher in the management hierarchy than Aerospace Corporation, which as technical director of the Bal-listic Missiles Division had responsibility for launch vehicles,

[62] They were incorporated June 4, 1960, as a nonprofit corporation which would not distribute gains or dividends to its members; funds would be solely devoted to furthering the corporate purposes determined by trustees under the charter. It would be exempt from taxation, and, consequently, would be precluded from engaging in propaganda, in-fluencing legislation, and involvement in political campaigns. *Ibid.*, p. 17.
[63] *Ibid.*

payload integration, and injection into orbit. This reversed their normal relationship. Space Technology Laboratories also extended its ties with NASA, the Navy, the Army, the Atomic Energy Commission, and other government agencies and industrial contractors.[64]

This was curiously reflective of the situation in late 1959. The Air Force was prepared to see a dilution in their former ties with Ramo-Wooldridge as a consequence of Defense Department decisions relating to roles and missions. The Air Force had emerged victorious in the interservice contest for space missions. They had received responsibility for the major part of space research and development and for all space booster programs. It also reflected the desire of the industries to divorce themselves from a stifling relationship with a single service in order to strike up ties with all agencies contracting for space projects.

The divorce of service suppliers and users, encouraged by the 1958 Reorganization Act, was thus paralleled by a reformulation of the relationship between the Air Force and their systems engineering staff, Space Technology Laboratories, and the transfer of the Huntsville team from the Army Ballistic Missile Agency to the National Aeronautics and Space Administration. The stage for a new confrontation was set, though this time the competition would include the vague distinctions between civilian and military space programs and the entry of a major civilian agency into competition for scientists, projects, and funds. Ironically, service rivalries in the ballistic missile field were superseded at the very time when their development agencies were beginning to reflect one another closely. Just as the Army began to neutralize the Air Force's political satellite, the airframe industry, by offering the prospect of an additional source of contracts, the Air Force began to develop its own equivalent of the arsenal development-production capability long considered a major technical, if not political, asset by the Army.

One may perhaps conclude that the broad base of technical

[64] *Ibid.,* p. 45.

competence in the technologies of ballistic rocketry and electronics, which were promoted by the diffuse efforts of the services during the 1950s, enormously increased the capacity of the United States to rapidly move into the space field in 1958, after a belated appreciation of its political and military significance. At the same time the dissolution of established industry-service-engineering staff alliances reinforced the trend toward a stronger centralized direction of military research and development programs from the Office of the Secretary of Defense. Consequently, technical competence could be more easily exploited even as the jurisdictional rivalries—which previously deflected service efforts from strategic requirements to technical gambits in the quest for dollars, missions, and prestige—were being slightly alleviated.

(8) CONCLUSION

Policy making in the innovation of strategic weapons is in its deepest sense political. Intellectual analysis may, to be sure, inform the selection of projects to be researched and developed, the determination of how many of which kinds of weapons to produce, the resolution of roles and missions disputes arising over the right to deploy novel systems, and the formulation of strategic conceptions governing their use. But the multiplicity of groups contributing to such decisions, the diversity of their objectives, and the uncertainties of technology, intelligence, and strategy all combine to insure that the relative power of the participants, as well as the logic of their arguments, will shape the outcome of policy deliberations.

At each stage in the Thor-Jupiter controversy, critical decisions were influenced by the interplay of power, for the difficult choices involved the reconciliation of goals in conflict, the coordination of rivals engaged in vigorous competition, and the adjustment of aspirations within a framework of limited resources. The issues could scarcely be resolved on their merits alone. None of the parties to the controversy could perfectly anticipate the weaponry that technology would disclose, that the services would require, that an adversary might develop, or that allies would permit to be emplaced on their territories. Consequently, the services were prepared to bargain for the promotion of their interests when efforts at persuasion did not suffice.

In this study attention has been drawn to the lobbying activities of the services on behalf of their institutional interests. Like the powerful lobbying groups in domestic legislative struggles, the services possess a measure of autonomy in the definition of their interests and the formulation of strategies to achieve them. Unlike associational interest groups the services must operate perforce within the bureaucratic setting of a formally hierarchical Defense Department.

The lobbying activities of the services pose managerial and political problems for the Secretary of Defense. The Secretary's efforts to define a coherent strategic policy, to clarify the procedures of defense policy making, and to shape the climate of opinion which informs the selection among strategic programs constitute, in turn, the primary determinants of the services' lobbying strategies.

Thus the dynamics of interservice politics are not to be understood in terms of the relationships among autonomous groups occasionally coordinating their activities as they pursue their independent interests. They rather involve the competitive as well as cooperative relationships among powerful, institutionalized interest groups formally subordinate to a civilian defense leadership that although legally empowered to coordinate and discipline the activities of the services is sometimes politically incapable of doing so.

Precisely this element of competitive lobbying by the services over the right to develop and deploy new weapons renders one descriptive model of the weapons innovation process somewhat dubious. It is frequently supposed that weapons decisions, since they are arrived at generally within the Executive branch and involve matters of considerable secrecy, are invariably resolved within the confines of a *closed* political arena. Nonetheless, the record of the Thor-Jupiter controversy raises many doubts about Sir Charles P. Snow's assertion that the "cardinal choices" of weapons policy are made in secrecy by a "handful of men," whose judgments are not informed by a "first-hand knowledge of what those choices depend on or what their results may be." [1]

[1] Sir Charles P. Snow, *Science and Government* (Cambridge, Harvard University Press, 1960), p. 1. An effective critique of Snow's contentions

One of the striking things about the Thor-Jupiter controversy was the very openness of many of the discussions and decisions leading to the development and procurement of IRBMs. The evidence of this case suggests that the process of competitive development of weapons by the services generates determined pressures for the broadening of participation in policy making, for the illumination of many of the financial and strategic costs and consequences of alternative proposals, and for the transmission of considerable secret information via leaks and counterleaks to Congressmen and the public, thus permitting the intra-Executive branch discussion of the issues to be monitored by a somewhat wider attentive and reasonably well-informed audience.[2]

In the Thor-Jupiter controversy, widespread participation in the policy struggles was encouraged by several factors. The pluralism of the services and their prolific contractual relationships with a host of industrial suppliers, university laboratories, and non-profit research institutes eager to refine or replenish the strategic arsenal, insured that the initiative for proposing novel weapon systems was diffused widely. In the innovation of major weapon systems, however, many novel proposals are conceived but relatively few are financed. Thus the ease of generating projects is counterbalanced somewhat by the potential vetoes which threaten service programs as costs mount and production decisions approach.

Securing the requisite program approvals for a major technical innovation entails consensus-building efforts of ever widening scope. Solicitation of support within a service gradually yields to negotiations among them. The difficulties of mobilizing such support increase, moreover, as one proceeds through the phases of research, development, and production to the

---

regarding the prophetic power of scientists in strategic issues is to be found in Albert Wohlstetter's essay, "Strategy and the Natural Scientists," in Gilpin and Wright (eds.), *Scientists and National Policy Making*, pp. 174–239.

[2] For an analysis of the role of the attentive public in the making of American foreign policy, see Gabriel Almond, *The American People and Foreign Policy* (New York, Praeger, 1960), especially chaps. VII and X.

deployment of a new system. At each of these stages in the Thor-Jupiter controversy, the costs of choice became more consequential and the interests to be reconciled multiplied. The sufficiency of persuasion diminished, and the imperatives of bargaining increased. The number of necessary concurrences grew as the implications of choice upon the existing distribution of power and responsibility among rival services, departments, industries, and even nation-states became more evident. Thus the fragmentation of power within the defense policy making system and the high stakes which important institutional interests invested in weapons decisions militated against leaving a monopoly of power over these "cardinal choices" to a "handful of men."

The pressures for broadened participation in these important decisions likewise posed incentives for public disclosures of classified information regarding the alleged advantages or deficiencies of rival projects. In the furious public relations campaigns waged by the services on behalf of their respective IRBM programs the Army and Air Force regularly divulged the shortcomings of their rival's technical approach and the failures of their development and test program. The temptation to reverse unfavorable decisions by bringing the issues to the attention of a wider circle of policy makers was sometimes compelling. Occasionally, as in the case of Colonel Nickerson, men of strong convictions took matters into their own hands by leaking secret materials to the press or Congress. The zeal of public information officers, the indiscretions of officials, and the improprieties or insubordination of staff officers provided at least an intermittent flow of information to Congress and the public about such sensitive matters as the technical design of weapons under development. By skillfully exploiting the divisions within the defense establishment and by capitalizing upon the relative openness of the Executive bureaucracies, conscientious Congressmen and industrious journalists were able to open substantial cracks in the "dike" of executive secrecy.

There is, of course, no assurance that in this process of "opening" the arena of policy making all the relevant facts or analyses are disclosed to Congress or the attentive public. Information leaked to outsiders naturally tends to reflect the peculiar bias of its source. Often it may be unreliable and misleading. Nor is there any reason to assume confidently that the distortions are necessarily corrected by the competitive efforts of rivals. What is evident is that secrecy regarding important weapons innovations becomes more and more difficult to maintain as the participants in such decisions become more numerous and as the implications of novel developments for the institutional interests of the services become widely appreciated.

Although the processes of mobilizing support or opposition for weapons policies tend not to be directed primarily toward the many decision making foci in Congress, Representatives and Senators occasionally emerged as advocates or critics of the various IRBM programs. Members of key committees were naturally most likely to become involved at an early stage. Privileged information such as was available to members of the Joint Committee on Atomic Energy and those who regularly participated in the executive sessions of the Armed Services Committees or Appropriations Committees allowed some individual members to act not only in the capacity of an informed and attentive public, but actually to play a decisive role in initiating dramatic new programs; to wit, Senator Jackson's interventions on behalf of both the Atlas and Polaris programs.[3]

At somewhat later stages, partisans of particular services were called upon to write letters, make representations, drop favorable comments in press conferences, and ask leading questions in committee hearings. Ardent support was also forthcoming from Congressmen whose districts stood to profit directly or indirectly from one of the programs. The force of their petitions was generally stronger against cancellation of a project than it was for innovation of a program.[4] Another rather inchoate group of Congressmen exerted occasional influence as a result of

[3] For a more general evaluation of Congressional participation in national security policy making, see Edward A. Kolodziej, *The Uncommon Defense and Congress 1945–1963* (Columbus, Ohio University Press, 1966).

[4] The deployment of subcontracts over a wide geographic area for the IRBM programs suggests that service leaders recognized advantages in the political leverage such grass roots support could engender.

their instinctively critical response to policies adopted by the Executive Branch. Their energies could be mobilized most readily by apparent or real failures. Their reactions were generally the most politically partisan. It was this group which agitated on behalf of drastic action to prevent the emergence of a possible missile gap after the Russian launching of ICBMs and earth satellites in the fall of 1957. Thus, as the participation of Congressmen tended to grow in the area of decision making in weapons innovation, their concern with strategic issues was supplemented by efforts to advance the proprietary interests of one service or another, and their partisanship appeared to increase. The myriad difficulties of consensus building were, to some extent then, compounded by the participation of legislators.

If Congress provided one set of potential critics of Defense Department decisions on weapons policy, the American system of contracting out certain responsibilities for the planning and evaluation of certain defense tasks to quasi-autonomous research institutions and to an extensive network of scientific and technical advisory committees located within the Executive branch supplied another. The links which this system provided between the "scientific estate" and the defense bureaucracies encouraged rather free discussion of weapons decisions by people who enjoyed extensive access to classified data yet preserved the unusual measure of critical freedom which their location outside the official chain of command and responsibility permitted.[5] Thus the Rand Corporation, the Weapon System Evaluation Group, the Killian Committee and the Gaither Committee all provided means of linking the realm of 'closed politics' with a broader, though still limited and discreet, public discussion of significant national security issues.[6] These outside experts could serve as critics, carefully dissecting recommendations emanating

[5] See Don K. Price, "Creativity in the Public Service." *Public Policy,* IX (Cambridge, Harvard Graduate School of Public Administration, 1959), p. 14.

[6] For an elaboration of this point, see Bruce L. R. Smith, "Strategic Expertise and National Security Policy: A Case Study," *Public Policy,* XIII (Cambridge, Harvard Graduate School of Public Administration, 1964), p. 104.

from a variety of points within the government. Their very pluralism assured the government of a broad base of scientific and technical advice, and, superimposed upon service rivalries, this provided additional insurance that criticism of weapons programs was persistent and far from perfunctory.[7]

Sometimes the arena of politics is broadened by those determined to reverse decisions by submitting them for review to a more sympathetic forum, sometimes by those eager to evade the responsibilities of decision-making by sharing the burdens of choice more widely, and sometimes by those anxious to secure the political judgment of Congressmen or the technical advice of non-governmental experts. In any event, the wider the circle of advisers, the more difficult it becomes to arrange a satisfactory policy consensus. This tends to increase the importance of triggering events as the catalysts of decision. New intelligence estimates of Soviet capabilities, technological breakthroughs on important components, or dramatic events on the international stage were thus of great significance in precipitating the decisions to initiate parallel IRBM programs, to place both Jupiters and Thors in production, and to exert pressure on NATO allies for the emplacement of those missiles on their territories. Additional catalysts of choice were provided by the annual budgetary cycle, and, indeed, by the very pace of technological progress which constantly threatened to obsolesce new weapons before they even became operational.

The uncertainties of technical innovation and the nature of the political process through which weapons innovation was managed during the 1950's inclined civilian defense leaders to resolve the "cardinal choices" by means of "minimal decisions." In the Thor-Jupiter case, officials regularly attempted to cope with the uncertainties of technology by traveling simultaneously down several paths, by foreclosing their options slowly,

---

[7] It would appear that during the period of the Thor-Jupiter controversy, these external critics were more zealous in exposing the gaps in America's preparedness posture than in calling attention to notable superfluities in the arsenals of the services. They tended, moreover, to share with the responsible officials a commitment to the basic premises underlying American National Security policy.

and by deferring the drastic choices as long as possible. The rationality of this approach may be debated. What is certain is the fact that it provided a convenient method of reducing the burdens of the predictive powers as well as the risk-taking proclivities of the key decision makers even as it offered a handy rationalization for postponing difficult jurisdictional decisions.

Regrettably the postponement of hard choices does not always facilitate their ultimate resolution. Thus Secretary McElroy's request for moral support from Congress in eliminating duplicative programs may have been less a confession of indecisiveness in the face of complex technical alternatives than it was eloquent testimony to the political pressures which could be exerted to continue weapons projects promising limited and very temporary strategic returns. This conclusion is also strengthened by Comptroller Wilfred McNeil's comment to the Jackson Subcommittee on National Security Policy Machinery: "We cannot expect to start development of ideas and have every one work out. So we ought to expect that a certain amount of the things that we do will not work out as originally planned. . . . I would only be critical if, when they are not going right, we haven't the courage to step up and stop it. That is the real thing that we should have been criticized for when I was there." [8]

Between the desire for economy and the interest in smoothing the ruffled seas of service conflict, something occasionally had to give. The additional $100 to $200 million required to finance the production of two land-based IRBMs was the price paid for the maintenance of harmony between the services.

In short, the evidence of the Thor-Jupiter case suggests that, at least in those instances where service rivalry is a significant factor in weapons innovation, participation is nowhere so limited, the absence of an attentive public so complete, secrecy so impenetrable, or the dichotomy between politicians and experts so stark as Lord Snow has portrayed them. But, of course, the simple fact that such decisions are not necessarily reached

[8] Senate Committee on Government Operations, *Hearings, Organizing for National Security*, I, 1961, p. 1068.

within the narrow confines of a very closed political system does not insure that they will be based upon appropriate criteria or that they will be informed by strategic insight.

THE CRITERIA OF RATIONALITY
IN WEAPONS DEVELOPMENT DECISIONS

One of the popular bits of contemporary "conventional wisdom" proposes that military technology restricts the freedom of democratic action. This is nonsense, as Don K. Price has noted, "because it is not technology that restricts freedom of action, but facts. Technology widens the range of possibilities that are open for choice, but only for those who know what they are doing. . . . The facts are inexorable; to control them we must make the right decisons at the right time." [9]

The problem is, of course, more easily stated than resolved. With regard to weapons innovation the importance of making the right choices in time is widely acknowledged. Agreement upon the appropriate criteria of choice is more easily obtainable in abstract discussions than in specific cases. A thorough discussion of the problems inherent in any attempt to establish standards of rationality in the development and production of novel weapons would go well beyond the scope of this book. The evidence of the Thor-Jupiter case may illumine a small portion of the larger problem. It also confirms its complexity.

Certainly the limits which political factors, such as interservice or interagency rivalries, impose upon the criteria of rationality are suggested by this study. In the management of research and development decisions, the vagaries of politics and the uncertainties of technology combine to render objectives hazy, evaluation of alternatives tentative, cost, time, and performance estimates of advanced systems highly questionable, and predictions regarding the strategic consequences of novel weapons hazardous. Such is the gestation period for important innovations in military technology that weapons conceived and

[9] Don K. Price, "Creativity in the Public Service," *Public Policy,* IX (Cambridge, Harvard Graduate School of Public Administration, 1959), p. 13.

developed in response to one set of political facts and strategic problems become operational years later in a political and strategic environment which in all probability has changed dramatically. It may be less rational to proceed in the making of weapons policy from self-confident assertions of precise goal priorities through bold means-end analysis of alternatives to clear cut choices, than to proceed by what have been termed "small, easily reversible steps" toward a number of goals whose exact rank on one's list of priority objectives cannot be stated with assurance.[10] Given the dynamics of the competitive arms race with the Soviet Union, however, it is not so easy to specify clearly those steps which are small and reversible.

The irreducible element of conjecture which surrounds all discussions of the future scientific, technological, and political environment suggests the difficulties of equating rational policy with a rigid adherence to a sequential process which begins with the definition of a single statement of strategic policy and proceeds then to deduce matériel requirements, research and development priorities, and budgetary decisions from it. Strategic policy, weapons developments, and budgetary constraints legitimately exert reciprocal influences upon one another within the equation of defense policy. Non-security values obviously limit military expenditures by constituting competing claims upon the scarce resources of the Federal budget. Budgetary ceilings may justifiably limit the pace of technological developments just as the unanticipated fruits of scientific research and engineering may substantially modify the strategic environment. The element of surprise in all scientific endeavors should be sufficient to induce caution in efforts to plan technological innovation with any exactitude.

During the research and exploratory development phase of the weapons innovation process, criteria of rational choice are especially elusive. The prospective costs and benefits of alternative concepts defy precise calculation. The intuitive hunches of those skilled in conjecturing about the technological and mili-

[10] Hilsman, "The Foreign Policy Consensus," *Journal of Conflict Resolution*, III (December, 1959), 364.

tary environments of the future may be as reliable guides to decisions as sophisticated analytic techniques, whose utility depend upon the very data which only experimentation can provide. But, if the technical uncertainties of rival projects are great at the outset, they can be reduced gradually through the information and experience accumulated in research and development programs. The costs of such exploratory development are relatively low compared to the dramatic increases in expenditures which occur at the stages of advanced engineering, production tooling, and the procurement of an initial operational capability.

Where military problems urgently demand solution, the support of parallel development programs may constitute a defensible method of overcoming technical difficulties efficiently. While postponing a choice as between rival approaches, technical uncertainties may be reduced, cost estimates improved, and strategic needs systematically assessed. A broad menu of technological possibilities may be assured even as the high costs of premature commitment to the production of any specific system may be avoided.[11] The hard choices cannot, of course, be evaded indefinitely. One must not only decide how technical competition is to be structured in order to achieve broad advances in technology, but must ultimately choose which projects to support for full-scale development. These are the most difficult decisions of all, because the financial costs of advanced development and production mount swiftly, and the implications of such decisions for the arms race, for the cohesion of the Western alliance, and for the coherence of America's military strategy may be both ominous and baffling.

One can make a defensible case for parallel approaches to

[11] The virtues and shortcomings of such a strategy are discussed in Warner R. Schilling, "The H-Bomb Decision: How to Decide Without Actually Choosing," *Political Science Quarterly*, LXXVI (March, 1961), 24–46; Richard R. Nelson, "Uncertainty, Learning and the Economics of Parallel Research and Development Efforts," *The Review of Economics and Statistics*, XLIII (November, 1961), 351–64; and Charles Hitch and Roland McKean, *The Economics of Defense in the Nuclear Age* (Cambridge, Harvard University Press, 1960), chap. XIII.

the development of technology as a means of hastening the learning process and hedging against the possibility that one or another approach will prove to be a blind alley. But few would countenance "wasteful duplication." Wasteful duplication is by definition irrational. What, however, constitutes duplication that is wasteful? Trade-offs between cost and time in programming weapons development are contingent upon the urgency with which particular innovations are required. In view of the inexperience of American engineers and industries with missile technology and the state of the art advances which were required if long-range ballistic missiles were to become efficient delivery vehicles, authorization for the Jupiter IRBM program may have been a prudent decision. Nor were the costs of competitiveness exorbitant in the realm of information sharing, when weighed against the technological benefits from the dual approaches to the IRBM system. The development of the ablation concept for shielding the incoming warhead from the heat generated by reentry may, in itself, have justified the additional cost of duplicate programs.

Criticism may, on the other hand, be directed at the somewhat haphazard way in which different technical approaches emerged as a by-product of Army-Air Force rivalry. In authorizing parallel programs, Secretary Wilson intuitively hedged his bets by authorizing competition between two proud and competent technical teams. This decision was not apparently informed by any clear conception as to how the technological yield of such competition could be maximized. Where the urgency of a specific requirement justifies parallel approaches, it follows that a systematic effort should be made to distinguish the technical approaches in such a way as to accumulate the maximum possible information relevant to the ultimate choice between competing projects. No such effort seems to have been made in the Thor-Jupiter case.

Duplication may also be wasteful if programs are continued beyond the point where choice between them is possible or their lack of strategic utility demonstrable. "The time to abandon programs," Vannevar Bush once asserted, 'is before they be-

come very expensive." [12] The Thor-Jupiter experience, however, confirms the judgment of the House Committee on
Government Operations which reported, "The time to choose is
brief and fleeting before projects become expensive, and there is
no really effective mechanism for clear-cut selection at an early
stage or otherwise." [13] Wasteful duplication is not necessarily
avoidable by postponing experimental work by competing technical teams. On the contrary, prolonged program definition
phases, while they may promote a refinement of designs and a
systematic evaluation of competing programs, may also foster
public relations contests of attractive brochures, presentations,
and unsubstantiated cost and performance claims. The requirement of long-term cost projections on competing projects, if
carefully scrutinized by a competent staff in the Office of the
Secretary of Defense (who are familiar with the certainties [14] as
well as the uncertainties of developmental costs) may also facilitate choice before the pressures for extending programs beyond
their useful lifetime become irresistible. The utility of such
procedures depends upon the precision and competence with
which designs and costs are estimated and appraised and the
humility with which such information is employed to influence
weapons planning.

Rational choices among competing projects would also be
facilitated by the postponement of decisions for production
tooling and their attendant "sunk costs." In the Thor-Jupiter
case, however, such pressures were peculiarly difficult to avoid,
since both missiles were regarded as interim capabilities useful
only for that relatively brief period before sophisticated and reliable ICBMs would be procured in quantity. Concurrency in
preparing the production facilities seemed, therefore, an appropriate method of preventing the entire investment in a transitional capability from becoming superfluous.

Duplication may finally be considered wasteful, as perhaps in
this case, if insufficient attention is paid to those design features

[12] House Committee on Government Operations, *Hearings, Organization and Management of the Missile Programs,* 1959, p. 151.
[13] *Ibid.*
[14] Among these certainties one would include the expectation that contractor estimates of cost incline generally to extreme optimism.

which facilitate the adaptation of costly new weapons to a changing political environment. The IRBMs were developed with specific reference to a *range of operation* which, in conjunction with the American system of overseas bases, seemed to guarantee their usefulness. There is little evidence available to suggest that comparable attention was paid to equally important design criteria such as the political suitability of highly vulnerable, slow-reacting, intermediate-range missiles in Europe. The space program ultimately provided a consumer of some of the booster vehicles, but this appears to have been a fortuitous and largely unplanned circumstance rather than the consequence of technical design for flexibility and multiple use. Neither the arrangements for control of the nuclear warheads to be used on the Thors and Jupiters nor the efforts made to insure the survival of the missiles against a surprise attack imply a serious evaluation of the utility of IRBMs against the problems of presidential decison making in a grave international crisis.[15]

The significance of political guidelines for design criteria appears absolutely crucial with respect to weapons destined for overseas deployment. The decision to produce both Thors and Jupiters was based upon unrealistic assumptions as to the willingness of allies to deploy strategic missiles upon their soil. More serious than this miscalculation was the fact that surprise and consternation greeted the first indications of European recalcitrance. Strategic policy within a multilateral alliance should be both militarily sound and politically acceptable. There is little evidence to suggest that prior to the American offer of IRBMs to the Europeans at the December, 1957, NATO Summit Conference, there had been either a sophisticated elaboration of the strategic implications of such an offer or joint discussions with major allies to discover a basis of agreement upon acceptable designs and deployment procedures for strategic missiles to be emplaced in Europe.

Allied influence on the design of intermediate-range ballistic

[15] See Wesley W. Posvar, "Strategy and Politics," reprinted in *Survival*, IX (March, 1967), 87–92, for some suggestions as to the kinds of design criteria based upon strategic analysis that might be appropriately given to engineer-scientists working upon new military technologies.

missiles was indirect and negative. The cool response given the American offer of Thors and Jupiters reinforced the growing preference for sea-based Polaris missiles under the unilateral control of the American president. General Norstad's proposals for follow-on MRBM systems reflected European tactical requirements and aspirations to share in the scientific and technical fallout accompanying such programs. The increasing priority attributed to arms control considerations, the desire to retain clear lines of command and control, and the pressures exerted by domestic groups in favor of the installation and maintenance contracts accompanying the deployment of ICBM systems at home combined to frustrate Norstad's plans. Even the participation of the British in the Thor program was that of a passive recipient rather than an active partner in development. To be sure, the level of technical knowledge and strategic sophistication about the new weapons was, for obvious reasons, less impressive among military leaders in Europe than in America. Still, the disutility of liquid-fueled, relatively slow reacting, unprotected, immobile IRBMs in Europe would surely have become apparent had the European allied authorities been more carefully consulted in advance.

Some Europeans, like the U.S. Army, were disposed to express their reservations about prevailing American strategy through the quest for independent strategic capabilities. It was unfortunate that the attempts in both cases to achieve a greater measure of influence and autonomy within the strategic framework compromised efforts to revise the basic strategy. The dilemmas encountered within the alliance, moreover, have proved unyielding to all attempted settlements.

NATO allies have discovered, as did the Army in their encounter with the Air Force, that though dependence is psychologically depressing if prolonged, the nature of modern weaponry tends to reinforce the necessities of centralized command and control over strategic capabilities.[16] As increasing centrali-

16 In the classic statement of this logic, Secretary of Defense McNamara contended: "There must not be competing and conflicting strategies to meet the contingency of nuclear war. We are convinced that a general

zation of such decisions within the context of increasingly inter-
connected military operations compounded interservice strains
at home, continued reliance upon nuclear retaliation combined
with the American monopoly of decision making in nuclear
weapons matters nourished the diplomatic problems of the Alliance in recent years.

Whereas interservice difficulties could be alleviated at home
through broadened participation in technological developments, through centralization of staff and command operations
at the level of the Joint Chiefs of Staff and unified and specified
commands, and through renewed efforts to create a balanced
arsenal and a pluralist strategy, such principles, for practical
purposes, have not been applicable for the Alliance. Objections
to an American nuclear monopoly, reservations toward the
basic strategy, and the emotional distress provoked by differentials in military power and prestige continue to sustain efforts,
particularly by the French, to acquire independent nuclear
capabilities.

While the appropriateness of applying the tactics of interservice politics to intra-alliance difficulties is beyond the scope of
this study, it seems reasonably clear that as long as the North
Atlantic area is considered a single strategic unit, the rationality
of weapons policies will be enhanced by providing regularized
procedures and forums for joint discussions of such matters. In
the Thor-Jupiter case, where European allies could express a
veto over deployment decisions with no corresponding responsibility for decisons related to weapons design, the consequence
was flagging confidence, occasionally acrid debate, and dual pro-

---

nuclear war target system is indivisible, and if, despite all our efforts,
nuclear war should occur, our best hope lies in conducting a centrally
controlled campaign against all the enemy's vital nuclear capabilities,
while retaining reserve forces, all centrally controlled. . . . A partial and
uncoordinated response could be fatal to the interests of all the members
of NATO. That is why we have consistently stressed the importance of a
single chain of command, to be employed in a fully integrated manner
against what is truly an indivisible target system." Robert S. McNamara,
Address at the Commencement Exercises, University of Michigan, Ann
Arbor, Michigan, June 16, 1962.

duction of a weapon which proved to be unwelcome in most Allied capitals.

Neither budgetary procedures nor organizational reforms can, of course, assure rational weapons policies. It is significant that in the report issued by the Jackson Subcommittee after their exhaustive investigation of the machinery for national security policy making, *personnel* was emphasized above *procedure*.[17] Such a judgment is confirmed by the Thor-Jupiter controversy. Given the political setting of weapons policy, successful innovation cannot be assured unless research administrators possess technical vision, political judgment, and entrepreneurial skill. And for those who, out of the welter of projects, must choose for production and deployment those which are technically reliable, strategically useful, and politically acceptable, political courage is as essential as scientific prescience!

MANAGERIAL CONTROL OF WEAPONS INNOVATION
AND SERVICE RIVALRY IN
THE EISENHOWER ADMINISTRATION

The Thor-Jupiter controversy is in a sense the story of the rise and demise of the Army's efforts to acquire an independent and meaningful role in the development and use of long-range ballistic missiles. From the vantage point of leaders in the Department of Defense, the controversy provided a test of their capacity to manage conflict within the context of a preferred set of weapons policies. Specifically it posed these demanding tasks for the managers of the defense establishment: (1) the maintenance of an environment favorable to the timely innovation of strategic weapons; (2) the selection, from a welter of competing proposals, of only those projects for advanced development, production, and deployment which promised strategic returns commensurate with their financial and political costs; and (3) the amelioration and resolution of jurisdictional conflicts among the services which arose out of the incorporation of novel weapons into the strategic arsenal.

The tools of management were various, and they were applied

17 Senate Committee on Government Operations, *Organizing for National Security*, III, 1961, p. 4.

with quite uneven results. Procedural and policy controls over service weapons programs included (1) the elaboration and implementation of strategic doctrine; (2) the negotiation of roles and missions "treaties" defining an acceptable division of labor among the service departments; (3) the centralization of managerial control over the missile programs; and (4) the use of analytic techniques for evaluating proposals, disciplining exaggerated claims, and illuminating technical and tactical alternatives.

Clearly the New Look doctrine conditioned the nature, the form, and the intensity of service politics in the Thor-Jupiter controversy. It also influenced the pattern of technological development more generally. The emphasis upon strategic retaliation, the faith in novel technology, the "long haul" perspective, the reliance upon nuclear weapons, and the depreciation of manpower and conventional capabilities prompted the services to emphasize the missile programs which came to dominate the landscape of military research and development history in the 1950s. The evidence of this study amply confirms Robert Buchheim's conclusion that the corollaries of such strategic perspectives were programs induced by haste, boldness in technological strategies, and a relative neglect of research and development fields separate from the mainstream of large systems.[18]

The initiation of missile development programs was encouraged both by these doctrinal incentives to buy into new technological fields at the expense of current preparedness or of the modernization of existing equipment and the relatively low costs of such programs in the planning and research stages. Rival projects thus proliferated. The exploration of parallel programs through the development stage offered a means of keeping the future open, technology fluid and up-to-date, and resources free from the heavier costs of quantity production until a choice could be reached. It also nourished a spirited competition among the Army and Air Force, and later the Navy, for the right to deploy intermediate-range ballistic missiles.

The Army was particularly zealous in its attempts to secure

[18] Robert W. Buchheim, "Problems of Planning and Decision in Military R & D." *RAND P-3021* (September, 1964), p. 3.

IRBMs. Its quest for such missiles appears directly related to the contraction of that service's budgets and roles and missions responsibilities portended by the New Look. While the organizational survival of the Army was scarcely threatened, its future status was obviously jeopardized. Under these circumstances the development and deployment of Jupiter missiles promised the Army an opportunity to express a variety of grievances against the Air Force, a prospect of enhancing its budgetary prospects, a means of expanding its operational responsibilities, an occasion for the exploitation of long-neglected technical resources, and a chance to reinforce its capabilities for fighting limited nuclear wars as well as slight possibility of obtaining responsibilities for the exploration of outer space.

The Air Force and Navy, while not initially as covetous of intermediate-range ballistic rockets as the Army, subsequently proved equally energetic in the promotion of their own programs. The Navy's interests were directed toward a sharing of mission responsibilities and the development of capabilities uniquely designed to operate in a naval environment. The Air Force's efforts were designed to resist encroachments on their established roles and missions, and to avert a dilution in the priority previously granted to their development program for the Atlas ICBM. In the activities of both services one may discern a confluence of strategic, budgetary, and proprietary interests comparable to those animating the Army missile program.

Clearly the New Look doctrine encouraged vigorous competitive efforts to develop strategic weapons systems. The New Look provided defense leaders with a blunt instrument for determining the basic reallocation of resources among the services and between various military missions. It supplied a yardstick for the elimination of some elements in the Korean War rearmament program. It narrowed the range of discussion, asserted the gross priorities as, for example between deterrence and defense, and served as a "shibboleth" for cloaking decisions and choking off debate. It did not constitute a terribly discriminating guideline for a number of fundamental weapons deci-

sions. Nor did it serve as a source of specific military and political design criteria for the weapons systems whose development the doctrine encouraged.

As a source of policy control over service rivalries, the New
Look merely defined the arena of interservice conflict. Doctrine
focused and sharpened the range of disagreements among the
services; it certainly did not eliminate discord between them.
Nor, of course, could any strategy, for the function of doctrine is
to assert the basic priorities, and to set priorities is to engender
rather than dissipate controversy. No strategic doctrine can
be sufficiently explicit and detailed to eliminate significant
conflicts when it comes to translating general objectives into
concrete programs. The New Look doctrine revealed a substantial reliance upon nuclear deterrence in preference to a strategy
depending upon the maintenance of a more balanced arsenal of
conventional as well as nuclear capabilities to cope with a variety of military contingencies. It provided no unassailable answers to such questions, however, as how much air-power was required for deterrence, or what level of expenditures for continental defense was called for, or which weapon systems could
best perform a given mission. On these matters a multitude of
imponderables insured that the intuitions of partisans would
not be susceptible to proof and that disagreements among qualified experts could not be overcome by doctrinal authority.

One other factor inhibited the utility of the New Look doctrine as a means of disciplining service programs. The premises
and objectives of the strategy were widely understood within the
Army, but they were not so widely accepted by Army leaders. In
such circumstances service doctrines and programs could be expected to have been closely adjusted to the national strategy and
the efforts of the other services only if service policies were carefully monitored and supervised by the Office of the Secretary of
Defense. Yet the prevailing dispersion of power within the Pentagon permitted no such detailed control of service programs.
This contributed to the ironical result that service doctrines
continued to proceed from different assumptions regarding the
nature of future military conflicts, while their weapons policies

made it appear that they were preparing to perform identical missions.

Rather than resolving roles and missions conflicts among the services, the New Look doctrine set the stage for spirited competition among the services over the disposition of a new generation of strategic delivery systems. Jurisdictional struggles among the services are actually a rather normal feature of American defense politics, since the services are somewhat autonomous, multi-purpose organizations sharing responsibilities for the maintenance of deterrence and the management of a host of other tasks related to American defense. "Treaties" defining the functional division of labor among the services can only be formulated in general terms in view of the confusing intermixture of roles and missions performed by the services. Where those roles and missions are nicely harmonized, advancing technology represents a dynamic element which can upset the balance and thus force the negotiation of a new treaty.

The relative autonomy enjoyed by the services makes bargaining over roles and missions necessary. The anxiety of the Eisenhower Administration over the costs of public disagreement among the services over the disposition of missile technology made such negotiations seem especially desirable in the Thor-Jupiter controversy. But several factors complicated the bargaining over roles and missions. First, the equivocal guidance of early directives relating to the permissible range of Army rockets and the precedent of the Navy's successful quest for access to the nuclear stockpile and strategic retaliation missions served to titillate Army Hopes, buttress Air Force fears, and nourish Navy interests. Secondly, the strategy of deferred choice between Thor and Jupiter development programs, while it permitted a buying of time, information, and technical experience to guide the ultimate decision between them, also encouraged the growth of vested interests, the mounting of furious public relations campaigns, the stimulation of hopes, and the commitment of service prestige to rival projects. Third, the services were represented in the Thor-Jupiter controversy by an extraordinarily able group of political and technological ntrepreneurs. Generals Medaris, Gavin, and Schriever, Admirals Rickover and Raborn, and many others were not only equipped with unusual technical or managerial competence; they were exceptionally adept as well in the solicitation of allies and the mobilization of consent for their weapons development proposals. Civilians like Trevor Gardner, James Douglas, Charles Thomas, and Wilbur Brucker played comparable roles and proved to be equally astute politically, equally skilled in partisan advocacy. It is significant that the competition for strategic weapon systems brought to the fore in each service men whose knowledge of technology was more extraordinary than their combat records. Equally significant is the fact that in the mid-1950's the Secretary of Defense possessed neither an equivalent zest for politics nor a comparable familiarity with missile technology.

If jurisdictional struggles are to be terminated and roles and missions conflicts resolved in a timely fashion, someone must assert "legislative leadership" in this realm of defense politics.[19] That is, someone must fit the rival ambitions of the services into a general program consonant with the priorities of the prevailing strategic doctrine. Then he must attempt to prevent the basic design of that program from being seriously compromised in the process of securing its approval. In the Thor-Jupiter controversy, neither the President, the Secretary of Defense, nor the Chairman of the Joint Chiefs of Staff appeared eager to assume this role of legislative leader.

Although the President considered himself the primary military expert within his Administration, he did not seek to exercise a detailed control over the proprietary issues raised by the development of missile technology. This is perhaps attributable to President Eisenhower's administrative style and his conception of the Chief Executive's Office.[20] Convinced that he had appointed the most capable men in the country to lead his Ad-

[19] For a discussion of legislative leadership in strategy-making, see Samuel P. Huntington, *The Common Defense*, pp. 188–96.

[20] See Richard E. Neustadt, *Presidential Power* (New York, John Wiley & Sons, Signet Ed., 1964), pp. 146–70 for an appraisal of Eisenhower's approach to the presidency.

ministration, he was not disposed to interfere in what he considered their business. Unlike some of his predecessors, most notably Franklin D. Roosevelt, he had little enthusiasm for jurisdictional rivalries among executive agencies or officials. He seems not to have welcomed such struggles as opportunities for exercising Presidential power but rather found them troublesome and annoying expressions of dissonance within the official family. Since neither Secretary of Defense Wilson nor Admiral Radford, the Chairman of the Joint Chiefs of Staff, provided bold leadership, however, the President's growing uneasiness over the public sparring among the Chiefs ultimately served as a catalyst of decision, and his support for the decisions embodied in the Wilson Memorandum on roles and missions was crucial in inhibiting the open expression of dissent by Army leaders.

Thus prolonged evasion of a decision on roles and missions was a consequence of disagreement among the Chiefs of Staff, the reluctance of the Chairman of the JCS to impose a decision, Secretary Wilson's hesitancy in exerting his authority until forced by events and budgets, and the general aloofness of the President. That negotiations, once joined, could yield a successful conclusion was demonstrated by the Wilson Memorandum. The settlement embodied in that document possessed a certain compelling logic, as well as a reflection of the relative power of the parties to the bargaining.

The Air Force was relieved of its anxiety that inroads were being made on its strategic retaliatory mission. To be sure, the Army lost control of a weapon which some considered promising. Yet the very breadth of Army interests in missile technology mitigated the resentment occasioned by the Wilson Memorandum. Compensation for the loss of the Jupiter was sought and obtained in the Nike-Zeus and Saturn booster engine projects. Their hopes for responsibilities in missile defense and the outer space field thus moderated their frustrations at losing the IRBM. The promise of the Navy Polaris program posed future problems in exercising command and control over strategic forces, but obstacles to cooperation did not appear insurmountable. In a sense, the services were all becoming more and more comparable to multiproduct firms competing within and among various industries. As the points of potential friction increased, the stakes in particular disputes declined. The intensity with which the services pursued specific weapons programs diminished as the scope of their interests expanded. This factor was likely to facilitate bargaining in the future.

One other feature of the bargaining over roles and missions worthy of mention was the tendency to express agreements in the language of technical limitations rather than that of strategic doctrine. The imposition of an arbitrary range restriction on Army rockets and the application of strict weight and fuel parameters for an Army field missile (Pershing) were illustrative of this tendency. Much of the debate over the relative merits of a mobile as opposed to a fixed-based IRBM also took place in something of a vacuum of strategic discourse. It is conceivable that the wheels of compromise were greased by avoiding an explicit discussion of strategic issues. Unfortunately there appears no sure way of untangling the complexities of those issues if explicit discussion is avoided. Again, it appears that the point of the inevitable bargaining which accompanied the resolution of the Thor-Jupiter controversy might have been rendered clearer by a Secretary of Defense confident of his grasp of the strategic issues and determined to provide legislative leadership in defense policy making.

Many of those who most loudly denounced the interservice haggling that accompanied this controversy seemed to assume that no such problems need have arisen had a missiles czar been appointed and granted sufficient authority to circumvent red tape, side-step the maze of technical advisory committees, and make timely decisions on missile development and production. Trevor Gardner was perhaps the most outspoken and influential advocate of such administrative arrangements. One can only speculate as to how the appointment of such a czar might have influenced the subsequent pattern of developmental decisions, for no such centralization was ever seriously attempted or achieved during the mid-1950s. To be sure, the coordinating committee structure which monitored progress on the long-

range missiles within the service departments and in the Office
of the Secretary of Defense was streamlined. A Special Assistant
for Guided Missiles was appointed by the Secretary in 1956.
Later his title was enhanced to Director for Guided Missiles
and his formal prerogatives were inflated. Neither incumbent
in these posts, however, ever managed to discover exactly the
dimensions of his authority, much less to exercise influence
commensurate with this authority.

At best the Special Assistant (later Director) for Guided Missiles helped to gather information for the various Ballistic
Missiles Committees, to convene and preside over sessions of the
OSD-BMC, to facilitate the accumulation of necessary concurrences, and to provide advice to the Secretary regarding the
progress and prospects of various developmental projects. At
worst, he and his staff constituted an additional layer of bureau-
cracy through which decisions had to be forced. The small size
and competence of the civilian and military advisers of the Special Assistant provided some insurance that he was more an expeditor than a deterrent to decision. The evidence available
hardly suggests that he was a central figure in resolving the
problems posed by competitive development programs for
IRBMs.

It is possible that a man of Trevor Gardner's temperament
with his evident relish for and skill at bureaucratic politics
might have transformed this position into one of seminal significance. This would necessarily have been contingent upon
the confidence of the Secretary, as well as his own energy. Surely
there was no dearth of formal authority in the Office of the Secretary of Defense to reach decisions on the development, production, and deployment of one or another IRBM. What was
frequently lacking was the disposition and confidence to exert
those powers which were obviously his. In addition to his legal
prerogatives, the Secretary was the inheritor of situational
power. Indeed, when Neil McElroy presented the Administration's proposal for the creation of the post of Director of Defense Research and Engineering in 1958, he argued that the
failure of the services to agree upon the correct assignment of

responsibilities for new weapons invariably forced the Secretary to arbitrate such questions. The Secretary, however, felt little confidence in his own competence to decide these questions, and apparently the advice and counsel of his Director for Guided Missiles did not steel his resolve for a particular course of action in the face of manifold uncertainties and powerful pressures.

But what of the case for delegating decision-making responsibilities over weapons research and development programs to a single individual—a "missiles czar" in this case? The proposal raises serious problems, for successful mangement in this area requires the careful balancing of two objectives. On the one hand, an atmosphere conducive to technical inventiveness and the thorough exploration of promising technologies must be maintained. On the other hand, full-scale development and production should be authorized for only those weapons systems which promise an increment to national security exceeding their monetary, political and strategic costs.

Clearly the case for a missiles czar or single manager of military research and development is weakest where the uncertainties of technology are greatest. As James Q. Wilson concluded in a survey of the relevant literature, the *proposal* of innovations is directly proportional to the diversity of effort and diffusion of power within an organization.[21] Since the appearance of gaps in technical capabilities must be considered among the serious threats to an adequate defense, the duplication of innovative efforts that sometimes results from administrative decentralization may be a price well worth paying for the encouragement of technical inventiveness provided by the spur of competition.[22]

The case for centralized decision making becomes stronger as one moves from the realm of research and exploratory development to the choices of weapons to enter the stages of full-scale development and production. As the costs of programs mount

---

[21] See his chapter entitled, "Innovation in Organization: Notes Toward a Theory," in James D. Thompson (ed.), *Approaches to Organizational Design* (Pittsburgh, University of Pittsburgh Press, 1966), pp. 193–218.

[22] See Ries, *The Management of Defense*, p. 207.

and the vested interests in their perpetuation grow, decisions become both more essential and more difficult. If the ease of project initiation is facilitated by a diffusion of power over developmental decisions, the difficulties of deciding which weapons the Defense Department shall finance, produce, and deploy are correspondingly increased.

Nor are these latter choices safely left to the discretion of a single central decision maker. The questions raised by the accelerated pace of weapons innovation in the 1950s were not simply problems which could be managed by delegating extraordinary powers to an expediter of crash programs. Basic issues of strategy and foreign policy were posed by the development of missile technology, and, as Roger Hilsman has observed, "producing policy is different from producing hardware and does not yield to the same expedients." [23]

Wise management in the development and selection of novel weapon systems requires the amalgamation of knowledge and judgment regarding a host of technical, political, and military questions. The painstaking accumulation of this knowledge and the careful balancing of myriad judgments involves, of necessity, a process of group policy-making. Some men become impatient with the delays this occasions. Others quail at the requirements of detailed justifications for their pet projects. Still others may resist having their views subjected to critical examination by other experts or having their proposals compromised to accommodate interests for which they bear no immediate responsibility. Thus the insistent pleas for the decisive executive, the efficient "missiles czar," who could presumably dismantle the intricate network of policy-making committees and issue crisp and authoritative commands.

Executive leadership in the office of the Secretary of Defense may have been somewhat faint-hearted in the course of the Thor-Jupiter controversy. Some of the innumerable committees which were accorded rights of consultation may have posed obstacles to intelligent decisions rather than facilitating wise and timely judgments. But this should not be allowed to obscure the

23 Roger Hilsman, *To Move a Nation,* p. 21.

fact that such committees may provide very effective forums for the collection and pooling of information, for testing the intelligence, reliability, and sense of proportion of experts, and stimulating mental effort while broadening the perspectives of those responsible for the drastic choices.[24]

Actually while demands for the appointment of a "missiles czar" were wisely resisted, some centralization of power over weapons decisions was affected by the organizational reforms introduced in 1958. Prior to 1958 the relative autonomy of the service departments allowed them to control their developmental priorities by emphasizing the functions they could execute independently and by neglecting those they shared with others. The competitiveness of this situation encouraged technical inventiveness. Short-term budget cycles prompted "foot-in-the-door" budgetary tactics, and various aspects of Defense Department management procedures allowed cost estimates on novel weapons projects to pass without receiving a careful evaluation for accuracy or sometimes even reasonableness. Relative to the problems of weapons development, the objective of the 1958 Defense Department reorganization was a strengthening of the Office of the Secretary of Defense for the supervision of weapons programs undertaken by the services, without completely undermining their independence. Those reforms did not contemplate the appointment of a single manager of defense research and engineering who would exercise arbitrary authority over all weapons developments. Rather they disclosed a substantial reallocation of power within the administrative structure in order to strengthen the hand of the Secretary. It was hoped that this would permit a more balanced dialectic between a central staff attempting a synoptic, comprehensive overview of defense requirements and the "disjointed incrementalism" which was more characteristic of the maneuvering of the services within a pluralist setting.

In one sense the creation of the Advanced Research Projects

[24] For a persuasive statement of the case for committees, see John K. Galbraith, *The New Industrial State* (Boston, Houghton Mifflin Company, 1967) , chap. VI.

Agency and the establishment of an office for a Director of Defense Research and Engineering multiplied further the agencies which might initiate projects. The Director was notably granted authority not only to monitor and supervise programs implemented by others, but he was to be granted operating functions through his power to purchase and contract. Meanwhile, service rivalries were to be mitigated by diluting their authority and vitiating their political resources for bargaining. The Advanced Research Projects Agency, the Director of Defense Research and Engineering, the unified and specified commanders, and the expanded Joint Staff were all the recipients of responsibilities previously exercised by the individual services. The lobbying power of the services was simultaneously diminished by diversifying their relationships to industrial suppliers and enforcing curbs upon them in their public relations and Congressional liaison activities.

The service departments unquestionably lost power to the Secretary of Defense, who in turn was to delegate much of this power to the newly created Director of Defense Research and Engineering. These changes reflected the conviction that decentralization of functions when it extended to the operating commands was troublesome because of the absence of a unified outlook among the services. Where such a unified outlook could be more readily insured, that is, within the Secretary's own Office, it was considered eminently desirable. The 1958 reorganization was to provide the technical competence in the Office of the Secretary which would underpin such decentralization. Yet while such changes could guarantee to the civilian leaders in the Defense Department a more substantial leverage on weapons policy decisions, this in itself could not insure that wiser decisions would result. The presupposition of such reforms was that officials in the Secretary's Office would be free of parochial loyalties in their evaluations of technical proposals and that their location at the top of the hierarchy would guarantee them the most complete information available and the most comprehensive viewpoint. These were assets that could be exploited only insofar as such officials employed appropriate analytic techniques with facility and with judgment. With respect to the field of weapons innovation in the mid-1950s, it is noteworthy that weapons were selected for development and production without an impressive system for analyzing such choices.

As President Eisenhower stated to Congress in 1958: "No military task is of greater importance than the development of strategic plans which relate our revolutionary new weapons and force deployments to national security objectives." [25] Yet the selection of IRBM projects was certainly marked by a considerable measure of intuition and improvisation. Analysis of the costs and of the consequences of alternatives appears to have been somewhat haphazard and far from systematic. Neither the planning nor the budgetary process provided adequate procedures for auditing the individual programs of the services against a comprehensive strategic concept. The National Security Council's "Basic National Security Policy" was invariably couched in hopelessly vague and ambiguous language permitting a variety of interpretations. Since it included no financial estimates of the required support, it was not directly related to the budgetary process.[26]

The Joint Chiefs of Staff annually produced a "Joint Strategic Objectives Plan" designed to elucidate the military support necessary for the implementation of the national security policy. It was, moreover, supposed to "provide planning guidance for the development of the forces needed in the Fiscal Year beginning four years ahead." [27] The JSOP was of little consequence in the Thor-Jupiter controversy, however, since the first one was not prepared until 1955–1956, and this initial effort consisted of plans devised unilaterally by the services and "pasted together" by the Joint Staff.[28] Thus, there was no insurance in the procedures of military planning that in the fash-

[25] See his "Special Message to the Congress on Reorganization of the Defense Establishment, April 3, 1958," *Public Papers of the Presidents, Dwight D. Eisenhower, 1958* (Washington, D.C., U.S. Government Printing Office, 1959), p. 278.

[26] Taylor, *The Uncertain Trumpet,* p. 82.   [27] *Ibid.,* p. 83.

[28] Charles Hitch, *Decision-Making for Defense* (Berkeley, University of California Press, 1965), p. 25.

ioning of a defense budget the combination of forces would be supportable by the financial outlays of the Department of Defense or in accord with an agreed-upon strategic concept.

Nor was this deficiency offset by the procedures of the budgetary process. The Budget Bureau was a "Presidential servant with a cutting bias," [29] more preoccupied with expenditure stabilization than the relationship between weapons policy and the nature of future military conflicts. The Budget Bureau assumed the role of the persistent critic, the skeptical auditor, the perennial catalyst of program reevaluations, and the vigorous challenger of departmental priorities. In addition to the influence the Director exerted on the general magnitude of defense spending through his personal influence with the President, he and members of the Military Division questioned particular items in the service budgets, forced department spokesmen to justify individual projects, promoted the resolution of stalemated proprietary issues, uncovered apparent inconsistencies in the programs of the various services, and sought to encourage more efficient military planning.[30]

The Military Division of the Budget Bureau had its offices in the Pentagon. The continuity of their personal, their considerable experience in costing military items, and the informal contacts which grew up over the years between service officials and the Bureau's staff insured them a respectful hearing in Defense Department budgetary deliberations.[31] Economy oriented in approaching expenditure requests for weapons development, they consistently adopted a skeptical attitude toward parallel programs. They were especially critical when the technical approaches were too nearly identical, when backup projects promised only a slight increment in military capabilities, or when the results of development would be useful for only very remote and unlikely contingencies.[32]

[29] Wildavsky, *The Politics of the Budgetary Process*, p. 160.

[30] Interview with William Schaub, former Chief, Military Division, Budget Bureau, August 25, 1965.

[31] See Senate Committee on Armed Services, *Hearings, Major Defense Matters*, 86th Cong., 1st Sess., 1959, p. 213.

[32] *Ibid.*, pp. 230–31.

Neither the Military Division of the Budget Bureau nor the Comptroller of the Pentagon regularly employed systems analysis or cost-effectiveness tests to evaluate comparatively the weapons proposals advanced by the services. Such tests were, to be sure, used in a rather crude fashion by the services themselves as they sought to rationalize allocative decisions between their myriad programs. Though functional budgeting had been neither refined nor implemented within the Defense Department, the Budget Bureau did occasionally review service programs "horizontally." When they did so, they pooled expenditure entries under " (1) strategic strike forces (2) ground and sea forces (3) forces and facilities supporting the entire services and (4) defense of the striking force and home base." [33] Such audits were potentially significant in light of the fact that the Joint Staff had not developed realistic military planning on a defense-wide basis. Nevertheless there is little evidence to indicate that the Budget Bureau exerted effective control over the big missile programs. Their high priority status tended to confer a measure of immunity from deep budget cuts. And without accurate forecasts of projected program costs for research and development, for the deployment of an operational force, and for maintenance, the Bureau's reservations about specific programs did not crystallize until the momentum behind them had become virtually irresistible.

Systems analysis was not a prominent feature of either defense planning or budgeting. Budgets were fashioned with an eye to inputs rather than outputs. The long-range cost implications of weapons decisions were not systematically examined. Competing weapons programs were not compared rigorously in terms of costs against the standard of a common mission. Little wonder that programs designed to serve the institutional interests of the services were not sufficiently questioned. Little wonder that the debates over the relative merits of the Thor and Jupiter too often focused upon the symbolic functions those weapons might perform rather than upon their real utility; that is, how many

[33] Senate Committee on Armed Services, *Hearing, Major Defense Matters,* 1959, p. 214.

of which systems would be required to accomplish which specific military mission?

It appears that the dearth of analysis in defense planning and the methods of presenting the defense budget also influenced the role played by Congress on decisions related to weapons innovation. Certainly the item-by-item presentation of the budget tended to focus the attention of Congressmen upon "nuts and bolts" rather than upon significant gaps or notorious superfluities.[34] That method of presenting the budget tended to obscure the point of the strategic debates from the legislators.[35] Though they were not well equipped to improve the rationality of executive choices, Congressmen could induce administrators to make unpleasant decisions. Secretary of Defense McElroy apparently welcomed Congressional demands for decisiveness on hard program choices. "It would not bother me," he conceded to Senator Stennis on one occasion, "if you held our feet to the fire and forced us in connection with this budget." Occasionally weapons policies were subjected to serious scrutiny by special blue ribbon panels. *Ad hoc,* short-term, authorized generally to analyze a single problem, possessed of the partial vision into the requirements of defense, and lacking permanent and intimate political ties within the Executive Branch, these panels' influence varied from case to case. With respect to decisions regarding the development and production of IRBMs, the influence of the Killian and Gaither committees was far from negligible. As President Eisenhower later conceded, the Gaither Committee's deliberations had a catalytic effect upon many in the Administration who were given to complacency. In addition "it listed a number of facts, conclusions, and opinions that provided a checklist for searching evaluation." [36] In heightening the general concern with Soviet space achievements and missile developments, their report may have reinforced the disposition

[34] This is not to say that Congress never played a significant role in such decisions. The Airpower Hearings and the Senate Committee on Armed Services' investigation of the space and missile program had a profound influence on subsequent decisions.

[35] Schilling, "The Politics of National Defense: Fiscal 1950," p. 265.

[36] Eisenhower, *Waging the Peace,* p. 223.

of the Defense Department to put both Thor and Jupiter missiles into production as an interim "fix" for the strategic deterrent force.

The Killian Report certainly triggered the decision to develop both land- and sea-based IRBM systems as a matter of national priority. It is possible that it inadvertently contributed to the ensuing jurisdictional conflict, for prior to the issuance of this report most of those with influence in the upper echelons of the Army supported the development of a mid-range (500 miles) ballistic missile. The urgency of IRBM development generated by the Killian Report created a climate of opinion congenial to the promotion of more grandiose ambitions.

In terms of the lobbying strategies of the services, the disjunction between planning and budgeting, the bluntness of analytic tools, the shortage of staff in the Office of the Secretary of Defense, the mirage of centralized control over the missile programs, the insufficiency of the strategic doctrine as a guideline for decisions between rival projects, and the long-deferred, *ad hoc* character of roles and missions decisions all promoted technical *faits accomplis,* "camel's nose" budgetary tactics, and the mobilization of support to precipitate or defer the hard choices related to the development, production, and deployment of the IRBMs.

From the standpoint of the Secretary's capacity to manage these multifarious activities, the diffusion of responsibilities for detailed planning and the absence of adequate procedures for allocating the defense budget tended to enhance the significance of lateral relationships and bargaining over the hierarchical elements of defense politics.[37] This may explain the fre-

---

[37] The development of the Planning-Programming-Budgeting System (PPBS) in the Department of Defense in the 1960s has been associated with a concurrent trend, namely, the growing centralization of power over defense policy in the Office of the Secretary of Defense. It does not follow, however, that those procedures can be implemented only in a hierarchical setting. On the contrary, since the principal result is to promote "open and explicit analysis" of the assumptions, factors, calculations, and judgments behind alternative programs, the techniques of analysis may be employed for purposes of advocacy by the services and commands just as ·

quency with which weapons emerged from the impetus of the technically feasible and the extent to which their military and political values were identified and rationalized *ex ante*.[38] It may well be true that "arms programs developed in an environment of technological innovation and international competition have a momentum of their own," and that "the direction the programs take is determined as often by the vagaries of technology as they are by the needs articulated by the political and military leadership." Those who provide policy leadership may indeed "find themselves 'riding herd' over forces that are hard to understand and difficult to control."[39] But the extent to which this was true in the Thor-Jupiter controversy was certainly related to the preference for intuitive, "seat-of-the-pants" judgment over the more rigorous, analytic techniques of systems analysis, cost-effectiveness criteria, operations research, and program budgeting.

THE MC NAMARA REVOLUTION, INTERSERVICE RIVALRY, AND THE MANAGEMENT OF WEAPONS INNOVATION

In view of the very considerable changes which Secretary of Defense McNamara introduced in the substance of strategic policy and the procedures of policy making, an analysis of the Thor-Jupiter controversy may appear to have little bearing upon contemporary defense problems. To be sure, the interservice rivalries that pervaded efforts to develop and deploy the intermediate-range ballistic missiles are not currently a prominent feature of defense politics. Few still bemoan the persistence

---

readily as they may be used by the Secretary of Defense to resist the pressures of the "special pleaders." See the testimony of Dr. Alain C. Enthoven, Assistant Secretary of Defense for Systems Analysis before the Senate Committee on Government Operations, *Hearings, Planning-Programming-Budgeting*, 90th Cong., 1st Sess., 1967, for an evaluation of the merits of PPBS in defense policy-making. For a slightly less sanguine view, see Dr. James R. Schlesinger, "Uses and Abuses of Analysis," Committee Print prepared for the Senate Committee on Government Operations, 90th Cong., 2nd Sess., 1968.

[38] For comparable conclusions, see Tarr, *Western Political Quarterly*, XVIII (March, 1965), 140.

[39] *Ibid.*

and ferocity of internecine strife among the services. Fewer still accused Secretary McNamara of an excessive faith in the promise of speculative military technologies.[40]

Certainly the dynamics of interservice politics and weapons innovation have undergone a dramatic transformation. An attempt to describe and explain that transformation far exceeds the scope of this book. Yet it is appropriate to suggest that such changes that have occurred appear to be explicable in terms of hypotheses elaborated and illustrated in the case materials. In short, the quiescence of interservice competition in weapons innovation reflects recent revisions in strategic doctrine, reforms in the procedures of policy making, and a redefinition of the climate of opinion that informs defense policy choices.

Secretary McNamara presided over a fundamental reorientation of U.S. strategy. He promoted the acquisition of a measure of strategic superiority sufficient to support a multitude of mutual defense commitments. He attempted to stabilize the deterrence equation by reducing the vulnerability of American retaliatory forces. Through the implementation of limited measures of arms control and the application of improved procedures for command and control, he sought to procure some insurance against inadvertent or accidental wars and against a dangerous diffusion of control over nuclear weapons. In his later years especially, he attempted to contain and even decelerate the arms race. Above all, he broadened the range of options available to those who formulate United States security policy by developing the more conventional resources of military power. Expensive as well as timely, these changes were accompanied by a substantial increase in the level of defense spending.

The Thor-Jupiter controversy, like so many other jurisdictional disputes over new weapons in the 1950s, was rooted in

[40] Criticisms of Secretary McNamara's management of weapons decisions may be found in Klaus Knorr and Oskar Morgenstern, *Science and Defense: Some Critical Thoughts on Military Research,* Policy Memorandum No. 32 (Princeton, Center of International Studies, 1965); and Hanson Baldwin, "Slowdown in the Pentagon," *Foreign Affairs,* XLIII (January, 1965), pp. 262–80.

the concatenation of a single weapon strategy, declining defense budgets, unlimited faith in technological breakthroughs, and a somewhat diffuse and fragmented pattern of decision making in the Defense Department. It is hardly surprising that the return to a strategy of "flexible response," a preoccupation with conventional options, the development of a balanced arsenal, rising defense budgets, and the greater degree of managerial control imposed upon the Department by Secretary McNamara combined to ameliorate or suppress strife among the services. Disputes continued to flicker, but they were neither as intense nor as public as they once were.

The pace and character of technological innovation were substantially influenced by revisions in strategic doctrine. The McNamara strategy initially encouraged an acceleration of the procurement schedules for strategic delivery systems as well as impressive efforts to improve and safeguard those systems. Special emphasis was devoted to securing retaliatory forces from surprise attack, e.g., the noteworthy investments in site hardening, the refinement of electronic intelligence-gathering techniques, and the invention of sophisticated penetration aids. The preoccupation with "assured destruction" and "damage limitation" was translated into rather specific design criteria emphasizing improved reconnaissance, greater accuracy in strategic delivery systems, better communications, and smaller warheads.

Participation in the qualitative arms race was by no means abandoned, despite the evident interest in controlling its pace. On the contrary, since 1962, annual expenditures for research, exploratory development, and advanced development—precisely the areas of new technology formation—have been increased by more than 25 per cent. During election campaigns in 1964 and 1966 various Republican candidates suggested that the Pentagon had developed no significant new weapon system during McNamara's tenure there. Such charges ignored progress in the development of the A-7 fighter bomber, the C-5A transport aircraft, Multiple Independently Targetable Reentry Vehicles (which enable a single ballistic missile to attack many separate targets), follow-on strategic delivery systems like the Minuteman I, Minuteman III, and Poseidon missile systems,

a Short-Range Attack Missile (SRAM), Fast Deployment Logistic Ships, the Airmobile Division, and the Sprint and Spartan
antimissile missiles, as well as the phased array radar which will
guide them.

The willingness to "seed" a variety of technological possibilities with research and development money was not always
matched by an equivalent enthusiasm for advanced engineering
and production work on specific weapons systems. Until September, 1967, for example, technical doubts about the efficacy
and operational utility of an Anti-Ballistic Missile system, reinforced by political reservations regarding the wisdom of procuring a system which could conceivably upset the strategic balance
and stimulate more vigorous competition for new offensive
systems, led the Secretary to resist the unanimous recommendation of the Joint Chiefs of Staff that an ABM be immediately
deployed.[41] The creation of additional conventional capabilities, stimulated especially by the war in Vietnam and by revisions in American strategic doctrine, also produced sharp
increases in the level of the defense budget in the mid-1960s.
The costs of maintaining more men in uniform and procuring
more conventional material was partially offset by a somewhat
more conservative investment in strategic weapon systems.

Interservice strife was not a prominent feature of defense
politics during the period of the massive buildup and qualitative improvement of strategic forces in the 1960s. This is not
particularly surprising in the light of the largesse which was so
widely spread smong all services and all functional commands.
Such strife that emerged has focused on strategic, tactical, and
role and mission questions related to the Vietnamese War. A
more prominent feature of contemporary defense politics is the
recurrent struggles which have marked relations between the
civilian Secretary and a United Jointed Chief of Staff on such
issues as the bombing strategy in Vietnam and the deployment
of an ABM system.

By altering the methods of policy analysis and the procedures

41 On September 18, 1967, Secretary McNamara announced the administration's decision to deploy a "thin" ABM system at a predicted
cost of $5 billion.

of defense planning and budgeting, Secretary McNamara shifted the balance of influence in the Pentagon away from the service departments to the Office of the Secretary of Defense. To an unprecedented degree Secretary McNamara and his staff succeeded in defining the strategic issues, in conditioning the terms of political bargaining, and in molding the climate of opinion which shapes the range of choice in defense policy making. In a sense, the interservice strife of the 1950s was simply displaced by conflict between civilian leaders in the Pentagon and the military professionals. Tolerance for intramural scuffling among the services did not increase; the Secretary's capacity to mute and discipline its overt manifestations did.

Secretary McNamara promoted the functional unification of the defense establishment in a subtle and rather oblique fashion. Although the traditional services were not formally assaulted, their independence and authority were significantly diminished. Some of the functions formerly performed separately by the service departments were delegated to new agencies. Thus communications, intelligence, and security responsibilities were consolidated in the Defense Intelligence Agency and the National Security Agency; procurement services in the Defense Supply Agency; common and long-line communications in the Defense Communications Agency.

The Defense planning and budgeting system was changed in 1961 to permit the application of systems analysis. At the direction of Secretary McNamara, Comptroller Charles Hitch installed the comprehensive Planning-Programming-Budgeting System. Through these new procedures of defense planning and budgeting the Office of the Secretary of Defense was able to substantially enhance its influence in the fashioning of strategic policy and the development of programs to support that policy. Strategic objectives or missions were defined with greater precision. Alternative methods of achieving the desired objectives were more systematically considered. More rigorous methods of quantitative analysis were employed to evaluate the costs and benefits of competing weapon systems. Systems were designed with reference to practical budgetary limitations, and the long-range cost implications of immediate choices were taken more clearly into account as cost projections were improved and the planning cycle extended into the future through the development of a defense-wide blueprint of tentative plans in the Five Year Force Structure and Financial Program.

The initiative and influence exerted by the Secretary of Defense and his staff within this system was enormous. Partly this was attributable to their own formidable executive talent, partly to their familiarity with the language of cost accounting and the methods of systems analysis, as well as to the opportunity afforded them to redefine the objectives of defense planning in terms of missions which transcended the activities of particular service departments.

A grudging acceptance of these reforms was secured through an agreeable bit of "horse trading." In return for the additional increments of power obtained by the Secretary and his civilian staff, the services and commands received generous donations of men, money, and weapons.[42] As Professor Schilling observed, "Who is going to object to systems analysis when the result is all systems go? Who is going to object to program budgeting when all programs get budgeted?" [43] It does seem doubtful that these changes in policy-making procedures could have been imposed upon the commands and the service departments during a period of declining budgets and shrinking roles and missions assignments.[44]

In the hands of an unusually competent, self-assured, and decisive Secretary, the Planning-Programming-Budgeting System was employed to rationalize many aspects of defense planning and to promote a greater consistency between plans and budgetary support. There is little doubt that such methods may have a felicitous effect upon weapons decisions. In the field of na-

[42] I am grateful to Warner R. Schilling for calling this to my attention.
[43] Panel discussion, American Political Science Association Annual Meeting, September, 1966.
[44] Systems analysis and cost-effectiveness studies are, of course, as useful when one must determine where cuts in defense spending may least harmfully be imposed as when the problem is deciding how additional funds may most effectively be spent.

tional defense the drastic choices frequently involve the selection of design requirements, objectives, and criteria for expensive weapon systems.[45] In recent years those decisions have been made with a greater effort to identify and evaluate in a systematic fashion the consequences of choice.

The new procedures of planning and budgeting also increase the constraints upon the independent activities of the services in the innovation of novel weapons. Bureaucratic, institutional, economic, doctrinal, and political obstacles may all hamper the innovative efforts of the services. These constraints were minimized by Trevor Gardner, Generals Gavin, Medaris, and Schriever, and Admirals Rickover and Raborn to the extent that authority and responsibility were coupled to some degree at the working levels of a defense establishment in which the services still enjoyed considerable autonomy. In the mid-1950s a service department could pursue a developmental project on the basis of urgency inspired by independent intelligence evaluations, it could finance the program out of a service budget only loosely audited against a comprehensive strategic concept; and it could employ both early successes in test programs and political support engendered by the diffusion of development and production contracts to sustain the life of projects initiated through "foot-in-the-door" tactics.

The need to halt a proliferation of nonessential weapons encouraged the erection of additional procedural hurdles to weapons innovation. A cursory look at the record would suggest that these have had their intended effect. Various criticism of the new procedures of policy-making or the manner in which they have been put to use have been expressed. Some have argued that the new methods of weapons selection have upon occasion been employed "at the expense of judgment and engineering and scientific intuition." [46] Others have been

[45] Albert Wohlstetter, "Strategy and the Natural Scientists," in Robert Gilpin and Christopher Wright (eds.), *Scientists and National Policy Making* (New York, Columbia University Press, 1964) , p. 194.

[46] Hanson W. Baldwin, "Slowdown in the Pentagon," *Foreign Affairs,* XLIII (January, 1965) , 277.

critical of the priority assigned to the "cost" part of the "cost-effectiveness" criterion, the significance attached to prolonged program definition phases, the profound influence of the Defense Comptroller or the Director of Defense Research and Engineering, the accuracy of long-range projections of the possible costs of new weapons systems, and the expansion of the number of necessary concurrences necessary to develop and deploy a new weapon system. "Never," as Hanson Baldwin put it, in the history of competition have so many been able to say no, so few to say yes." [47] Doubts have been expressed as to whether a high-risk project such as the Polaris proposal could survive cost-effectiveness tests as they were applied in the Mc-Namara Pentagon.[48]

It is beyond the scope of this book to analyze the validity of these assertions. The somewhat heated debate which has accompanied the incorporation of the new procedures of PPBS into defense policy making has, however, clarified several points. Systems analysis cannot substitute for wise judgment. Nor have its sensible proponents ever claimed that it could. Systematic analysis may, on the other hand, serve to sharpen the intuitions of decision makers. Reliance upon systems analysis by no means eliminates the adversary relations among the services. It may, however, refocus the strategic dialogue among the services upon the real issues. The systems analysis approach to weapons decisions may be biased, as some have charged, in favor of qualitative improvements in existing weapons rather than for innovations of entirely novel weapon systems. It is far from evident, however, why " 'open and explicit analysis' should be any more biased in this direction than judgment or intuition or experience unsupported by analysis." [49] Systems analysis provides no infallible method for discovering wise strategic policy. It does, however, offer a useful

[47] *Ibid.*, p. 270.
[48] Knorr and Morgenstern, *Science and Defense*, p. 21.
[49] Alain C. Enthoven, "The Systems Analysis Approach," in a Committee Print, *Selected Comment on Planning-Programming-Budgeting*, prepared for the Senate Committee on Governmental Operations, 90th Cong., 1st Sess., 1967, p. 5.

tool for identifying the relative merits of various alternative defense postures. Systems analysis will not necessarily insure timely disclosures of the weapons the United States may need to maintain an adequate defense. It may be employed to great advantage in distinguishing between essential and marginal projects. As James R. Schlesinger has noted, "The volume of government resources that may be lavished on the care and feeding of white elephants is simply staggering." [50] It may be especially efficacious in "uncovering cases of gross waste: points at which substantial expenditures may contribute little to any stated objective." [51] The potential utility of such analysis in the Thor-Jupiter case is self-evident.

Actually, the increased authority of the Office of the Secretary of Defense and the techniques of systems analysis might as easily facilitate as inhibit the pace of military-technological innovation. As well as informing the content of strategic doctrine, systems analysis may simply reflect the assumptions or premises of a specific doctrine. The systems analysis undertaken in the Office of the Secretary of Defense will presumably be influenced by the doctrinal prejudices of the Secretary as well as the institutional interests which are grounded in his Office. During the 1960s, much of the systems analysis which has undergirded the important weapons decisions has been responsive to a new doctrinal consensus on the major strategic issues. Several features of that climate of opinion have had a direct bearing on the weapons innovation process. In the first place, the Secretary and his staff have expressed a greater Missourian skepticism toward novel weapons projects. This attitude was formed by understandable apprehensions that the services and defense suppliers were inclined to grasp at straws in promoting any and every technical possibility. In order to reduce expenditures on nonessential projects, there emerged a tendency to promote a vigorous developmental effort only on those projects for which an explicit military requirement could be stated.

Secondly, perspectives regarding the likelihood and the de-

[50] Schlesinger, "The Uses and Abuses of Analysis," p. 10.   [51] *Ibid.*

sirability of strategic weapons innovations underwent a substantial metamorphosis. Many prominent defense officials expressed the conviction that a technological plateau had been attained which rendered radical scientific or technological breakthrough extremely unlikely.[52] This conviction was perhaps reinforced by the anxiety shared by scientists and strategists alike that a perpetuation of the arms race would disclose increasing hazards while new weapons promised little additional security to the United States. Thus the conscious effort to manage and contain the arms race. The implication of such perspectives on the weapons innovation process are obvious.

Scarcely a year has passed since Mr. McNamara departed from the Pentagon. It nonetheless seems clear that many of the reforms he introduced will prove to be durable features of defense planning. A new Administration now confronts new dilemmas of national security policy. They must adjust strategic policy to new conditions of political multipolarity. They must make the fateful choices produced by advancing technology. They must adjust to a public mood of growing skepticism about the contribution additional arms may add to the nation's security and a mood of diminishing indulgence regarding the requests of military and industrial groups for new weapons. New men, eager to affect significant changes in strategic policy, will predictably seek to facilitate the implementation of their preferred policies by altering the methods by which policy is made. Thus the forces which condition the intensity of institutional strife within the Defense Department as well as the rate of technical innovation in military weaponry are being dramatically transformed anew.

52 See, for example, Jerome Wiesner, *Where Science and Politics Meet* (New York, McGraw-Hill, 1965, pp. 279–96.

INDEX OF NAMES

SUBJECT INDEX

AC Spark Plug Co., 126

Advanced Research Projects Agency, 181, 225, 226-33, 234, 237, 238, 239, 243, 278

Advent Communications Satellite Project, 247

Aerojet-General Co., 107

Aerospace Corporation, 246, 247

Aircraft Industries Association, 88

Air Force: Strategic Air Command, 7, 39, 61, 98, 102, 128, 192, 197n; postwar ballistic missile research, 24-26; roles and missions, 26-27, 37-39, 69, 82-84, 97, 117-20, 270-73; basic doctrine, 1953, 37; Continental Air Defense, 39; procurement priorities under the New Look, 39-41, 268; Tactical Air Force, 40, 41, 223; Military Air Transport Service, 41; and IRBMs, 52, 55-64, and *passim;* Strategic Missiles Evaluation Group, 57-58; requirement for tactical ballistic missile, 59, 62n; perspectives on overseas bases, 61, 62; authorization of Thor, 71; political resources of, 90-92; strategy for controlling IRBM deployment, 96-103; and Navy Polaris program, 97; administrative arrangements for Thor program, 98-99; Air Material Com-

mand, 98; Air Research and Development Command, 98; Ballistic Missile Division, 98 ff.; Ballistic Missile Center, 99; SAC-MIKE, 99; industrial contractor network, 99-100, 155-63, 244-49; "philosophy of concurrency," 100-101; missile testing policy, 141-43; technical competition with Army: engine procurement conflict, 135-38; information sharing on technical design, 138-43; turbopump failure controversy, 139-43; rival approaches to reentry problem, 143-46; operational concept for deployment of IRBMs, 146-52; and Holaday *ad hoc* Committee, 170; discussions with UK over Thor deployment, 191; opposition to ARPA, 231-32; and transfer of Army missile engineers to NASA, 240-44

Armed Forces Policy Council, 117

Army: Ordnance Technical Intelligence Branch in Europe, 23; Army Air Corps, 24; roles and missions, 26-27, 37-39, 44-45, 48, 69, 82-84, 97, 117-20, 270-73; reaction to New Look strategic doctrine, 27-37, 267-68; Weapon System Evaluation Group, 34n; Sky Cavalry, 36; doctrine (Field